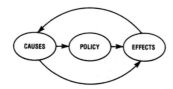

Policy Studies Organization Series

Analyzing Poverty Policy

Analyzing Poverty Policy

Edited by
Dorothy Buckton James
Virginia Polytechnic Institute
and State University

Lexington Books
D.C. Heath and Company
Lexington, Massachusetts
Toronto   London

Library of Congress Cataloging in Publication Data

Main entry under title:

Analyzing poverty policy.

Includes index.
1. Economic assistance, Domestic—United States—Addresses,
essays, lectures. 2. Public welfare—United States—Addresses,
essays, lectures. I. James, Dorothy Buckton
HC110.P63A72   338.973   75-748
ISBN 0-669-99499-5

Published simultaneously in Canada

Printed in the United States of America

International Standard Book Number: 0-669-99499-5

Library of Congress Catalog Card Number: 75-748

To Pat and Pete

Contents

Introduction

Until this decade there has been only modest research involvement by political scientists in the area of poverty and welfare policy. While public and scholarly concern for poverty issues developed rapidly during the 1960s, sociologists, anthropologists, economists, and specialists in fields such as health, law, and housing made most of the major contributions. Yet, with the shift in focus toward policy studies, during the past few years more political scientists have become interested in research on poverty and welfare questions.

There are several ways in which the particular expertise of political scientists can contribute to a fuller understanding of poverty and welfare questions. Political scientists can analyze the significance of the political values that underly various programs and influence the institutional structure that creates, administers, and interprets them. They can indicate the implications of the American political context (including the nature of public opinion toward the poor, the consequences of interest group activity, the decentralization of the political system, and the significance of specific institutional structures) for poverty and welfare policy. They can evaluate the impact of existing programs and the potential impact of alternative choices.

The 18 chapters in this book attempt to analyze these questions. Originally 14 authors contributed brief articles for a symposium issue of the *Policy Studies Journal* on ''The Political Science of Poverty and Welfare.'' These articles have been completely revised and greatly expanded for this book, and four new chapters have been written (those by Robert Albritton, Elmer and Mary Rusco, Stephen Sachs, and Richard Shingles). In spite of the diversity of topics and authors' viewpoints, three themes seem to run through the contributions to this book: the incremental nature of change in poverty and welfare policy (as opposed to the comprehensive change implied by a rational decision-making model); the inadequacy of information on which to plan policy or evaluate its effectiveness; and the lack of coordination of regulations, institutions, and officials dealing with questions of poverty and welfare policy. These three problems reflect the decentralized nature of the American political system.

In the United States decision making has been decentralized through the dual impact of federalism and the provision of separate institutions sharing power. Thus, federalism has created multiple decision-making centers by providing 50 state governments in which poverty and welfare policy is formulated and administered, as well as the national government and a bewildering array of local governments (roughly 38,000 not including school districts and special districts). Moreover, in *each* government (national, state, and local), power is shared by separate institutions—executives, legislators, judges, and bureaucrats. Conflict is inevitable within this system because *each* of these officials in *each* of these governments has a *different constituency*. (For example, the constituency of the President is national; United States senators and governors have statewide constituencies; members of the United States House of Representatives are elected from congressional districts; the district lines of state legislators are drawn differently from those of congressmen; and bureaucrats are either appointed or gain their positions through civil service regulation and their constituencies are highly specialized clientele groups.) Even when the constituency is similar (as with United States senators and governors), the officials are elected on different issues and given different responsibilities.

This multiplicity of decision-making centers makes it very difficult to gain adequate information or to coordinate poverty and welfare policy. Because the variety of decision-making centers provides myriad points from which groups can veto the policy initiatives of others, the government is so structured that it enables groups to protect their interests by limiting each other's initiatives. Consequently, the decentralization of American politics is a bulwark of the *status quo* such that change can only occur incrementally, particularly in the area of poverty and welfare policy.

The chapters by Dale Rogers Marshall, Leonard Rubin, Richard L. Fogel, Frederick R. Eisele, and Robert B. Albritton in part I consider the fragmentary nature of our knowledge about the scope and causes of poverty and the impact of implementation of federal poverty and welfare programs. Dale Rogers Marshall reviews the literature on implementing federal poverty and welfare policy. Leonard Rubin considers the political implications of information gathering in three antipoverty programs. Richard L. Fogel's focus is the General Accounting Office's evaluation of social services. Frederick R. Eisele reviews the fragmentary nature of our knowledge about implementation of welfare policies affecting the elderly. Robert B. Albritton proposes a sophisticated technique (the application of systems dynamics concepts in computer simulation) to provide a more effective means to describe and explain welfare policy.

Chapters by James E. Anderson, William J. Hagens, and Joseph A. Cepuran in part II consider different aspects of the problem of coordinating poverty and welfare policy. James E. Anderson considers national policy, William J. Hagens focuses on the state level, and Joseph A. Cepuran considers the dysfunctional impact of revenue sharing on existing poverty and welfare policy.

A number of aspects of OEO (Office of Economic Opportunity) programs are analyzed in parts III and IV. In part III Lawrence Neil Bailis,

Richard D. Shingles, and Terry L. Christensen consider the impact of community action agencies. Lawrence Neil Bailis indicates the lessons of the 1960s but stresses the need for a wide range of detailed and objective case studies to provide more adequate information. On the basis of one such case study Richard D. Shingles offers some cautionary notes about some of the assumptions of the community action program and those who have written about it. Terry L. Christensen emphasizes the urban bias of existing evaluations of the community action program.

In part IV Elmer R. and Mary K. Rusco analyze the impact of OEO services on American Indians, while Paul B. Fischer analyzes their impact on bureaucratic segmentation. The chapter by Harry P. Stumpf, Bernadyne Turpen, and John H. Culver, and those by Stephen L. Wasby and Stuart S. Nagel focus on aspects of the OEO legal services program. The former considers it broadly; Stephen L. Wasby analyzes Supreme Court responses to the cases recently raised by OEO lawyers and welfare rights organizations, and Stuart S. Nagel applies a simple decision theory approach to the question of how to provide legal counsel for the poor.

The chapters in Part V propose alternatives to present American poverty and welfare policy. Stephen M. Sachs prefers an effective employment program based on self-management. Marian Lief and Howard A. Palley prefer a national income and services policy. Each chapter is presented in the hope of stimulating further thought, debate, and research in the area of poverty and welfare policy.

**Part I
Inadequate Information**

1

Implementation of Federal Poverty and Welfare Policy: A Review

Dale Rogers Marshall

Political scientists have given more attention to the formulation of federal policy than to its implementation. Thus, we know more about the legislative process than we do about what happens after the legislative drama fades and the bureaucrats go to work to implement the legislation, to translate the ideas into action.

This chapter focuses on the implementation of federal social policy, that is, poverty and welfare policy broadly understood, and reviews some of the central issues and recent literature. Special attention is given to the ways that cities implement federal social policies. Since implementation is a relatively new topic of study it crosses traditional fields within political science, such as public administration and state and local politics. The study of implementation contributes to the field of public administration since policies are implemented primarily by executive agencies and involve extensive intergovernmental relations. Implementation studies also add to our understanding of state and local politics because the implementation of much federal policy is dependent on state and local governments. The study of implementation is also central to the emerging interdisciplinary field of policy analysis. The central issues discussed here are: What changes have resulted from the implementation of federal social policies? What are the characteristics of the implementation process that explain the results? And what factors explain variations in implementation by different cities?

Results of Implementation

The rapid growth of social programs in the 1960s was accompanied by an increased interest in finding out what effects the programs were having, or to put it another way, in evaluating the results of policy implementation. This interest led to the growth of research designed to evaluate the impact of public policy. As each new program was announced there was a dash to capture the accompanying evaluation money and soon afterwards a spate

This chapter relies heavily on research being done in collaboration with Rufus Browning and David Tabb at San Francisco State University, supported by the Institute of Governmental Affairs, University of California—Davis and the Institute of Governmental Studies, University of California—Berkeley.

3

of conflicting published reports on the merits of the programs. Kenneth Dolbeare has traced the evolution of policy impact studies and the methodological difficulties involved.[1]

Many of the studies, regardless of the specific social policy under consideration, tell the same sad story. One knows how the story will end before beginning. A new program is announced with great flourish at the White House; a new team of bright young administrators is assembled and barnstorms the country exuding enthusiasm. But as the results start to come in and problems increase, the program declines and slowly disappears from view. The conclusion is that the policy does not make significant changes in the distribution of benefits. In Edelman's terms, the policy is found to be primarily a symbolic gesture that eases discontent but does not significantly change the existing social and political structure or who gets what.[2]

Studies reaching generally pessimistic conclusions about the results of social policy seem to predominate. Edward Banfield argues that social policies by inevitably failing to meet the expectations they create and thus increasing discontent have done more harm than good.[3] Daniel Moynihan calls the war on poverty a failure and blames the fuzzy ideas of reformers for unclear goals that increased conflict and hastened the demise of the program.[4] Frances Fox Piven and Richard Cloward reach similarly pessimistic conclusions but for different reasons.[5] They conclude that the war on poverty temporarily stimulated valuable unrest that led to some desirable reforms in welfare but these positive results were not strong enough to overcome countervailing forces that gradually succeeded in eliminating the positive programs. Ira Katznelson, like Piven and Cloward, says the war on poverty served to quiet discontent and thus protect the political system from basic changes.[6] Theodore Lowi also is critical of federal social policies.[7] His main argument is that in response to pressure from interest groups, the national government has abdicated its responsibilities to promote justice. This tendency is aggravated in social programs like the war on poverty that call for increasing participation in policy administration and thus make strong central administration even more difficult. Other studies that reach negative conclusions about the results of social policies include Martha Derthick's study of new towns in-town,[8] Francine Rabinovitz's and Helene Smookler's study of new communities,[9] and Robert Alford's review of policies in several fields including health and social welfare.[10]

However, there are other studies which find that some positive results have occurred. Robert Levine's assessment of the Economic Opportunity Act is that it was neither a complete success nor an absolute failure.[11] Martha Derthick in *The Influence of Federal Grants* stresses the significant changes brought about in the Massachusetts welfare system by federal welfare policy.[12] Harrell Rodgers and Charles Bullock argue that the results of civil rights policies vary according to types of policies.[13] Richard

Cole finds that various social programs to increase participation, such as neighborhood councils and multiservice centers, have positive effects on municipal services and citizen attitudes.[14]

The conflicting assessments of the results of social programs highlight the complex problems involved in evaluating policy impact. First, evaluators use different standards in evaluating results. The diverse judgements reviewed above indicate that the public must give close attention to what evaluators mean by the terms "success" or "failure." Different evaluators use the terms differently. The studies often disagree less about what the results are than about the appropriate standard to use in evaluating results. Some analysts use very demanding standards. They look to see if the programs have resulted in major improvements, and if they have not, the analysts conclude that the policy falls short of the standards and is a "failure". Other analysts use looser standards. They look to see if the programs have resulted in at least some positive changes and if they find any positive effects at all, these analysts typically conclude that the policy is a "success". The first type of analyst has high expectations that are repeatedly dashed; the other type has lower expectations and finds it amazing that any positive change occurs at all.[15]

A second problem in evaluating social programs is that the goals of the programs are typically unclear, conflicting, and shifting. These characteristics mean that evaluators cannot simply use program goals as the standards against which to measure results. The analysts must first try to specify what the goals seem to be and decide how to deal with conflicting goals.

A third problem is specifying the effects of programs. The effects may be direct and immediate and/or indirect and long run. Which types of effects should an evaluator look for? All the types of effects may be extremely weak, hard to measure, and difficult to link to the independent effect of the policy. For example, the increased strength of minority organizations in a given city that had a model cities program may have been the result of the program or of other social forces operating, such as the national civil rights movement or the preceding partisan activities in the city that trained strong minority leaders.

In addition to the methodological problems in evaluating social programs, there are bureaucratic and political problems. Organizations resist the time and effort required to do systematic evaluations; decision makers may not be willing to expend the necessary resources and may ignore results they do not like.

These methodological, bureaucratic, and political problems in evaluating social problems are described more fully in several interesting books. Alice Rivlin in *Systematic Thinking for Social Action*,[16] Peter Rossi and Walter Williams in *Evaluating Social Programs*,[17] and Walter Williams in *Social Policy Research and Analysis*[18] review existing evaluations of social programs such as the war on povertry and equal opportunity efforts and suggest ways of overcoming the existing problems. Joseph Wholey et al. analyze evaluations done by the Department of Housing and Urban Development, the Office of Economic Opportunity, the Department of Health, Education, and Welfare, and the Department of Labor, and propose reforms that would facilitate a comprehensive federal evaluation effort.[19] In a later article Wholey reluctantly concludes that many programs cannot be evaluated effectively because they lack clear goals, clear statements of cause and effect (in other words, expectations that a given action will have a certain kind of impact), and effective management willing or able to use the findings of evaluators.[20]

One effort to overcome these problems is the development of social indicators that can be used to measure impacts of policies. Peter Rossi et al. in *The Roots of Urban Discontent* make a major effort in this direction by attempting to measure differences in the way blacks are treated by city government in 15 large American cities.[21]

In spite of conflicting evaluations and the problems involved, there is a growing body of literature that evaluates federal social programs. I have previously reviewed some of the literature on the war on poverty.[22] Other recent reviews of the war on poverty include books by Sar Levitan[23] and by J. David Greenstone and Paul Peterson.[24] Greenstone's and Peterson's book, *Race and Authority in Urban Politics*, is a comparative study of the war on poverty in New York, Chicago, Los Angeles, Philadelphia, and Detroit. It explains variations in the amount of community participation in these five cities (Chicago had the least; Detroit and New York had the most). According to Greenstone and Peterson the political structures and electoral and organizational interests alone could not explain the differences. Instead, they argue that the ideology of groups is very important in explaining the patterns of participation in the different cities. By ideology they mean the role interests of groups that shape their attitudes toward race and authority. They conclude that in New York and Detroit the black groups and their allies have gained power in poverty policy making.[25] They argue that participation of the poor in poverty programs has been an effective strategy for redistributing power because it follows the American tradition of self-development of ethnic groups.[26] The literature on model cities is not yet as extensive as the war on poverty literature. The consulting firm of Marshall Kaplan, Gans and Kahn has done numerous studies of model cities.[27] Many of those studies focus on the planning process as does the work by James Sundquist.[28] George Washnis's book, *Community Development Strategies*, studies eight Model Cities: Boston, Chicago, Dayton, Indianapolis, Newark, New York, Savannah, and Seattle.[29] It concludes that the program has had a favorable effect on local governments, encouraging them to expand services to disadvantaged areas, and institute social planning, coordination, evaluation, and citizen participation. He thinks that the caliber of the administrators is important in explaining variations in the success of the program in the various cities. Additional assessments of the war on poverty and model cities can be found in the special issue of the *Public Administration Review* published in 1972.[30] *The Politics of Economic and Human Resource Development* also reviews social programs, namely, the Economic Development Administration, job corps, Appalachia programs, and model cities.[31]

A wide range of the 1960s social programs is assessed in an interesting collection of articles in *The Great Society: Lessons for the Future*.[32] The conclusion is that the record is mixed, there are both successes and failures, "as any sensible person should have expected."[33] The editors conclude this evaluation by saying that, in spite of failures, the legislation was not a mistake because we cannot wait until conditions are ideal but instead must be willing to continue to act even though we do not have clear goals, or knowledge of how to reach the goals, or enough resources, or effective administration. The problem cannot be solved better by local governments or the free market so we must act and learn from the partial successes as well as the failures.

Characteristics of the Implementation Process

A second major issue in the study of implementation concerns the characteristics of the implementation process itself. The conflicting evaluations of the effects of programs have led to more interest in the implementation process, in tracing why programs turn out the way they do.

Some social scientists view implementation as primarily a technical, mechanical, or routine process. The term *implementation* itself connotes the rational carrying out of a decision by subordinate, neutral instruments or tools.[34] Jeffrey Pressman and Aaron Wildavsky describe the implementation of the Economic Development Act (EDA) in Oakland as a complex chain of reciprocal interactions. They argue that originally the participants agreed on goals so no major value or interest conflicts were involved.[35] But the long chain of decision points meant that an immense number of clearances were necessary and these resulted in long delays during which the participants changed and the original agreements eroded. So the complexity of joint action resulted in program failures for primarily technical reasons. Robert Levine, too, emphasizes the technical aspects of implementation. He says that implementation of federal programs has relied too heavily on the central administration of rules. Due to the resistance of organizations to rules, centrally administered rules cannot effectively compel local jurisdictions to comply with national policy.[36]

James Sundquist's book, *Making Federalism Work*, also stresses the structural blocks to implementation by focusing on the organizational impediments to coordinated policy implementation.[37]

The position in these studies is similar to organizational theorists' emphasis on the limited capacity of an individual organization to process information without distortion.[38] The policy studies imply that the problems could be alleviated by changes in the policy design to eliminate the technical problems. For example, Pressman and Wildavsky suggest shortening the chain of decisions; Levine proposes policies that do not rely on decentralized administration of centrally formulated rules but on manipulations of incentives; and Sundquist proposes structures that will facilitate coordination.

This optimism is challenged by a conflicting view of the implementation process that sees it primarily as a political process and maintains that the major impediments to implementation are not technical but political. The implementation process is seen by this group of social scientists as involving basic differences in preferences about outcomes and in beliefs about how to achieve desired outcomes. Jeffrey Pressman's study of federal programs in Oakland emphasizes the political characteristics of the implementation process, using an analogy with foreign aid that has built-in conflict between the needs of the donor and recipient.[39] Similarly Stephen Mittenthal's and Hans Spiegal's study of the model cities planning process in Oakland, New Haven, and the South Bronx reveals the political struggle between neighborhoods and city hall for control of policy implementation.[40] The implication in these studies is that improvements in implementation depend upon changes in the demands being generated by the participants in the political conflict.

Both the technical and political views of implementation stress the wide gulf between the expected and the actual results of policies. Both stress the amount of distortion that occurs. There seems to be an emerging consensus that implementation results from the complex interaction of multiple factors including technical and political factors.[41]

Graham Allison has developed some useful labels to show the multiple processes involved in policy formulation in foreign and military affairs. The three major processes according to Allison are: rational actor, organizational process, and governmental politics. The organizational process model indicates that decisions are the result not just of rational calculations but of the interests, procedures, and repertoires of the organizations involved in the decisions. For example, the State Department, the Defense Department, and the CIA disagreed over the alternatives open to the United States once the installation of Soviet missiles on Cuba was discovered. They had contrasting estimates of what needed to be done and which organizations should do it. These estimates were linked to their organizational interests[42] and shaped the substance of the decisions. The governmental politics model indicates that decisions also reflect the outcome of bargaining among the participants that is shaped by their power and skill in the bargaining process.[43] For example, Allison describes in detail the "bargaining, pulling, hauling, and spurring" that went on within President Kennedy's Executive Committee before the decision to blockade Cuba was reached.[44]

No conceptualization of the multiple processes in policy implementation has achieved as much prominence as Allison's but recent works on policy implementation show many parallels with Allison. They show that policy implementation is every bit as complex as policy formulation. Let me review two of these.

Martin Rein and Francine Rabinovitz suggest a theoretical perspective on domestic policy implementation.[45] First, they review three approaches to implementation calling these the administrative, competitive, and the executive management approaches. The *administrative* approach sees implementation as the administration by subordinates of directives from their superiors. The *competitive* approach views implementation as an area where the conflicts of different interest groups are settled. The *management* approach sees implementation as the result of executive initiative. Then Rein and Rabinovitz present a fourth view that synthesizes the three preceding views and tries to go beyond them.

They view implementation as a process in which purpose is redefined at each stage in the process. They say that implementation is government choices shaped by actors who participate in a circular process involving reciprocal power relations and negotiations.[46] At each stage in the interaction three imperatives are operating and, when they are in conflict, must be resolved. The *legal imperative* stresses the importance of compliance with legislative mandates; the *consensual imperative* stresses the need to take into consideration the wishes of various interest groups inside and outside the government; and the *rational imperative* says that the executive and his/her bureaucracy must take into account other standards such as professional norms, organizational needs, and feasibility.

The resolution among these imperatives is primarily determined by three factors: the purposes of the policy (how clear and consistent they are, how much importance is attached to them); the resources committed to implementing the policies; and the complexity of the implementing process.[47] They hypothesize that low saliency programs with unclear goals will be implemented in a complex and circular process, while high saliency programs with clear goals will be implemented in a more central and hierarchical fashion.[48] In illustrating this perspective on implementation the authors review past experiences with the implementation of domestic policy from urban renewal to economic development to poverty programs.

Gene Bardach also stresses the complexity of factors shaping implementation. He conceptualizes implementation as a process involving the operation of numerous interrelated games.[49] The outcomes of these games shape the nature of the program elements that actually occur. Bardach explains implementation as a process of putting together a program using components controlled by different people whose decisions about contributing depend on the outcome of a series of complex games.[50] He classifies the implementation games that arise in the competition for control over the policies, resources, and services of the new programs as follows: easy money, bureaucracy, pork barrel, piling on, tenacity, odd man out, up for grabs, and reputation. These new games often have new stakes, rules, and players. In addition, Bardach considers control games, delaying games, and attempts to fix games.

These studies and others such as Helen Ingram's treatment of implementation as a process of bargaining, with a succession of bids and counter-bids between the participants with different goals,[51] and the work by Donald Van Meter and Carl Van Horn,[52] all agree that implementation in a decentralized political system with a multiplicity of competing groups is just as complex as the other parts of the policy-making process, involving both technical and political aspects. It is shaped by the competition between mobilized groups, their resources, and strategies,[53] and is characterized by unclear and contradictory goals, lack of knowledge and resources, and many unintended results.

Variations in Implementation

A third issue in the study of implementation is what factors explain variations in the way different cities respond to federal policy. As social scientists become more familiar with the general results and processes suggested above, they are trying to make finer distinctions and better explanations of the patterns. Attempts are being made to explain why one type of policy is implemented differently from another kind of policy and why one city implements a given policy differently from another city. Social scientists are trying to answer questions such as: How will city x's implementation of a given policy differ from city y's implementation? What criteria distinguish the cities that will best implement a given policy?

The "determinants" literature on local policy output suggests a range of variables that presumably influence the way a local government implements federal policy.[54] These include socioeconomic and electoral characteristics, group demands, city government structure, and attitudes of decision makers. There is space here to review only a few of the hypotheses about the influence these factors have on cities' implementation of federal social policy.

The most widely accepted hypothesis is that socioeconomic characteristics have a major impact on city response. Michael Aiken and Robert Alford's studies of public housing, urban renewal, and poverty conclude that the poorer, larger cities are more responsive to federal social policy.[55] A review of model cities programs in 148 cities finds that medium-size cities show the best results.[56] Other studies conclude that the size and proportion of black population accounts for the major variations in implementation.[57] Less attention has been given to the importance of electoral characteristics but Ralph Kramer finds that where political power is concentrated, partisan, and influenced by minority votes, implementation of the Economic Opportunity Act was characterized by strong conflict.[58]

Many studies emphasize the importance of group demands in explaining implementation, but no consensus exists on whether strong ethnic coalitions facilitate or impede implementation. Some studies emphasize the positive contributions of ethnic coalitions. James Vanecko's study of the war on poverty, for example, concludes that conflict between minorities and city hall results in more effective programs.[59] Paul Peterson finds that higher levels of conflict in poverty programs were associated with stronger demands for basic changes in city services for the poor.[60] Bennett Harrison's study of model cities employment finds that where black political power is higher employment of ghetto residents increases.[61] Fred Wirt, too, stresses the beneficial results of strongly organized minority demands.[62] But other studies conclude that cooperation between minority groups and government officials results in better programs.[63] *Making Federalism Work*, for example, extolls the virtues of strong city hall involvement in model cities programs and advocates a balance between community participation and central coordination.[64] Similarly, the Marshall Kaplan, Gans, and Kahn studies of model cities conclude that when resident groups dominate the implementation process, the results are not as satisfactory as when there is parity between the residents and the staff. They argue that local performance is best when residents and staff have approximately equal influence over the programs and this situation is most likely to occur where resident groups are cohesive and politically integrated but where the level of demands and conflict is not too high.[65] Richard Cole comes to the same conclusion in his study of 26 different kinds of citizen participation programs. He says that moderate group demands and participation are associated with more material benefits and satisfaction for participants.[66]

A number of hypotheses have been suggested about the importance of city government structure for output. J. David Greenstone and Paul

Peterson maintain that reformed governments disperse power via broad participation in poverty programs but do not disperse material perquisites as effectively as nonreformed governments.[67] Bennett Harrison says the more bureaucratized a government is and the greater the centralization of power in the mayor, the less willing a city is to hire ghetto residents for model cities jobs.[68]

The attitudes of decision makers or levels of professionalism have also been used to explain variations in city policy implementation. Martha Derthick finds that the personal preferences of welfare administrators are the major source of variations in Massachusetts' administration of welfare policy.[69] Joel Handler and Ellen Jane Hollingsworth come to similar conclusions about welfare implementation in Wisconsin.[70] The model cities studies also emphasize the importance of the support of the chief executive; when the executive is actively involved in facilitating the program, the results are better than when that backing is absent.[71]

In addition to hypotheses about local factors shaping policy implementation, there are also hypotheses suggesting that federal factors are important in influencing variations in implementation.[72] Important federal factors include the type of policy and the strength with which it is implemented by the federal agencies, in other words, the amount of resources put into implementation and the strictness with which federal officials supervise the local governments. An important book on variations in local distribution of resources finds that federal programs in education that require compensatory distribution result in educational outcomes that differ from the outcomes in streets and libraries where no such federal requirements exist.[73] This finding seems easily transferable to social policy.

Little systematic study has been made of the relative influence of federal versus local factors in policy implementation. Both Martha Derthick and Frederick Wirt argue convincingly that local factors are at least as important as federal factors. Martha Derthick attributes the failure of the "new towns in-town" policy to the federal government's inability to control local governments.[74] Wirt says that the implementation of civil rights legislation in the South depended on the clarity of the federal regulations, the vigor of the federal regulators, and the strength of the local forces being regulated and benefitted by the regulation.[75] Studies looking at federal/local interaction in social policy raise questions about the changing nature of the American federal system and of the appropriate balance between the power of the national government and local governments.

Review of the hypotheses about variations in city implementation of federal social policies calls attention to the normative implications of the various generalizations. Each hypothesis implies ways of improving implementation that can be inferred from the variables which are emphasized. For example, analysts who stress the positive importance of group demands imply that strengthening this factor would improve policy implementation; those who stress the importance of governmental structures imply that reorganizing structures would make a real improvement in policy implementation; those focusing on attitudes of decision makers imply that changing the decision makers would help; and those who emphasize federal factors imply that this is where the major changes should be made. Thus, even studies that do not seem to be oriented to reform have implications for reform. Explanations of policy implementation can be used to suggest which factors are the most important to reform.

Review of the hypotheses also calls attention to the shortcomings of the "determinants" literature on local policy output. Results vary according to the indicators used;[76] causal linkages and reciprocal relations are sometimes ignored in favor of correlations;[77] and many questions about the quality of life and the distribution of resources within a given city are not addressed by these studies.[78]

Conclusion

Review of the literature on the implementation of federal social policy reveals that our knowledge, like our policy, is very fragmentary. But in spite of the literature's limitations, it has contributed to a greater awareness of the importance of implementation's results, processes, and variations. We know a lot more about these issues than we did a decade ago, and many aspects of the implementation of categorical grants for social programs have become familiar. Some of the interesting analytical tasks that remain are:

1. We need more specification of the various criteria that can be used to evaluate policy results and appreciation of the shortcomings of various types of evaluations. We must educate ourselves so that we can critically assess experts' conclusions about the success or failure of various programs.

2. We need more appreciation of the complex implementation process. We should be able to recognize that poor implementation may reflect many factors beyond simple bungling or evil intentions, including the technical and political complexity of large postindustrial social systems.

3. We need to specify theories of implementation that can account for the variations (or distortions) which occur. We want to know why different cities implement the same social policy in differing ways and why one type of policy is implemented differently from another type of policy. In other words, we want to be able to determine the relative importance of the various factors that shape the implementation process and results, so we

can attempt to change those factors that will have the greatest positive results.

However, now that the pattern of the implementation of categorical social grants has become familiar, the content of federal social policy is undergoing major changes. Categorical grants are being cut and replaced by revenue sharing and block grants. *The New Federalism* by Michael Reagan describes the rationale behind this change to federal grants with fewer strings and thus less federal control over local policy implementation.[79] Studies of these new grants are beginning to be published. David Caputo and Richard Cole report on the use of general revenue sharing in cities over 50,000.[80] Richard Nathan is directing a Brookings study of revenue sharing in selected cities, counties, and states.[81] Randall Ripley has done a study of the initial implementation stages of the Comprehensive Employment and Training Act, a block grant for employment programs.[82] And Steven Waldhorn compares the categorical with the postcategorical era.[83]

Some expect the new social policies to be very different from their predecessors; some expect them to be very similar. In either case, they raise issues of implementation—issues of results, process, and variation. And attention to these issues will contribute to the unending human quest to understand the social system that shapes our behavior but that our actions can also shape. Study of social policy implementation, like policy formulation, is an attempt to increase our understanding of, and thus our control over, decisions about the distribution of social benefits in our society.

Notes

1. Kenneth Dolbeare, "The Impacts of Public Policy," in C.P. Cotter, ed., *Political Science Annual: An International Review,* Vol. V (Indianapolis: Bobbs-Merrill, 1975).

2. Murray Edelman, *The Symbolic Uses of Politics* (Urbana: University of Illinois Press, 1964).

3. Edward Banfield, *The Unheavenly City Revisited* (Boston: Little, Brown and Co., 1974).

4. Daniel Moynihan, *Maximum Feasible Misunderstanding* (New York: Free Press, 1970).

5. Frances Piven and Richard Cloward, *Regulating the Poor* (New York: Vintage Books, 1971).

6. Ira Katznelson, "Participation and Political Buffers in Urban America," paper presented at the Annual Meeting of The American Political Science Association, Washington, D.C. (September, 1972).

7. Theodore Lowi, *The End of Liberalism* (New York: Norton, 1969).

8. Martha Derthick, *New Towns In-Town* (Washington: The Urban Institute, 1972).

9. Francine Rabinovitz and Helene Smookler, "Rhetoric and Performance: The National Politics and Administration of U.S. New Community Development Legislation," paper presented at the Conference on Human Factors in New Town Development, University of California, Los Angeles (June, 1972).

10. Robert Alford, "Local Autonomy and the Quality of Life," paper presented at the European Urbanism Conference, Los Angeles (June, 1972).

11. Robert Levine, *The Poor Ye Need Not Have* (Cambridge: Massachusetts Institute of Technology Press, 1970).

12. Martha Derthick, *The Influence of Federal Grants* (Cambridge: Harvard University Press, 1970).

13. Harrell Rodgers and Charles Bullock, *Law and Social Change* (New York: McGraw Hill, 1972).

14. Richard Cole, *Citizen Participation and the Urban Policy Process* (Lexington, Mass.: Lexington Books, D.C. Heath, 1974).

15. Jeffrey Pressman and Aaron Wildavsky, *Implementation* (Berkeley: University of California Press, 1973).

16. Alice Rivlin, *Systematic Thinking for Social Action* (Washington: Brookings, 1971).

17. Peter Rossi and Walter Williams, *Evaluating Social Programs: Theory, Practice, and Politics* (New York: Seminar Press, 1972).

18. Walter Williams, *Social Policy Research and Analysis: The Experience in The Federal Agencies* (New York: American Elsevier Publishing Co., 1971).

19. Joseph Wholey et al., *Federal Evaluation Policy* (Washington: The Urban Institute, 1970).

20. Joseph Wholey, "Many Useless Evaluations of Federal Programs Churned Out" in *Search: A Report From The Urban Institute,* Vol. 4, Nos. 3-4 (August, 1974).

21. Peter Rossi, Richard Berk, and Bettye Eidson, *The Roots of Urban Discontent* (New York: John Wiley, 1974).

22. Dale Rogers Marshall, "Public Participation and The Politics of Poverty," in Peter Orleans and William Ellis, Jr., eds., *Race, Change, and Urban Society,* Urban Affairs Annual Review No. 5. (Beverly Hills: Sage Publications, 1971).

23. Sar Levitan, *The Great Society's Poor Law* (Baltimore: Johns Hopkins Press, 1969).

24. J. David Greenstone and Paul Peterson, *Race and Authority in Urban Politics* (New York: Russell Sage Foundation, 1973).

25. Ibid., p. 293.

26. Ibid., pp. 296 and 315.

27. Marshall Kaplan, Gans, and Kahn, "The Model Cities Program: A Comparative Analysis of City Response Patterns and Their Relation to Future Urban Policy," Office of Community Development, Department of Housing and Urban Development, no date. See also Neil Gilbert and Harry Specht, "Planning for Model Cities: Process, Product, Performance and Predictions." Sub-study of the Model Cities Evaluation by Marshall Kaplan, Gans, and Kahn, San Francisco, undated (mimeographed).

28. James Sundquist, *Making Federalism Work* (Washington: Brookings, 1969).

29. George Washnis, *Community Development Strategies:* Case Studies (New York: Praeger, 1974).

30. "Citizen Action in Model Cities and CAP Programs: Case Studies and Evaluation," *Public Administration Review,* Special Issue, 32 (September, 1972).

31. Randall Ripley, *The Politics of Economic and Human Resource Development* (Indianapolis: Bobbs-Merrill, 1972).

32. Eli Ginzberg and Robert Solow, eds., *The Great Society: Lessons for the Future* (New York: Basic Books, 1974).

33. Ibid., p. 220.

34. Rufus Browning and Dale Rogers Marshall, "Implementation of Model Cities and Revenue Sharing in 10 Bay Area Cities," paper presented at the Annual Meeting of the American Political Science Association, Chicago (September, 1974).

35. Pressman and Wildavsky, p. 93.

36. Robert Levine, *Public Planning* (New York: Basic Books, 1972).

37. James Sundquist, *Making Federalism Work* (Washington: Brookings, 1969).

38. Anthony Downs, *Inside Bureaucracy* (Boston: Little, Brown, 1967); James March and Herbert Simon, *Organization* (New York: John Wiley, 1958); Charles Lindblom, *The Intelligence of Democracy* (New York: Free Press, 1965).

39. Jeffrey Pressman, "City Politics and Federal Programs," dissertation, University of California, Berkeley, 1972.

40. Stephen Mittenthal and Hans Spiegel, "Urban Confrontation: City versus Neighborhood in the Model Cities Planning Process," Institute of Urban Environment, School of Architecture, Columbia University, 1970.

See also Dale Rogers Marshall, *The Politics of Participation in Poverty* (Berkeley: University of California Press, 1971).

41. Rufus Browning, Dale Rogers Marshall, and David Tabb, "City Implementation of Federal Social Policies," Research Proposal, 1975 (mimeographed).

42. Graham Allison, *Essence of Decision* (Boston: Little, Brown, 1971), pp. 122-23.

43. Ibid., p. 145.

44. Ibid., p. 210.

45. Martin Rein and Francine Rabinovitz, "Implementation: A Theoretical Perspective" (Manuscript, 1974).

46. Ibid., p. 9.

47. Ibid., p. 53.

48. Ibid., p. 44.

49. Gene Bardach, "The Implementation Game" (Manuscript, 1974), p. 138.

50. Ibid., p. 144.

51. Helen Ingram, "Impacts of Environmental Policy," paper presented at the Western Political Science meeting (San Diego, April, 1974), p. 3.

52. Donald Van Meter and Carl Van Horn, "The Policy Implementation Process: A Conceptual Framework," *Administration and Society,* Vol. 6, no. 4 (February, 1975).

53. Dale Rogers Marshall and Janell Anderson, "Implementation and The Equal Rights Amendment" (Manuscript, 1975).

54. Brett Hawkins, *Politics and Urban Policies* (Indianapolis: Bobbs Merrill, 1971); Robert Fried, "Comparative Urban Performance," European Urban Research, September, 1973. Richard Hofferbert, "State and Community Policy Studies: A Review of Comparative Input-Output Analysis," *Political Science Annual* (Indianapolis: Bobbs-Merrill, 1972). John Kirlin and Steve Erie, "The Study of City Governance and Public Policy Making", *Public Administration Review,* Vol. 32 (March/April, 1972).

55. Michael Aiken and Robert Alford, "Community Structure and Innovation: The Case of Public Housing," *American Political Science Review,* Vol. 64, No. 3 (September, 1970).

56. Marshall Kaplan, Gans, and Kahn, *The Model Cities Program: A Comparative Analysis of City Response Patterns* (mimeographed), 1973.

57. David Austin, "Resident Participation: Political Mobilization or Organizational Co-optation?" PAR, Special Issue (September, 1972);

Melvin Mogulof, "Citizen Participation: The Local Perspective" (Washington: The Urban Institute, March, 1970); Cole, *Citizen Participation*.

58. Ralph Kramer, *Participation of the Poor* (Englewood Cliffs, N.J.: Prentice-Hall, 1969).

59. James Vanecko, "Community Mobilization and Institutional Change: The Influence of the Community Action Program in Large Cities," *Social Science Quarterly*, Vol. 50, No. 3 (December, 1969), pp. 609-30.

60. Paul Peterson, "Forms of Representation," *American Political Science Review,* Vol. 64, No. 2 (June, 1970).

61. Bennett Harrison, "Ghetto Employment and the Model Cities Program," paper presented at the Annual Meeting of the American Political Science Association (Washington, D.C., September, 1972).

62. Frederick Wirt, *Politics of Southern Equality* (Chicago: Aldine, 1970).

63. U.S. Congress, Senate Subcommittee on Employment, Manpower and Poverty of the Committee on Labor and Public Welfare, *Examination of The War on Poverty: Staff and Consultant Reports* (90th Congress, 1st Session, 1967); Howard Hallman, "Federally Financed Citizen Participation," *Public Administration Review,* Special Issue, 32 (September 1972), pp. 421-28.

64. Sundquist, *Making Federalism Work.*

65. Marshall Kaplan, Gans, and Kahn, "The Model Cities Program."

66. Cole, *Citizen Participation,* p. 119.

67. J. David Greenstone and Paul Peterson, "Reformers, Machines, and the War on Poverty," in James Wilson, ed., *City Politics and Public Policy* (New York: John Wiley, 1968).

68. Harrison, "Ghetto Employment."

69. Derthick, *The Influence of Federal Grants.*

70. Joel Handler and Ellen Jane Hollingsworth, *The Deserving Poor* (Chicago: Markham, 1971).

71. Gilbert and Specht, "Planning for Model Cities."

72. Pressman and Wildavsky, *Implementation*; Levine, *Public Planning;* Lowi, *End of Liberalism;* Rein and Rabinovitz, "Implementation."

73. Frank Levy, Arnold Meltsner, and Aaron Wildavsky, *Urban Outcomes* (Berkeley: University of California Press, 1974), p. 223.

74. Derthick, *New Towns In-Town,* p. 83.

75. Wirt, *Politics of Southern Equality.*

76. John L. Sullivan, "A Note on Redistributive Politics," *American*

Political Science Review, Vol. 66 (December, 1972), pp. 1301-5; Brian Fry and Richard Winters, "The Politics of Redistribution," *American Political Science Review,* Vol. 64 (June, 1970), pp. 508-22.

77. Edward Fowler and Robert Lineberry, "Comparative Policy Analysis and the Problem of Reciprocal Causation," in Craig Liske, William Loehr, and John McCamaut, eds., *Comparative Public Policy* (Beverly Hills: Sage Publications, 1974).

78. Robert Alford, "Local Autonomy and the Quality of Life."

79. Michael Reagan, *The New Federalism* (New York: Oxford University Press, 1972).

80. David Caputo and Richard Cole, *Urban Politics and Decentralization* (Lexington, Mass.: Lexington Books, D.C. Heath, 1974).

81. Richard Nathan, Allen Manvel, Susannah Calkins, and Associates, *Monitoring Revenue Sharing* (Washington: Brookings, 1975).

82. Randall Ripley, "Evaluating Implementation: The Case of CETA," paper presented at the Annual Meeting of the Midwest Political Science Association, Chicago (May 1975).

83. Steven Waldhorn, "The Role of Neighborhood Government in Postcategorical Programs," in J. Sneed and S. Waldhorn, eds., *Restructuring the Federal System* (New York: Crane Russak & Co., 1975).

2

Politics and Information in Three Antipoverty Programs

Leonard Rubin

The Politics of Information: Clarifications

Information is necessary to formulate and administer public policy, if only to identify the problems to be confronted and to provide a basis for estimating costs and results. But only rarely is such information sought and provided without reference as well to other, more political, considerations. Undoubtedly, there are many ways of thinking about the relationships between politics and information.[1] I am going to consider what I call the politics of information in terms of three components: political purposes in seeking information; political conditions affecting who provides the information; and political influences on the use of information.

First, information is often sought for political advantage: to advocate, defend, or attack a policy, program, or stance on a particular issue. Whether the information obtained can then be used depends both on the political position of those who sought it and on the nature and quality of the information provided. A research design, to be acceptable, must get at the substance of the policy problem and accommodate political exigencies. But in the effort to meet the needs of those who seek the information, research may be attempted that involves particularly difficult strategies or that results in conclusions that are too politically challenging.

Second, political conditions may determine whether information on social policy is provided primarily by a technical staff within an agency or through contracts and grants. Crucial to such determinations is the degree of political stability and the political character of an agency or of programs it administers—sometimes the two are related. As political stability increases so, too, does reliance on technical staff within an agency for research, analysis, and evaluation.

Third, the particular information that gains primary recognition indicates which political influences are ascendant and what attitudes are most acceptable in the circumstances. How forcefully information is put forth may be indicative of the strength in political position of those using it, or it may indicate the degree of partisanship or the intensity of the feelings of those involved. In any event, knowledge is sought and provided in the hope

This chapter represents the views of the author only. I am indebted to Professor David L. Paletz of Duke University for excellent substantive and editorial commentary. Wayne Finegar, long involved in applied research, has offered very useful observations.

21

that it can be acted upon; and knowledge of problems constitutes a challenge to policy makers to confront those problems. But where politics has
the effect of inhibiting action or where it affects the usability of knowledge,
knowledge itself becomes part of politics and tension is created when the
extent of what is known is at odds with what can be done.

These three components of the politics of information are by no means
mutually exclusive. Rather, they combine variously, depending on the
nature and complexity of the politics in which a policy issue is involved. To
give some insight into the dynamics of the politics of information, I use
illustrations from three antipoverty programs. The examples are chosen to
represent different types of bureaucracies with different degrees of political
stability and different political characters.[2]

**Employment of the Disadvantaged and the Manpower
Administration**

Most of the employment programs for the disadvantaged poor went to the
Manpower Administration in the Department of Labor. These programs, to
provide training or retraining, supportive services, and placement, were
newly initiated with emphasis on the poor in the mid-sixties. They involved
a measure both of social and economic intervention and also a client
population quite alien to the purposes, style, and clientele long associated
with this old-line agency that had previously been involved primarily with
unions and the regular labor force but not much with the poor who constituted the marginal labor force. The clientele of the established programs,
in comparison with the poor who were the new clientele, were well organized, wielding considerable political and economic influence. The staff
already within the department were differently oriented from much of the
new staff associated with the antipoverty effort and had more direct formal
and informal connections with the main lines of decision making in the
upper echelons of the department and with established committees in
Congress. The attempt to organize the old and new staffs together to cope
with the new responsibilities resulted in considerable organizational and
program instability within the Manpower Administration and considerable
unease among the personnel.

These conditions were reflected in the reporting systems designed to
provide information on the ways in which money was spent and on the
results achieved in the areas of job training, placement, and supportive
services. These reporting systems may be studied to provide insight into
three aspects of the politics of information: who provides the information
and how; what the political purposes are; and how the information is
actually used.

Established leadership in the Manpower Administration retained, at considerable cost, a large accounting firm to construct an information reporting system for manpower programs. The system that was developed focused on such items as the number of training slots needed; the number available; type of training, placement, and other services provided; number of completions; and number of placements. These data were provided by Department of Labor staff from program reporting forms. However, reasons for successes and failures were not included and, therefore, the sort of information needed to improve programs was not routinely provided.

This reporting system was close in character to the sort already in use for the older politically established programs which themselves seemed to work well for those who became unemployed after having been steadily employed—not just in the marginal labor force. This system, relatively politically neutral, became the major source of data for the review and generation of manpower programs by policy makers. Commitment to it on the part of decision makers grew with each decision taken: the choice of contractor; the spending of considerable amounts of public money; and instituting and using the system. All this reflected and added to the inertia of established manpower programs and agencies.

The reporting system did show that manpower programs for the poor were largely ineffective; but it did not show how and why. As a result many programs were cancelled or subsumed within other programs. Effective revision of programs was rare. Overcoming the disadvantages associated with poverty was proving to be difficult, and so was the attempt to translate marginal labor into regular work. The newer portion of the staff, directly concerned with the antipoverty effort, recognizing this much, sought information to document the problems and to provide a basis for devising effective programs or improving existing ones. Since the dominant information system did not provide the necessary data and analyses, these had to be sought elsewhere.

Considerable resources were provided for contracts and grants to individuals and research groups to provide information that would be germane to the problems of employment among the poor. Research reports ranged over a broad variety of topics from labor economics to social psychology. But the contributions of the information to solving employment problems of the poor were often small and difficult to assess: too often information was not effectively disseminated; the applicability of some was problematic, given limited resources and the extent of intervention comtemplated; where it was used for policy, appropriations rarely sufficed. To stimulate and broaden interest in research results and to increase their impact, the director of the Office of Manpower Research negotiated a contract for an evaluation of the experimental and demonstration research program.[3] The evaluation was critical of the fact that the results of the research, while often of worth, were not more generally disseminated and effective, and remedies were suggested. Reactions to the evaluation were mixed but so, too, were reactions to the critical implications of research results.

One of the earmarks of the war on poverty was the immense amount of exploratory and evaluative research that was produced under contracts and grants—produced, that is, by persons or staffs working outside of the formal lines of influence that obtain within the institutions of the system. Such staffs may be free to be critical but they have little power.

The reasons are, of course, political. The research reports produced were often critical of policies and not much restrained by political concerns in their analyses of the relationships between questions of employment and the host of other issues raised in antipoverty research. Information resulting from the second information system was often seen as threatening to established programs and policies. It is also true that knowledge stemming from research on employment and poverty may have shown the task of solving the problems to be so great as to result in a paralysis of policy given political limitations on the commitment to solve them.[4] The impulse to avoid the findings of research that might serve to complicate issues and threaten political compromises and established policy commitments was evident not only in the bureaucracy but also in Congress, where supporters of the antipoverty policies wished to prevent critical issues from being raised that might serve the ends of those who opposed the extant programs.

It is interesting to consider that where programs are relatively experimental and where changes in ways of conceiving policy are thought to be too challenging to established political lines, relevant information is likely to be held at arm's length. In other words, where policies and programs are being developed and where political support is tentative, the free flow of a broad spectrum of information is least acceptable, albeit extremely important in the early stages of policy development. Nor, apparently is it difficult for a congressional committee to have generated information that is challenging and then to fail to use it in the actual legislative processes of authorization and appropriation.[5]

Legal Representation for the Poor and the Neighborhood Legal Services

The Neighborhood Legal Services (NLS) program was established within the Office of Economic Opportunity (OEO) as an offshoot of the Community Action program. The program to provide legal services to the poor had the support of the American Bar Association—support that remained firm throughout the history of the program. The immediate political environment within the OEO was sympathetic, though the OEO was often involved in difficult political circumstances. The Legal Services program itself was divided between providing services, like getting redress for clients with specific complaints, and more general law reform work. The latter was far more politically percussive, involving as it did class actions aimed at getting judgements on statutory or constitutional grounds. This division of functions became an issue: which should the program emphasize and espouse as its main objective?

Eventually the issue was decided in favor of law reform, perhaps because the attorneys who provided services most ably were also the most active in law reform and received support from such legal services backup centers as the Center on Social Welfare Policy and Law at Columbia University.[6] Law reform activities also acted as a catalyst for political action: the National Welfare Rights Organization received great impetus from the activities of legal services attorneys. This effect, together with the success of the attorneys in obtaining redress and their energy and expertise in pushing for law reform begat political reactions, like those of Governor Reagan of California. In brief, legal services attorneys were exerting pressure on political decision makers to readjust budget decisions, alter administrative practices and change statutes governing public policy on poverty issues (in Texas this involved the state constitution) in ways that did not jibe with the views of the political leaders or of administrators committed to established practices. As a result the Legal Services program was seen increasingly as a political threat, and moves to curtail or dismantle it materialized, creating serious concern from 1969 on among those involved in the program.

One expression of this concern may be seen in a decision to obtain through contract an overall evaluation of the program to identify its strengths and weaknesses and to provide, it was hoped, a factual basis for defending the program against emasculation and for showing the worth and propriety of its efforts. The evaluation process was under the direction of a separate OEO staff that was interested in careful research. Obviously they were not seeking an antipathetic evaluation or evaluator, and they worked with NLS staff, accommodating the objectives of the evaluation to the needs and concerns of the NLS. The fact that the goals of the Legal Services program were being subjected to increasing political pressure and that the evaluation was not isolated from the political circumstances was recognized and responded to by the eventual contractor, although this does not mean that their analyses were actually biased by political factors.

In the spring of 1970 OEO accepted a proposal for the evaluation research that manifested in three ways a position more than moderately sympathetic to the Neighborhood Legal Services program. First, the introduction to the proposal emphasized the importance of the program and the pertinence of its work in terms that were positive rather than neutral and that went beyond the requirement to demonstrate an understanding of the program. Second, an extensive list of consultants, competent in special aspects of the research and knowledgeable in the area being investigated, emphasized those who were actively involved in poverty law work, including prominent poverty law attorneys—persons whose activities indicated their sympathies. There can be no doubt that such consultants could contribute to the perceptiveness and pertinence of the research—sympathy and objectivity are not mutually exclusive. But in the world of contract research part of the means to success is the ability of those who write proposals for research to discern and accommodate the attitudes and needs of those who request proposals. This proposal, more than the others that were submitted, displayed such ability, in addition to giving the usual evidence of technical expertise, methodological objectivity, and professionalism, which, of course, carry great weight.

Third, the research strategy chosen, and accepted by OEO evaluation staff, indicated that the proposal was suited to the concern of NLS staff to show the worth and propriety of their efforts, including law reform activities. The strategy chosen—the most ambitious of types of approaches to evaluation—was to attempt to measure the impact, on some scale of success-failure, of the goals of service and law reform. There is no space for the details here; it must suffice to say that for technical and substantive reasons appropriate measures could not be devised and the strategy proved to be unworkable. Midway in the research the contractor and the monitors, fulfilling their obligations as researchers, substituted a less ambitious and less politically useful strategy, one that eschewed examination of the goals and focused instead on comparing legal services with other types of programs for their relative efficacy and costs in helping the poor with their legal problems. Given the biases of the Nixon administration and the resulting pressure to dismantle not only the NLS but the OEO as well, perhaps no information would have been significant enough to turn the political balance in favor of the program as then constituted. Apparently, as with much of the Manpower research, the evaluation of the NLS has not been put to much use.[7]

Income Security for the Aged and the Social Security Administration

We have been concerned so far with programs that have contemplated considerable social and economic intervention without having a secure political base. The administering agencies were, as with the Department of Labor, an old line agency with other primary commitments and established political support or, as with the Office of Economic Opportunity, one committed solely to new poverty programs with limited political support. Poverty policy served the needs of a population that was, by and large, politically inert, having too small an economic base and too little demonstrated power at the polls to exert much consistent political influence.

By contrast, the Social Security Administration is politically stable, and the programs it administers have general political support. The population it serves is a voting population with a clear pecuniary interest in social security programs that through cash benefits provide a measure of economic security for disabled and retired workers and their dependents or survivors. Although social security programs result in considerable economic intervention they have no direct authorization to intervene in social and political aspects of policy issues, providing no supportive, legal, or training services. Social security programs are labeled as social insurance rather than as social welfare programs. The character of the cash benefit program was hammered out in the 1930s and so were many of the major political issues raised with regard to it. Revision of the program in response to emerging needs in the population has been gradual though continual, with the basic character of the program being carefully preserved, and carefully excluded from the array of specifically antipoverty programs of the 1960s.

Nevertheless, social security programs play a large role in antipoverty efforts, because relatively large proportions of social security beneficiaries are poor when they enter the system, and oftentimes those who are not poor when they become beneficiaries find that their retirement income hardly keeps them out of poverty. But, the role played by cash benefits as a type of antipoverty policy is peculiarly difficult, both politically and administratively, for several interrelated reasons.

Social security benefits are earned: the amount of benefits is calculated on the basis of amount of earnings in covered employment averaged over the number of years that a worker is considered to be in the labor force for his or her working life. Social security benefits are secured by the social security trust fund reserves and payroll tax on workers and employers; the tax is a specified percentage of a fixed portion of covered earnings. This policy reflects the attitude of a majority of workers and political and policy leaders, who hold that benefits are something that should be earned and that it is proper that relative success in work should result in higher benefits. Although the policy also provides that earnings are replaced at a higher rate for low earners, benefits are nevertheless higher for more successful workers. Moreover, given the regressive nature of the tax that supports the funding system, lower earners pay a higher proportion of their earnings. It is this system that passed its political crises 40 years ago, and since then its basic structure has not been politically challenged (though problems are arising that may affect the political stability of the program).

However, this does not mean that the system has always rested easily and suffered no challenge at all.[8] The workers who become entitled to benefits have, for the most part, already played out the better part of their working lives. Those who were poor or nearly poor as workers usually remain so as beneficiaries and, while poverty is forestalled or alleviated for some, others may even become poorer when they can no longer work. It is generally conceived that the system cannot be expected to make up such disadvantages after the fact. But this view is challenged in two basic ways: first, by arguments, usually based on research, which maintain that payment by workers of a regressive tax means that workers are involved in the system prior to becoming entitled to benefits and that the regressive tax adds to the burden of the relatively unsuccessful workers; second, by arguments, based on research that elaborates the conditions under which the beneficiaries live who are socially and economically disadvantaged, which maintain that such conditions among the program clientele cannot be accepted. These arguments and the information accompanying them do not go unnoticed. The question here is how these politically difficult issues are dealt with by the Social Security Administration, recognizing the human misery created by poverty.

The Social Security Administration does maintain a modest grant and contract program that funds research on the program and on the client population by external researchers. But most of the data and analysis for policy review and program monitoring are produced within the Social Security Administration by the Office of Research and Statistics—in contrast to the two agencies already discussed. Orientations in research are taken from questions raised in Congress and in the research itself, from the views of a statutory Advisory Council, from observation of changes in the program or beneficiary population, and from issues raised by outside researchers or interest groups. The research produced by the Office of Research and Statistics is used both to provide evidence of needed changes in the program and to serve as a guide in establishing alternatives and choosing from among them. In addition, this in-house technical staff relates economic and sociological material to the structure of the program and its functions. In all this, disadvantaged groups in the client population receive considerable attention.

The role of the technical advisory staff in the Social Security Administration benefits from the general political stability of the agency and its programs. For this reason the value function of the technical advisory staff, expressed through the specification and analysis of key issues, for instance, of those relating to poverty and disadvantage, may be more acceptable to policy makers and political leaders than is perhaps generally the case for programs or agencies with less political support. Because political commitment to social security is strong, information and analyses that clearly define the politically difficult issues of poverty for social security do not often generate serious political repercussions and are not seen as so politically threatening that the results of the research are shelved.

The conditions of poverty and related program issues are the subjects of research, position papers, and open discussion. But between the resulting knowledge, clearly put, and the resistance to action to solve the problems, a tension exists by virtue of the political limitations on the possibilities for action. To act on these issues is seen as politically risky by those who fear that change may undermine the important functions performed by the program. There is, as well, an ideological element in the resistance to program changes, an element antipathetic to changing the program from one of social insurance to one of social welfare, from one in which benefits are earned to one in which payments are based on need. Whether or not an active pursuit of program changes to cope better with poverty among the aged would produce a political reaction that would do more than just reject the changes, that would in fact jeopardize social security programs, is a key question.

What is at issue here is that a program not designed to cope with a particular problem is nevertheless faced with that problem, in this case the fact that a considerable proportion of beneficiaries are poor or near poor—an issue heightened by the antipoverty war. The results of research have been reflected in program changes intended both to cope with disadvantages that contribute to the likelihood of poverty for particular groups and to prevent poverty from increasing among beneficiaries. But, and now we come to the crux of the matter—the issue of political limitations—program changes that would broadly reduce the incidence of poverty or near poverty are not seen by policy makers as proper to the program. As it is, the fear of political risks may be enough to stifle any real effort among policy makers and political supporters to include the results of research in actual policies. In the case study of social security the tensions between knowledge and action, resulting from political constraints, are pitched lower than in the other case studies but apparently relative political stability does not eliminate them.

Concluding Note

As we have seen, what has been called the gap between thought or knowledge and action is not easy to bridge.[9] Information is sought for a variety of purposes in the pursuit of public policy but always in a political context that influences those who want the information, those who provide it, and the use to which it can be put. Moreover, in the politics of information, questions of substance, method, and style in research and its results often appear as political issues. Yet, there has been and still is a frequently made assumption that knowledge will generate solutions to policy problems. Included in this assumption is the view that social research can provide the knowledge from which appropriate policies and programs can be drawn or according to which existing policies and programs may be reviewed and evaluated. Indeed, information about poverty and on antipoverty policies has been one of the major products of the war on poverty. But because politics is involved, the gap between knowledge and action is not, in reality, often bridged in such fashion. Rather, as argued here, there is not just a gap between knowledge and action: in politics there is tension between them.

Resources for Research

Very considerable resources for the study of politics have been generated by the politics of information but have been largely ignored.

Research reports abound in agency libraries. The reports themselves often contain valuable information on the substance of policy issues and the populations involved. Sometimes the research performed is amenable to secondary analysis, particularly when surveys have been used. But also, the research reports identify participants—researchers, sponsoring agencies, and contract monitors, consultants, and colleagues who provide guidance and commentary.

Those involved in applied research are often very willing to discuss the circumstances in which they work and their perception of political factors in the initiation, formulation, and use of their research, including, perhaps, pertinent documents from their files. Interviews with bureaucrats may not be so free-wheeling but they may provide valuable data on political dispositions and how these influence decisions to seek certain information, the selection of a provider, and the reception given to the research. Again, it may be possible to identify related documents, especially with external research reports that include contract and grant numbers which may serve to locate appropriate files, though obtaining bureaucratic papers can be difficult. Additionally, interviews with members of Congress and with congressional staff will afford opportunities to trace reactions on the Hill to policy issues and related research.

Particularly for those interested in the judicial review of the substance and administration of public policy or in the political aspects of the practice of poverty law, records of NLS offices and backup centers and the insights of attorneys into political influences on their endeavors constitute a valuable resource for research. For political scientists who are further interested in relationships between law and social science and lawyers and social scientists, one unusual source of data exists.[10] In 1969 the NLS contracted with the Bureau of Social Science Research, a private nonprofit research organization, to provide social science support to NLS attorneys. The Bureau of Social Science Research established the Legal Action Support Project, which became involved in many aspects of poverty law and a variety of cases representing different legal strategies. The records of the project and the experiences of those involved with it, social scientists and lawyers, and the record of the reactions of courts to the use of social science data constitute an intriguing resource.

In the case of social security, resources generated cover a comparatively long legislative and administrative history, one accompanied by an extensive literature of documents, commentary, and critique.[11] Thus, it may be possible to use these resources to study the politics of information through a greater variety of political circumstances and styles than it would be in some other cases.

Notes

1. There is a growing literature on the usability of research in public policy, most of it by economists and sociologists who have been involved in applied research. Political aspects of the question have been raised only rarely and then only cursorily. For an excellent account of an early use of social research see, Barry D. Karl, "Presidential Planning and Social Science Research: Mr. Hoover's Experts," *Perspectives in American History,* Vol. 3 (1969), pp. 347-409; a series of essays on the usability of research in setting policy on cable television are gathered together in Rolla Edward Park, ed., *The Role of Analysis in Regulatory Decision Making* (Lexington, Mass.: D.C. Heath and Co., Lexington Books, 1973). Other works on usability that mention political issues or political feasibility are: Yehezkel Dror, *Ventures in Policy Sciences: Concepts and Applications* (New York: American Elsevier Publishing Co., 1971); Irving Louis Horowitz, ed., *The Use and Abuse of Social Science* (New Brunswick, N.J.: Transaction Books, 1971); Peter H. Rossi and Walter Williams, eds., *Evaluating Social Problems: Theory, Practice, Politics* (New York and London: Seminar Press, 1972); Robert A. Scott and Arnold Shore, *Sociological and Social Experimentation: Observations on the Application of Sociology to Applied Problems,* Mathematica Policy Analysis Series: Comments and Papers on Current Research, No. 4 (Princeton, N.J.: Mathematica, Inc., 1974); Walter Williams, *Social Policy Research and Analysis: The Experience in the Federal Social Agencies* (New York: American Elsevier Publishing Co., 1971).

2. Material for the illustrations is drawn from personal observations made by the author while working in these areas. Experience was qualified

and corrected by interviews with congressional and agency staff members and with persons involved in applied social research.

3. Harold E. Sheppard, "The Experimental and Demonstration Program of the U.S. Department of Labor, Office of Manpower Policy Evaluation and Research" (Washington, D.C.: The W.E. Upjohn Institute for Employment Research, 1966, unpublished report). The view that I present on the effectiveness of research in contributing to the development of policy and programs is shared by Paul Barton, formerly director of the Office of Policy Development in the Department of Labor. For his perception of the situation see his chapter, "Social Science and Social Policy," in *Solving Social Problems: Essays in Relevant Sociology,* eds. Marcello Truzzi and Philip B. Springer (Pacific Palisades, Calif.: Goodyear Publishing Co., Inc., 1975), esp. pp. 14 and 17.

4. See, Thomas R. Dye, "Policy Analysis and Political Science: Some Problems at the Inter-face," *Policy Studies Journal,* Vol. 2 (Winter, 1972) pp. 104-5.

5. U.S., Senate, Committee on Labor and Public Welfare, Sub-Committee on Employment, Manpower and Poverty, *Examination of the War on Poverty,* 90th Cong., 1st Sess., 1967. It is interesting to compare these volumes with deliberations and action in both the Congress and the bureaucracy. Interviews with Sub-Committee staff, research contractors, bureaucrats, and consultants support the generalizations on the politics of information offered in this case study.

6. For a good brief account of the history see, Joel F. Handler and Ellen Jan Hollingsworth, *Organizations and Legal Rights Activities,* Institute for Research on Poverty Discussion Papers, No. 232-74 (Madison: University of Wisconsin, 1974), pp. 20-34.

7. John D. Kettelle, *Evaluation of OEO Legal Services Program* (Paoli, Pennsylvania: John D. Kettelle Corp., 1971). For a study of the problems in the evaluation see, Fred D. Baldwin, "Evaluating the OEO Legal Services Program," *Policy Sciences,* Vol. 4 (September, 1973) pp. 347-64. For interesting comments on evaluation research see, Carol H. Weiss, "The Politics of Impact Measurement," *Policy Studies Journal,* Vol. 1 (Spring, 1973), pp. 179-83.

8. One such major critical review of the program is, Joseph A. Pechman, Henry J. Aaron, and Michael K. Taussig, *Social Security: Perspectives for Reform,* Brookings Studies in Social Economics (Washington, D.C.: The Brookings Institution, 1968). In addition to The Brookings Institution, two of the other organizations that have been active in supporting research on poverty which has included effects of social security are The National Bureau of Economic Research and The Institute for Research on Poverty at the University of Wisconsin.

33

9. See, Robert Lane, "Social Science Research and Public Policy," *Policy Studies Journal,* Vol. 2 (Winter, 1972), pp. 109-10.

10. Ibid., p. 108.

11. For example, see, U.S., Department of Health, Education and Welfare, Social Security Administration: Office of Research and Statistics, *Basic Readings in Social Security* (Washington, D.C.: U.S. Government Printing Office, 1970). In 171 pages, the bibliography remains basic but not complete.

3

Social Services' Impact: Information for Legislative Action

Richard L. Fogel

Assessing the effectiveness of a federal program is by no means a clear-cut task, particularly in the area of social action. With rising federal costs coming under increasing scrutiny, the need for dependable program evaluation is greater than ever.

This need exists not only for executive branch agencies to obtain data so they can administer their programs more effectively but also for congressional legislative and appropriation committees so they can have better information available to them when making policy and resource allocation decisions.

Program evaluation generally asks this question: Is the program achieving the objectives sought by the Congress and the executive branch and is it achieving them at the lowest practicable cost? Arriving at a satisfactory answer presents difficulties since the approach taken can influence the outcome tremendously. Whether the assessment is based on a political test or that of a more objective researcher, the results are difficult to pin down. In the social area no observer approaches the task free of political bias.

Whether it is good, bad, or indifferent, program evaluation is going on all the time. The challenge is to provide decision makers with the best analysis possible within the current state of the art.

In its role as the investigative and auditing arm of the Congress, the General Accounting Office (GAO), headed by the comptroller general of the United States, does extensive program evaluations of federal government programs. The basic purpose of such evaluations is to provide the Congress with independent, objective assessments of how executive agencies are carrying out their programs. GAO also makes recommendations to executive agencies on how they can improve their programs' operations. By continually watching over the operations of executive agencies, the GAO assists the Congress in carrying out its legislative oversight role—a key process if the Congress is to make knowledgeable decisions.

But GAO is by no means the only group that evaluates such programs. Executive agencies themselves do extensive assessments of their operations, often because legislation requires such evaluations. The basic goal of all such efforts is to provide decision makers with information on program performance so that better-run programs will result.

Formidable problems confront the GAO and others evaluating social programs. Two of these seem to occur no matter what program is being reviewed. The first problem is the lack of clearly, specifically stated program goals and objectives. In many programs neither the legislative process nor the subsequent administrative process developed goals and objectives of necessary clarity. If intended accomplishments are not stated there is nothing against which to measure program outcomes.

The second problem is the lack of useable program performance data.[1] This is not entirely the fault of the legislative or administrative process. In social programs there are few criteria for measuring performance. Planners and managers of programs attacking social ills do not have an over-abundance of information on how to achieve results most effectively.

Recently the Comptroller General wrote to Congress and the Office of Management and Budget of the Executive Office of the President suggesting that improvements in evaluation could be brought about in part by developing legislation that is specific. Too often the Congress requests periodic reports from agencies without determining whether the reports will contain the information it needs. Prime responsibility for making the evaluation rests with the agencies administering the programs, but Congress should attempt to specify kinds of information and tests that will enable these agencies, the GAO, and Congress better to assess how well the programs are working and whether alternatives may offer greater promise.

Regardless of the problems, information on program results must be developed so better decisions can be made regarding the allocation of our country's resources. The need for such information is especially critical when looking at social programs because of the controversy over their usefulness and the amount of funds they should receive.

The federal government provides two basic types of public assistance—money and social services—to certain groups of individuals who generally are economically deprived. They include the aged, blind, and disabled, and certain dependent children and their families. The welfare programs, authorized by certain titles of the Social Security Act, are administered at the federal level by the Department of Health, Education, and Welfare (HEW). The states receive federal funds from HEW to provide money and social services to those in need. Because the states receive federal funds, they must adhere to certain rules and regulations established by HEW as to how the welfare programs must be operated. These regulations are basically designed to insure fair, equitable, efficient, and effective use of federal funds. HEW's primary job is to see to it that the states carry out its rules and regulations adequately and, if they do not, to assist them in changing so they do comply.

Many recent decisions regarding the welfare program—changes in the

Work Incentive program (WIN), enactment of a ceiling on social service expenditures, and changes in federal social service regulations—were made without the benefit of adequate information on the program's impact. GAO's recent work in the social service area was designed to provide such information.

Do social services help recipients of Aid to Families with Dependent Children (AFDC) get off welfare or reduce their dependency on welfare? Is that goal realistic? Are services provided to those who could benefit most from them? These are the questions GAO tried to answer in its June 1973 report to the Congress, "Social Services: Do They Help Welfare Recipients Achieve Self-Support or Reduced Dependency?"[2]

The questions are not easy to answer, but answers have to be found if Congress, the Executive branch, and the public are to assess fully the role of social services in the nation's welfare program, especially in light of the current debate as to the relative merit of money payments versus in-kind services (such as food stamps, medicaid, and various other types of social services). What follows is a discussion of GAO's evaluation of social services.

Lack of Clearly Defined Goals

One of the difficulties in determining the impact of the program is that goals have not been defined clearly. Neither Congress nor the Executive branch developed criteria by which to measure the success of the program. Would the program be successful if 4 percent of the recipients who achieved self-support or reduced dependency did so because of social services? Should the number be 20 percent? No one could say. By using GAO's data, responsible parties could begin to develop criteria to judge the results.

What did GAO mean by social services? They included any type of service provided to AFDC recipients under provisions of Title IV, Parts A and C, of the Social Security Act. They ranged from counseling regarding money management or family planning to providing job training or job placement services under the program.

GAO classified services as either developmental or maintenance. *Developmental* services were those that could directly assist recipients in achieving self-support or reduced dependency. Such services usually included counseling or referrals to job training programs, job training, or job placement. *Maintenance* services were those that could help recipients sustain or strengthen family life. Services such as day care therefore could be considered developmental or maintenance, depending on whether the recipient needed them to obtain or retain employment.

Impact of Services

Given GAO's objectives and classification of services, what were the results of the review? Work in Baltimore, Denver, Louisville, New Orleans, and Oakland, based on random samples of ADFC recipients who got off welfare and of those still receiving it, showed that:

1. Social services had only a minor impact on directly helping recipients develop and use the skills necessary to achieve reduced dependency or self-support. Only 4.5 percent of those no longer needing AFDC and 2 percent of those still receiving it were directly assisted by services in achieving self-support or reducing dependency. One of the basic congressional goals for social services—that they help people get off welfare—has not been achieved.

2. It is unrealistic to expect that social services can play a major role in helping recipients achieve reduced dependency or self-support, considering the nature of services provided, the method for determining who should receive certain services, and present economic constraints.

3. Social services, however, have positive aspects. Developmental services directly helped some recipients obtain employment. Maintenance services helped many AFDC recipients cope with and overcome specific day-to-day problems, strengthen their family life, and increase their self-confidence. Over the long run these benefits are necessary if recipients are ultimately to benefit from developmental services.

Inadequate Resource Allocation

Just as important for improving the services program, GAO's work also showed that local welfare departments do not have adequate systems to assess recipients' potential for self-support. They cannot insure that their service resources are allocated for the maximum benefit of recipients. By developing better ways to allocate resources it should be easier eventually to assess the impact that those services had on the recipients.

Recognizing that social service resources are limited, that not all AFDC recipients have a potential for self-support, and that certain services might be able to help recipients achieve self-support, several questions can be asked about AFDC recipients eligible for services.

1. Who is presently employable?
2. Who has the potential to become employable?
3. Who requires services to become employable?
4. Who is most likely to benefit from services?

GAO found that local welfare departments do not provide their caseworkers with a means to answer such questions objectively and uniformly. Answers must be found if services are to be more effective.

The Denver Department of Welfare developed and tested an approach (which GAO called the inventory approach) that gives caseworkers a more systematic and analytic means to assess recipients' potential. Accordingly, it could improve the effectiveness of the allocation of social service resources. A modified version of the approach is being used in Nevada. GAO's validation of Denver's statistical tests showed that the approach can accurately predict employment potential. GAO also used the approach to help determine the potential of AFDC recipients in its review.

How does the inventory approach work? By analyzing 20 characteristics and circumstances, such as physical condition and interest in employment, AFDC recipients' strengths, problems, and potential for self-support can be measured. Under each of the categories descriptive terms are listed and are assigned a number from zero to six depending on the severity of the problems. After visiting the family's home, a caseworker selects the term under each category that best describes the situation. By adding the scores for each of the 20 categories an overall score can be computed—the lower the score, the higher the potential for self-support.

GAO made statistical tests to identify additional recipient characteristics (i.e., not included in the inventory approach) that could assist caseworkers in identifying recipients likely to benefit from social services and to reaffirm the potential usefulness of other characteristics. The findings showed that additional characteristics to help identify recipients likely to have potential to achieve self-support and possibly benefit from receipt of appropriate services are:

1. Length of time on welfare
2. Number of children in recipient's household
3. Number of such children under age six
4. Age of recipient

Recommendations

To improve the program's administration GAO recommended that the secretary of Health, Education, and Welfare:

1. Initiate a number of demonstration projects using the inventory approach, or similar approaches, to assess the potential of all welfare recipients and to allocate service resources accordingly.
2. Establish an appropriate time period—probably two years—for com-

pleting these projects and, analyze the data to determine which approach would most effectively allocate resources.

3. Report to the Congress at the end of the test period on actions to be taken to improve the allocation of service resources as a result of the study.

4. Develop by July 1974, in conjunction with the secretary of Labor, a system so certain characteristics of recipients—indicative of high potential to achieve self-support or reduced dependency—serve as the basis for determining which recipients will be afforded priority in receiving WIN services. Among the characteristics that should be used are time on welfare, educational level attained, and previous employment experience.

The department agreed to implement the recommendations.

GAO also recommended that the Congress direct the Executive branch to develop criteria for measuring the effectiveness of social services, with a goal of incorporating such criteria in federal regulations.

Conclusion

Program evaluation is a fundamental part of effective program administration. The lack of meaningful evaluation in the social welfare field has often resulted in development of policies based mostly on intuition, rather than on proven results. The current debate over the usefulness of many social welfare programs points up the need for reliable information on the successes and failures of such programs.

In the final analysis the hard choices will be political, but political leaders and the public need increased awareness of the arguments of the choices that must be made. Those who make such decisions should at least be equipped with good information.

Notes

1. Subcommittee on Fiscal Policy, Joint Economic Committee, U.S. Congress, "The Effectiveness of Manpower Training Programs: A Review of Research on the Impact of the Poor," (November 20, 1972).

2. U.S. General Accounting Office, "Social Services: Do They Help Welfare Recipients Achieve Self-Support or Reduced Dependency?" B-164031(3) (June 27, 1973).

4

Policy Strategies for Older Americans

Frederick R. Eisele

Poverty has always been heavily felt among older Americans, but in previous generations there were so few old people that they were more or less "invisible." There was also little public concern then for the general welfare of anyone who was dependent—for anyone who could not "pull his own weight"—even if his dependency was obviously no fault of his own. As a result there were few social programs providing for the needs of old people; and there was even less reliable information about those needs.

In the intervening years, especially since the Great Depression, a great deal has changed: Today, there are three times as many people over 65 as there were in 1900, while major social legislation has now provided a floor of support for this dependent sector of the population. A good deal of information is just becoming available about the problems of those who now amount to 10 percent of the population (see Appendix 4A).

Although much had been done by 1975, the needs of the elderly are far from adequately met. A good 20 percent still live in poverty, and elderly persons who are minority group members account for a disproportionate share of the impoverished. One of the most rapidly increasing strata of the older population is comprised of the especially vulnerable, those over 75 years of age. These are people plagued by chronic illness and dwindling reserves and many of them will spend their final years in poorly run, impersonal nursing homes.

The plan of this chapter is to look closely at the nature of dependency in older people and at the policy response to the problem by reviewing the highlights of the past half century through a history of the system of public policy for the elderly.[1] The focus is on three major policies, really subsystem strategies, designed to better the welfare of the elderly—income maintenance policies, health care policies, and social services policies.

Policy History

Without reconstructing a history of public and private actions toward old people one might have the erroneous impression that institutions and practices "just happened." As we hope to show, things "happened" (or did not) because people tried very actively to *make* them happen. The notion of a policy history introduced here is important for another reason.

Recently, a political historian coined the term *policy inheritance*, by which he meant the continuing influence of past decisions on present and future decisions.[2] We rarely start from scratch in anything—least of all in public policy. Rather, we build from and rely heavily on what went before, on the consequences of inherited decisions.

Reviewing the history of any policy area requires understanding of the original issue to which the policy was a response. The question arises as to why there is *any* policy toward the aging. Since aging is a normal process, why should government, or anyone, have to intervene? Part of the answer was suggested above—because isolation, health, and economic losses leave old people dependent upon others (usually adult sons and daughters with children of their own) who usually do not have the resources to provide what is needed. Therefore, the government has, gradually, been asked to step in with some form of collective support. Almost every industrialized nation in the world found this step necessary, and most took it long before the United States.

After such a decision to intervene is made—and we shall see below how this happened in the 1930s—several other decisions necessarily followed. Among the most important was that of deciding how to define the problem in the first place. In other words, before government decided how to intervene, officials had to define specifically the situation to be remedied—specify its causes, the key goals and strategies for achieving them, and the costs and benefits.

Who Shall Be "Old"?

For example, one of the basic questions for policy planners was how shall "aged" be defined? If public provision was to be made for a certain category of persons, then it was critical to determine who was (and who was not) in the category. The criteria of *eligibility* selected for most public benefits for the aged has been, not surprisingly, age; for most programs, the age chosen was 65. This figure has become so widely adopted (e.g., by industry as a mandatory retirement age) that we tend to think of "aged" as a homogeneous block of everyone over 65. In fact, the issue is far more complex. Under certain conditions one may be eligible for benefits at 62. Many workers are now encouraged to choose early retirement at 55. The Department of Labor defines the "older worker" (blue collar) as 45 years of age. Many analysts have suggested abandoning the 65 eligibility level altogether in favor of a graduated scheme that would better reflect the complexity of reality. Obviously, people do not become aged all at once on their 65th birthday. Rather, the process is gradual, occurring over several decades. Bernice Neugarten has proposed that we consider "the aged" to be composed of at least two groups: the "young-old" (55-74 years) and the "old-old" (75+ years).[3] Older persons who are also members of ethnic minorities (such as black, Indian or Spanish-speaking) present an even sharper disparity in regard to the eligibility criterion of 65 years. Because of their history of unequal opportunity these minorities have shorter life expectancy levels; many do not survive to 65 to collect the benefits they have earned. People in the second half of life also differ among themselves in another important way: their composition is constantly changing. In other words, every year a new set, or *cohort*, of people turns 55 years old. Gradually, these newcomers reflect the differing values and outlooks of their generation.

Clearly "the aged" are far from being a homogeneous group. In fact, there is psychological evidence that as individuals get older, they become more differentiated from one another, and therefore in many ways, impossible to treat with equity as a group. The point here for those who are concerned with policy is that aging programs must deal with differences and accommodate the changing needs of the new elderly. As an illustration, think of the different kinds of programs that will be necessary for today's college students when *they* are 55 and over, around the year 2010. If nothing else, older people will be far more educated than their predecessor elderly were.

The Policy Inheritance

With these problems and definitions as background, let us review the policy history in more detail. The components of a policy history, are far more complex than the chronology of legislation. The story really begins in the early decades of the twentieth century, when a small group of reformers began to push for a public, social insurance policy that would, among other things, provide a modest pension for all retired workers. For a variety of reasons—chief among them being the opposition of the life insurance industry, as well as labor—this early movement never succeeded in its goal of national legislation.

The Depression of the 1930s was a turning point in the development of policy. The elderly were among the hardest hit in the sense that they were least able physically to withstand the stresses of rapid change. Thousands of middle aged workers 45 and over never again held full time jobs: by the time the Depression had bottomed out, they were in their middle fifties with skills that were largely obsolete. Thousands of workers in their fifties and sixties did not survive the rigors of migration forced by the hopes of job markets in other states.[4] In the early 1930s many older migrants from the drought-stricken Midwest to southern California found hope in a social movement whose goal was to secure $200 per month for everyone over 65 years. While this "Townsend movement" had little organizational staying power, and failed to have the political impact that it potentially might have had, it did attract national attention.

It was during this period, when the plight of the older worker was becoming increasingly apparent, that President Roosevelt set into motion a policy planning group that brought about passage of the Social Security Act in 1935. This was the first effort in the United States to provide a minimum retirement income for all workers; the act has been the backbone of most policy toward older Americans ever since.

Subsequent development of policies and programs was, however, sporadic for the next 20 years. It was as if social security filled the basic need, and little more was necessary. The quiescence of this period may be accounted for by a number of factors: the preoccupation with war or its threat between 1940-52; the general inattention to social legislation during the Cold War "celebration of capitalism" period; and the failure to develop any sustained, serious social movement of and for older citizens.

Rediscovery of the Elderly

In the late 1950s and early 1960s, however, political changes became apparent. A Senior Citizens for Kennedy movement in 1960 grew in the next decade into an important interest group: the National Council of Senior Citizens. Another organization, the National Retired Teachers Association and the American Association of Retired Persons, increased its membership more than ten-fold in the same period.[5] The United States Senate initiated what was to become the Special Committee on Aging in 1959, and in 1961 the first White House Conference on Aging was held, focusing attention on the neglect of this sector.

A key reason for these developments was a growing concern over the costs of health care, which were disproportionately high for older Americans. Heirs to the same group that had tried to introduce a public social insurance policy for retirement in the 1910s were in the late 1950s seeking to develop legislation that would provide minimum insurance for rising medical costs. In their move toward some form of national health insurance, they were vigorously opposed by the powerful American Medical Association, which labelled health insurance a form of "socialized medicine," effectively stigmatizing the issue in an era preoccupied with anticommunism. The health insurance reformers then hit upon a strategy that would defuse the explosive issue of national health by proposing a scheme to provide health insurance only for a subset of the population, one which was obviously in need and undisputedly "deserving": the aged.[6] The strategy was to use the elderly as a foot-in-the-door to national health insurance for some time in the future. This approach was successful. Enormous opposition from the medical establishment was finally overcome, and the Medicare program was passed as Title 18 of the Social Security Act in 1965.[7]

This same period saw a reawakening of national concern toward some of the issues of the 1930s. The "War on Poverty" launched in the Kennedy-Johnson years was concerned with the disadvantaged in general, which came to include the elderly.[8] In 1965 President Johnson signed into law the Older Americans Act, which for the first time set up a federal agency exclusively concerned with this constituency, the Administration on Aging. Two years later, in line with current trends, Congress passed the Age Discrimination in Employment Act, designed to protect older workers from premature layoff.

Yet, neither of these laws was fully implemented nor enforced. The first languished for several years for lack of serious funding, while the second was buried in the Department of Labor without sufficient manpower to initiate serious court actions until some four to five years later. Possibly, Washington's preoccupation with Vietnam was a factor in this temporary decline in interest.

The 1971 White House Conference on Aging, while largely symbolic, did mark a regeneration of national concern. In the following year there were very significant increases in social security benefits—over 50 percent in the preceding four years. In the next two years a major pension reform bill was signed into law and a national research institute for aging was created. And, a most important shift—as far as individual older Americans were concerned—came with the 1973 comprehensive services amendments to the Older Americans Act. This marked the opening of a new policy front, one aimed at providing social services as an important complement to Social Security's income and medical insurance programs.

Three Policies, Three Strategies

For purposes of analysis, the above history can be reconstructed along lines of three successive policies, essentially three basic strategies toward achieving the overall goal of bettering the lot of older Americans. Initially, an income policy was developed (the 1935 Social Security Act), aimed at relieving undisputed poverty among those who were no longer able to work because of age. Thirty years later this was supplemented by a health policy (Medicare and Medicaid), which sought to enable individuals to enjoy adequate health care without suffering devastating financial losses from spiralling medical costs. Very recently, a social services policy was introduced (the Comprehensive Services Amendments to the Older Americans Act) designed to complement the first two policies in important ways.

Each of these policies may be considered a subsystem of a larger policy system for the aging. The notion of a policy system—a complex set of interrelated actors and actions that emerges around a single focal area—has been aptly applied to the area of aging.[9] The "aging policy system" consists of the interest groups, the legislation, the executive agencies, and the professionals that have emerged in regard to aging in recent years. Each of these elements has diverse multiple goals, but inasmuch as they focus on the aged, they constitute a system.

The above policy-strategies, then, are each subsystems of the overall aging policy system. We will analyze, in a very general fashion, each subsystem in terms of the following successive stages in the policy process: planning, implementation, and evaluation. The planning phase includes the originating problem and how it was conceptualized. Implementation refers to how the policy response was administered after it was mandated, and the shifts it underwent as it was executed in different settings. Evaluation focuses on the impact of the policy or of its programs in terms of effectiveness in solving the original problem.

Income Maintenance

The most important subsystem of the aging policy system—income maintenance—was the first to be developed. The originating problem is not complicated: final separation from work, whether voluntary or not, entails sharp and sudden decreases in income at an age when a good decade or more of life usually remains. There is no effective way in which the average wage earner can prepare for the economic losses of retirement, without outside support. Savings, for example, are usually seriously eroded by inflation, and at any rate, savings from even 40 years of work are limited for a future whose duration is unknown. As a result, there has always been a disproportionate number of older workers living in poverty.

The policy response to this chronic situation, which was aggravated by the Depression, was to develop a federal subsidy directly to retired workers and their families, financed from a payroll tax. The formal name of this program is Old Age, Survivors, and Disability Insurance OASDI, one of several programs administered by the Social Security Administration. Its objective was to maintain a minimum income and thereby to help maintain independence. Since its first benefits were paid in 1937, the Social Security Administration, and especially the OASDI program, has been relatively nonpolitical. It was launched by executive initiative and went through Congress with little opposition. The Social Security Administration became a large and very well-entrenched bureaucracy with a great deal of autonomy.

There were few problems in implementing the programs of this country's major income maintenance policy. Monthly checks were mailed to individuals in amounts based on their previous earnings, and extensive local office administration moved the system smoothly. Most importantly, most older Americans were provided with the minimum income necessary for food and shelter. Some, with savings, private pensions and other income, lived quite comfortably. In general, the first 35 years of income maintenance policy under social security were relatively effective, untroubled, and unchanged.

Change came in the 1970s. There were many more retired beneficiaries and they had higher expectations than in the past. Over the years the payroll tax had increased from 1 percent to 5.8 percent, while the taxable base rose from the first $3,000 to the first $13,200. New legislation was trying to keep abreast of change: benefits were increased by over 50 percent between 1968 and 1972, and in 1975 benefits were indexed to the Consumer Price Index. This meant that beneficiaries' payments would be adjusted automatically to inflation for the first time. Starting in 1974 a new, complementary program was introduced to the country's general income maintenance policy: Supplemental Security Income, (SSI). This was a federal-to-state, low-income support program for the blind, disabled, and those over 65 years. As a complex program designed to increase cash income for the aged poor, it was a helpful move, enrolling people who had not been receiving OASDI, but its implementation has been complicated and its impact unclear. A year after its introduction Senate hearings were being held to determine what some of the major problems were.

In its fortieth year of operation, the country's major income maintenance policy and its primary implementor, the Social Security Administration, were increasingly coming under fire. Some of the assumptions made a generation earlier were losing their relevance. Among the targets of complaint were: the regressive nature of the tax schedule (the poor and middle class were overtaxed in relation to the rich); the retirement earnings test (earnings over $2,400 per year of persons between the ages of 65 and 72 were taxed); and the disadvantageous benefit schedule for working spouses. Yet, the sheer magnitude of benefits and the unquestionable popularity of its intentions at least continued to keep the Social Security Administration well beyond the range of any independent policy evaluation.[10]

Health Care

Related to the problem of income loss for older Americans is their loss of health. Although illness is not synonymous with aging, the later years (especially after age 75) are characterized by an increase in chronic impairments, the discomfort of which may be relieved, but rarely cured. In the 1960s surveys showed that persons over 65 were twice as likely to have chronic illness, and likely to be hospitalized twice as long as those under 65. A typical health deficit is bone brittleness, not uncommonly resulting in hip fractures. Because mending is very slow in old age, hospitalization and posthospital care are long and costly.

Two major obstacles to adequate health care for these older citizens have been its cost and its accessibility. Expenditures for hospitalization, doctors fees, drugs, and ancillary health services have skyrocketed in the past 20 years. In 1975 the per capita cost for health care for persons over 65 was well over $1,000 per annum. Furthermore, health facilities are doctor-centered rather than user-centered, and most physicians seek to practice where profits are greatest rather than where needs are most acute. Mal-distribution of facilities (such as clinics and hospitals) and of physicians in relation to people is a special problem for the elderly, inasmuch as they are more dependent upon public transportation for access.

As a subsystem, health care policy has much in common with income maintenance policy because recovering lost health largely requires costly medical institutions and is therefore a financial problem for individuals. One direct link between income and health is work-related health insurance, which is often nonrenewable upon retirement. The major health care programs (Medicare and Medicaid) are forms of insurance. Most health care programs differ from income maintenance, however, in that they are far more involved with the profit-seeking private sector represented chiefly by physicians, proprietary hospitals, the pharmaceutical companies and the health insurance companies, Blue Cross and Blue Shield. For this reason health care has always been much more politicized than any of the other policy subsystems. For example, the American Medical Association spent millions of dollars in an unsuccessful lobbying campaign to defeat health insurance for the elderly.

The most direct policy response to the health care problems of older Americans was Medicare, Title 18 of the Social Security Act, passed in 1965. Basically, this was a federal health insurance program designed to pay for the major portion of hospital and physician costs. A 20-year struggle was required for its passage; yet, ironically, the group most opposed to it—the American Medical Association—ended up benefitting enormously. In spite of some confusion in implementing medicare in its early years, there was general agreement toward the end of its first decade that millions of elderly had benefitted from it in important ways.

The other major health program affecting older Americans—Title 19 (Medicaid) of the 1965 amendments to the Social Security Act—met with less success. Medicaid was a federally funded, state-administered medical insurance program. It was also a welfare program inasmuch as recipients had to submit to an income-based means test to become eligible. As a form of "welfare medicine" Medicaid represented the largest involvement of government in the private medical sector to date.[11] One result was that regulatory policy, seeking to control and account for the flow of federal and state dollars, inevitably increased and became more complex to meet an increasingly complex situation.

One aspect of Medicaid revealing a major administrative difficulty became so bad that it emerged as a political problem: the "nursing home scandal." Briefly, the regulations for Medicaid payments to nursing home operators (and physicians and druggists) did not include adequate or enforceable controls. In part, this lax system of accountability for reimbursement was a result of the fact that Medicaid was administered through state governments that could set their own regulations. What happened was that unscrupulous nursing home operators saw a golden opportunity to enrich themselves through padded bills, pernicious cost cutting and political kickbacks to state politicians (for overlooking inspector-reported violations of health and safety standards), all at the expense of aged, destitute patients, and, of course, the taxpayers. In 1974 and 1975 most of these practices were publicly exposed through the press and a series of reports produced by the Senate Special Committee on Aging;[12] but given the past record, there was no guarantee that they would or even could be curtailed.

One piece of evidence in support of such a pessimistic view emerged during hearings on nursing home questions in New York City. After hearing extensive documentation and testimony about current patient abuse and dubious financial practices, the Stein Commission learned that the same abuses and even some of the same individuals had been named in a report made 15 years earlier, but that political authorities and taken no action. Apparently, the big-time nursing home chain owners had been making sizeable political contributions high enough in the state political systems to ward off any serious threat to their operations.

The nursing home industry scandal has many lessons: the high social costs of private profits, particularly when an exploitable minority has no effective advocates; the inevitability of fraud when federal subsidies are allocated with inadequate procedures for accountability; and the costly complexity of enforcing regulatory policy.

Social Services

The third policy subsystem considered here, and the most recent strategy in the public responses to problems of aging, consists of social services. These may be defined as a variety of community-based supports to individuals and families that sustain their well-being and thereby that of the community in general.[13] Because of their increasing losses—in health, income, mobility, and often in morale—older people need a wide variety of services, from information on how to get services, transportation, or nutrition' to legal advice.

While there is little overlap between this policy subsystem and the income maintenance subsystem (since the latter is a direct cash transfer from government to individual), there is a growing convergence between social services and the health care subsystem. Gradually key aspects of health care are becoming demedicalized, that is, taken out of the costly, exclusive domain of medical professionals and institutions. Instead, there is growing support for community health services that can be delivered by nurses, paraprofessionals, and health aides. For the elderly this movement is important because many of their needs require neither sophisticated medical technology nor highly skilled professional care. Rather, other arrangements such as regular visits by home health aides can provide quality care at low cost.

A coordinated, national policy of social services for the elderly began only in 1973, with the passage of the "new" Older Americans Act, entitled "Comprehensive Services Amendments for Older Americans." The key provision was Title III, which mandated the establishment of Planning and Service Areas for each state. From these emerged the Area Agency on Aging plan, a federally supported, services planning and coordination program operating at the substate (usually county) level. The Area Agencies are not service providers unless absolutely necessary, but rather service coordinators, in the sense that they are mandated to build upon existing service agencies and to expand their coverage to include the elderly. Variation among Area Agencies of course is enormous, ranging from sophisticated operations in urban and suburban areas to relatively undeveloped and poorly organized rural areas.

Evaluating the effectiveness of a social services policy is complex. The widely diffused nature of programs and the indirectness of the services delivered make their impact on people's well-being very difficult to assess. For example, evaluating Title VII of the Older Americans Act—the Congregate Meals program, whereby older persons can purchase at very low cost (or have free) several hot meals a week—is complicated because the program goals are not only nutritional improvement, but social and psychological well-being derived from before-and-after meals socializing.

While the data are not yet available from the evaluation of the nutrition and other programs, it has become clear that they are increasingly popular. Even if evaluation research turns up a "no effects" finding that it is impossible to determine whether the service programs have had any impact, good or bad, the political feasibility of terminating the programs has decreased with the passage of time.

Conclusion

There are always two views about any policy problem. There is the knowledge that "experts" have, what they define as problematic in a particular situation, and what those experiencing the problem themselves define as problematic. The two are not necessarily the same. The task for the policy analyst is to see this divergence clearly and to develop policies that come as close as possible to fulfilling real needs.

We have looked briefly at some of the problems of planning, implementing, and evaluating three policy subsystems in regard to the aging. A key issue for policy analysis in each of these areas is obtaining adequate information about program effectiveness so that modifications can be made to improve policy. Such information is generally acquired through evaluation research.

The purpose of evaluative research is to help make better decisions. But research findings may be either applied or ignored by decision makers. In other words, programs are born and survive or die not only on the basis of their effectiveness, but also, perhaps largely, because of the political clout of the interest groups involved in the policy system. The rapid expansion of programs for the elderly in the past decade relative to previous decades occurred in large part because of the organizational abilities (and therefore political potential) of interest groups for and of the elderly. In all probability, however, current and future programs for the aging will expand in spite of the increased political sophistication of the elderly lobby. This has to do with the expanding population of old people and with the natural propensity of bureaucracies to expand operations, especially likely with popular causes such as that of the aged.

Yet, evaluation research should be as important for popular as for unpopular programs. In fact, it may be more important, because the tendency to be "soft" where popularity displaces effectiveness could waste public dollars for years. The need for good policy evaluation in the future will increase as programs grow. This is particularly true in the policy subsystems of health care and social services, which will be most likely to feel the demand for "more and better." While the future is impossible to predict, one forecast for the elderly population seems reasonable: that the aged then, having much more than a half century of policy history behind them, will have greater public awareness and support than did those elderly of the mid-twentieth century, to whom the above policy strategies were introduced for the first time.

Notes

1. The notion of a policy system for the elderly has been developed by Dale Vineyard, "A Policy System for the Aged: Some Preliminary Observations," unpublished paper, Department of Political Science, Wayne State University, 1974.

2. On this, see Hugh Heclo, *Modern Social Politics in Britain and Sweden: From Relief to Income Maintenance* (New Haven, Conn.: Yale University Press, 1974).

3. See Bernice L. Neugarten, "Age Groups in American Society and the Rise of the Young-Old," in F.R. Eisele (ed.), "Political Consequences of Aging," *The Annals of the American Academy of Political and Social Sciences,* Vol. 415 (September, 1974), pp. 187-198.

4. For more on this, see A. Holtzman, *The Townsend Movement: A Political Study* (New York: Bookman Associates, 1963); and J.K. Putman, *Old Age Politics in California: From Richardson to Reagan* (Stanford, Calif.: Stanford University Press, 1970).

5. See Henry J. Pratt, "Old Age Associations in National Politics," *The Annals of the American Academy of Political and Social Science,* Vol. 415 (September, 1974), pp. 106-119.

6. See Theordor Marmor, *The Politics of Medicare* (Chicago: Aldine, 1973).

7. Richard Harris, *A Sacred Trust* (New York: New American Library, 1966).

8. For background to this, see James L. Sundquist, *Politics and Policy; the Eisenhower, Kennedy and Johnson Years* (Washington, D.C.: Brookings, 1968), ch. 7.

9. Vineyard, *A Policy System for the Aged.*

10. Robinson Hollister, "Social Mythology and Reform: Income Maintenance for the Aged," *The Annals of the American Academy of Political and Social Science,* Vol. 415 (September, 1974), pp. 19-40.

11. Robert Stevens and Rosemary Stevens, *Welfare Medicine in America: A Case Study of Medicaid* (New York: Free Press, 1974).

12. U.S. Senate Special Committee on Aging, *Nursing Home Care in the United States: Failure in Public Policy* (Washington, D.C.: November, 1974).

13. See Alfred, J. Kahn, *Social Policy and Social Services* (New York: Random House, 1973).

Appendix 4A:
Information on Aging

Reliable information about the elderly should become more accessible than it has been when the National Clearinghouse on Aging (within the Administration on Aging) becomes operational in 1976 or 1977. In the meantime, the following suggestions might be helpful:

Among government publications, the Social Security Administration has had the longest history of involvement in monitoring the distribution and change of a variety of income and health indicators among the aged. Its research reports, data series, and surveys concerning Social Security and Medicare programs are important background for almost any policy research; and its 1963 and 1968 *Survey of the Aged* provides the most comprehensive set of national data available. Current issues and new developments are presented in its monthly *Social Security Bulletin.* For more issue-oriented information, the best source is the publications (memoranda, hearings, and special reports) of the U.S. Senate Special Committee on Aging. For example, between 1969 and 1970 over a dozen documents on such topics as health, home ownership, and pensions appeared in the series "Economics of Aging: Toward a Full Share in Abundance." This committee has also put out on an approximately annual basis a useful miscellany of position papers, hearing summaries, etc. under the title *Developments in Aging.*

Relevant to policy on aging is a series of background papers to the 1971 White House Conference on Aging, dealing with such topics as income, retirement, planning, and services, although these are now difficult to obtain. The conference's recommendations appeared under the title *Toward a National Policy on Aging,* which is worth reviewing as a summary statement of issues. The Administration on Aging—created in 1965 and located in HEW—issues a monthly information magazine; often the 50 state units on aging also distribute similar general purpose publications for state-level developments.

Among nongovernment publications, the research-oriented American Gerontological Society issues the *Journal of Gerontology,* which includes an extensive bibliography, including "social" topics, broadly defined, although its emphasis is in the biological sciences. The society's more general *Gerontologist* does publish policy-relevant research and discussion and, increasingly in recent years, has taken an advocacy role on behalf of the elderly and for aging research funding. The society encourages research, and through its Committee on Research and Development has issued several research policy reports. Another private group, the National

Council on Aging, sponsors *Industrial Gerontology,* which abstracts articles on income maintenance-related topics such as unemployment and
retirement.

An indispensable review and evaluation of social sciences work in aging
is Mathilda W. Riley et. al., *Aging and Society* (New York: Russell Sage
Foundation, 1968), Vol. I, a research inventory, properly cautions the
reader as to the special methodological difficulties in age-related data, and
to the shortcomings in studies available up to the mid-1960s (e.g., the
age-and-cohort confound). A second volume on the professions involved
with the elderly might also be of interest to those concerned with problems
of organization and delivery of services.

For a more recent survey, see Robert H. Binstock and Robert B.
Hudson, "Political Systems and Aging," ch. 14, in E. Shanas and R.H.
Binstock (eds.), *Handbook of Aging and the Social Sciences* (Chicago:
Rand McNally, forthcoming).

5

Simulation of Welfare Spending: Some Approaches to Public Policy Analysis

Robert B. Albritton

One of the most important tasks of political research is to develop substantive theories that describe and explain political phenomena. This is an especially vital function for policy analysis although efforts in this area are notably meager. Public policy formulation requires accurate models to inform policy decisions, for example, models indicating which changes in a variable or parameter produce measurable changes in outputs, and to predict precise amounts of outputs likely to occur. Without explicit models of policy systems, decision makers engage in planning and programming on the basis of *implicit* models of social processes that are frequently inaccurate or characterized by a high degree of uncertainty. The result is that a host of "satisficing" decisions fail to produce consistently satisfactory results.[a]

Theoretical work in public policy is severely restricted by overreliance on correlational analysis. Although valuable as an exploratory tool, limitations of the methodology for representing dynamics of complex social systems are generally acknowledged.[b] Perhaps the most severe limitation of correlational procedures is their incapacity to express relationships precisely between variables in a model. Without precise formulations of variable interactions, a model is limited to rather vague statements concerning outcomes of specific policy actions (an "increase" in variable A is "associated" with an "increase" in variable B). Thus, research that relies solely on correlations is unlikely to provide methods and models of social processes that contribute substantially to more effective policy decisions.[c]

---

[a] For example, after several years of programs to provide housing for low-income people, results have included the destruction of stable neighborhoods, concentrated poverty densities (with attendant social ills), and a net reduction in low-cost housing.

[b] Limitations include the problems of spurious inferences, inflated correlation coefficients from the presence of multicollinearity, and an inability to treat cross-sectional and longitudinal variance simultaneously. Limitations of cross-sectional analysis are suggested by Otis Dudley Duncan, Ray P. Cuzzort, and Beverly Duncan, *Statistical Geography* (Glenoe: Free Press, 1961), pp. 160-161.

[c] Analysis of unstandardized regression coefficients is more profitable if correlation coefficients are generally high. See H.M. Blalock, Jr., "Causal Inferences, Closed Populations, and Measures of Association," in H.M. Blalock, Jr., ed., *Causal Models in the Social Sciences* (Chicago: Aldine Publishing Company, 1971), pp. 139-151.

The successes of Jay Forrester et al. in developing dynamic models of urban and world systems offer alternative approaches to the familiar inputs-outputs models of policy analysis.[1] By applying systems dynamics concepts in computer simulations, Forrester has analyzed dynamic growth processes in a variety of systems.[d] The fundamental difference between this method and the Easton-Dye society-politics-policy models is the assumption that system *structures* (i.e., specific arrangements of relationships among component variables) are as significant for determining behavior as the components themselves. Adapted to techniques of computer simulation, this conceptual framework allows a researcher to visualize and test dynamic relationships among variables, even those characterized by complex interactions such as variable feedback within a system. In addition, the methodology facilitates trial-and-error testing of controlled interventions in which variable values and parameters are manipulated to produce alternative outcomes.

Forrester's use of systems dynamics for analyzing social processes appears especially suited to policy analysis. When policy makers have little knowledge or awareness of complex linkages that convert inputs into policy, they may be led to focus attention on apparent causal linkages that are proximate in time and space only to discover, too late, that actual linkages are located in a distant sector of the system. Visualizing policy system dynamics in computer simulations gains greater conceptual clarity of actual variable interactions and provides important clues to causes of policy failures. Although considerable lip-service is paid to systems approaches in policy analysis few efforts have been made to construct these more elaborate and useful models of policy systems.

Welfare Spending Model

Application of systems techniques to an analysis of welfare policy requires a model that includes formal statements about relationships of essential components to each other and to the environment. Isolating these components and their relationships is essentially the task of combining extant theories with intuitive understandings of historical welfare processes.

Although the body of welfare theory is not large, considerable research suggests that welfare policy is a function of the extent of poverty in America. According to this notion, essential components of welfare policy are the factors that give rise to poverty conditions. Race, class, prejudice, economic and geographic isolation, lack of education and training, domi-

---

[d] Forrester has also been able to show that policy making can produce outcomes exactly the opposite of those intended in managerial organizations. See "Counterintuitive Behavior of Social Systems," *Technology Review* (January, 1971), pp. 55ff.

nant norms, and some features of the economic system are all leading contenders as explanations of welfare policy in the American states.[2] While theories of this type are very useful for explaining poverty, there is little evidence to support the notion that welfare dependency is primarily a function of the number of people who are poor. By any definition of poverty, only slightly over half the poor benefit from the welfare system. Because the system defines eligibility according to criteria that have little bearing on needs of the persons involved, poverty is related only indirectly in a statistical sense to welfare dependency.[e] For this reason variables associated with origins of poverty are not relevant to this analysis.

More significant for welfare policy analysis are studies that show the impacts of federal grant-in-aid assistance on welfare spending by governments at state and local levels. Seymour Sachs and Robert Harris note substantial declines in explanatory power of socioeconomic variables that coincide with increasing importance of federal and state assistance to lower levels of government.[3] In the area of welfare policy, Jack Osman found that increases in federal welfare participation stimulated increases in welfare spending by states.[4] The most important implication of these findings is support for the "marble-cake" quality of policy development at state and local levels.[5] Models that ignore federal initiatives as explanations of state policy actions are clearly omitting one of the most important components of state welfare policy.

The key mechanism for administration of welfare policy in the American states is the complex set of arrangements between state and federal governments that has been established to provide income and other assistance to certain categories of the poor. Terms of intergovernmental agreements require states to furnish aid to poor persons who qualify by reason of old age, blindness, permanent and total disability, or the presence of dependent children. States administer this assistance according to a plan that binds them to administrative procedures and eligibility requirements set by federal law and regulations. In return, the federal government agrees to pay a large share of the costs of welfare assistance in each state. Exponential growth of welfare budgets in recent years is an outcome of provisions in federal-state agreements obligating the federal government to pay its share of spiraling welfare costs regardless of what states choose to spend. From a state perspective, policy initiatives to curb welfare costs are frustrated by federal requirements that leave little discretion over one of the largest items of expenditure in most state budgets.

---

[e] The most conservative estimate of numbers of persons below the poverty line for 1972 is 24,460,000 persons. In that year approximately 13,301,000 received welfare assistance of all types. This is a direct result of excluding poor persons who hold jobs (the "working poor") from receiving welfare benefits. In addition to being poor, welfare is generally available only if a person is *also* aged, blind, disabled, or supporting dependent children.

Rapid growth in welfare spending during the past decade is accompanied by dramatic changes in patterns of welfare policy. In 1960, for example, nearly half of all welfare expenditures by state and local governments went for Old Age Assistance (49.5%), somewhat less went for Aid to Families with Dependent Children—AFDC (28.3%), with the rest distributed among other categories of welfare assistance. Yet, a decade later, AFDC-related spending equaled spending for all other categories of income assistance combined. This striking shift in welfare spending policy resulted from phenomenal increases in numbers of dependents in the AFDC category while numbers of recipients in most categories either remained stable or declined. By 1970, 73 percent of all welfare dependents were AFDC related and the rising caseload trend in this category continued into the 1970s.

Although all spending by state and local governments is responsive to factors that exert inflationary pressures on all spending in the public sector, much of the increase in the welfare area can be attributed to changes in policy structures at the federal level, for example, a series of amendments to the Social Security Act, adopted in 1965, which extended coverage to persons formerly ineligible for AFDC assistance, initiated a massive program of medical coverage for welfare recipients, and provided the first increase in federal support for AFDC grants since 1958. Effective July 1, 1965, states were permitted to provide retroactive assistance to AFDC families with children over 18 years of age who were still attending school, to AFDC families with minor children earning income, and to persons residing in state-operated facilities for persons suffering from tuberculosis or mental illness. Retroactive features of the legislation produced significant caseload increases in states that took advantage of this option in 1965, well before the effective date of most other provisions. Increases in federal support of welfare grants added further impetus to the caseload spiral when they became effective in the following year.

Much of the increase in welfare spending since 1965 is a direct result of adoptions of Medicaid assistance programs by various states that provide payment for comprehensive medical assistance rendered to welfare recipients.[f] Within five years its expenditures ($5.5 billion by 1970) exceeded those for any of the categories that provide income support, including AFDC. Incentives for states to adopt the new program were great, not the least of which was a stipulation that federal reimbursement to participating states should be not less than 105 percent of state medical expenditures for welfare recipients in 1965. In addition, states were virtually coerced into adopting Medicaid since legislation provided for termination of all federal medical assistance payments to states that failed to provide basic Medicaid services by 1970. Even so, adoption of the program at the state level was not universal, with some states holding out until the deadline.[g] The net effect of Medicaid plus modifications of the basic income assistance programs was a whopping increase in levels of welfare spending at state and local levels and expanded welfare assistance financing to meet the needs of the poor in future years.

How can this knowledge be used to construct a model that represents "reality" and that can be manipulated by a computer to approximate system dynamics described above? Figure 5-1 introduces a model of welfare dynamics that includes selected salient variables of welfare policy since 1960 and structural arrangements that purport to describe and explain welfare activity during this period. Salient variables are identified as AFDC caseloads, federal welfare assistance to state and local governments, and the central focus of analysis—total welfare spending by state and local governments. Medicaid spending is a function of the number of welfare recipients, that is, AFDC caseloads, as a pro rata spending increase for each case and is included as part of the federal assistance factor.[h] Inputs of the 50 states to the operation of welfare policy are represented by introducing data on population size for each state as the "raw material" or "demands" that, when converted by structures of the welfare system, result in welfare spending by state and local governments.

The relationship of federal participation to state and local welfare spending policy is complex. Terms of federal-state agreements provide that state funds shall be spent before the federal government will honor claims for payment of its welfare assistance obligations. The "promise to pay" of the federal government, however, operates as an incentive for state and local governments to spend for welfare purposes in expectation of reimbursement. Federal welfare assistance thus exerts its influence on welfare spending by state and local governments *prior* to actual distribution of federal funds. This effect of federal reimbursement *in being* is represented in the model by arrows that indicate causal impacts on AFDC caseloads and welfare spending by state and local governments (Figure 5-1).

But federal welfare spending is also an *effect* of prior spending for welfare purposes by state and local governments. States submit claims for

---

[f] Adoption of the program *required* states to provide at least six basic medical services, including hospitalization and primary physician care, to all persons receiving aid under any of the categorical assistance programs. States are permitted to provide assistance under Medicaid to persons who qualify for categorical assistance under income standards but are not otherwise qualified to receive aid.

[g] As late as 1968, 11 states had not yet elected to provide medicaid assistance: Alabama, Alaska, Arizona, Arkansas, Florida, Indiana, Mississippi, New Jersey, North Carolina, Tennessee, and Virginia.

[h] When data are aggregated at state level, variation in utilization of medical services by individuals is obscured. Assuming that welfare populations in various states have approximately equal needs for medical care, the aggregated data will show additional spending due to Medicaid as a pro rata increase in cost per case.

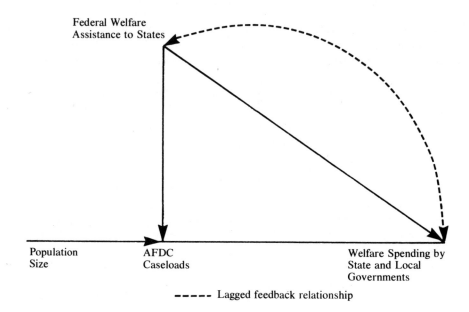

Federal Welfare
Assistance to States

Population
Size

AFDC
Caseloads

Welfare Spending by
State and Local
Governments

‑ ‑ ‑ ‑ ‑ Lagged feedback relationship

Figure 5-1. Model of Welfare Spending Processes

payment of federal obligations on a quarterly basis under terms of federal-
state agreements. These claims are audited by the federal government, a
process that delays federal payments, and several more months may elapse
before actual reimbursement occurs. This process implies a lag of several
months to a year from time of expenditure to time of reimbursement. In
order to take account of this feature of the federal role in welfare policy, a
one-year lag representing effects of state and local welfare spending on
federal welfare assistance is incorporated in the model as a feedback
relationship.

Specification of the Model

Simulation of the welfare spending model (Figure 5-1) requires explicit
statements of relationships between variables in the form of mathematical
equations or other statements subject to manipulation by the computer.
These statements or equations must be sequenced to conform with processes of the model and iterated (repeated) successively within the computer. Examination of the output enables a researcher to determine logical
consistency, stability, and correspondences to reality of the model. If, after
several iterations or repetitions, values of variables increase, decrease, or
oscillate in explosive fashion one may infer that: (a) social processes de-

scribed by the model are unstable; (b) the formulation of the model is unstable; or (c) the model is just plain wrong.

Forrester's work with urban systems suggests that equations representing systems dynamics contain two types of variables. The first are steady-state components that he designates "level" variables. The second type are those that define transactions occurring within the system or "rate" variables. Dynamics of a system are the interactions of these variables, that is, changes in level variables are a result of rate variables and changes in rate variables are a result of fluctuations in level variables. No level variable can affect another level variable except through an intervening rate variable. Likewise, no rate variable can affect another rate variable except through a level variable.[6]

Least squares regression equations of the form: $\hat{Y} = a + bX + e$ approximate this relationship. If X and Y are understood as "level" or steady-state variables and b is assumed to be the transaction or "rate" variable, relationships of b, X, and Y in the equation for the regression of Y on X are analogous to Forrester's concept of interactions between "level" and "rate" variables in dynamic systems. Since least squares equations are conducive to this interpretation, ordinary least squares estimates of parameters for each of the model's variable linkages provide explicit statements of underlying system dynamics amenable to treatment by computer simulation.

When the "estimating" equations that represent the two-variable relationship between population size and AFDC caseloads (based on 50 states) are derived for each year of the period 1960-70, the series of regression coefficients shows evidence of profound disturbance visible as trend (Table 5-1). A measure of slope in the series of coefficients indicates that the trend is pronounced. Difference of this measure from zero indicates approximate error in estimating parameters attributable to trend. Ignorance of trend factors is generally a serious weakness of many cross-sectional analyses. In this case, if one were attempting to predict AFDC caseloads from parameters estimated at t_1, for example, error would increase at an exponential rate until t_n, at which point the prediction would very likely be far off the mark.

There are several strategies for coping with trend. One strategy is simply to control for trend by removing it from the time series. A second strategy is to treat trend as a function of time in a differential equation.[7] Neither of these strategies attempts to *explain* trend or identify its source. In fact, trend in a series of coefficients signifies effects of a variable not included in the model. The preferred strategy for coping with trend is to identify the disturbing variable and include it in the estimating equation.

The source of trend in the relationship between population size and AFDC caseloads proves to be effects of federal welfare assistance on the

Table 5-1
Multivariate Analysis of Population Size and Federal Welfare Assistance as Predictors of AFDC Caseloads, 1960-70

	Bivariate Coefficients of Regression of AFDC caseloads on Population size[a]	Intercepts of Multivariate Estimation Equation	Multivariate Coefficients of Regression of AFDC Caseloads on Population Size	Multivariate Coefficients of Regression of AFDC Caseloads on Federal Welfare Assistance	Multiple R
1960	15.16485	−484.99064	10.00323	0.52197	0.94
1961	18.40012	−2,638.18309	15.05025	0.32958	.92
1962	20.24305	−4,676.60873	15.41258	0.39639	.91
1963	21.72996	−6,504.27321	16.67961	0.34902	.93
1964	25.10600	−13,740.97525	16.57023	0.54579	.95
1965	26.99912	−13,283.53988	12.27410	0.82983	.96
1966	29.31794	−14,863.01708	9.83844	0.94174	.96
1967	33.64175	−16,475.73494	16.73689	0.63626	.96
1968	39.50420	−6,436.28603	10.05017	0.79415	.98
1969	46.45018	−4,618.40721	13.33835	0.74411	.99
1970	60.75253	−10,716.72574	20.06189	0.77800	0.99
Slope of Series =	3.87234		0.18856	0.04638	
Series Mean =	−30.66452	−8,585.34016	14.18325	0.62426	

Source: U.S. Department of Commerce, Statistical Abstract of the United States (Washington, D.C.: U.S. Government Printing Office, 1961-74 editions).

[a]Correlation coefficients for each year: $r > 10.90$.

relationship. When this variable is included in the equation determining AFDC caseloads, the series of regression coefficients representing the relationship between population size and AFDC caseloads becomes stable and the slope of the series is reduced toward zero (Table 5-1). This finding is consistent with intuitive perceptions of the welfare system in which pressures, needs, or "demands" of state residents are combined with federal incentives resulting in a program of assistance to AFDC and other categories of recipients.

A similar trend is observed in the relationship (series of regression coefficients) between AFDC caseloads and welfare spending by state and local governments (Table 5-2). This trend is also reduced toward zero when federal welfare assistance is included in the estimating equation. No significant trend is observed in the feedback relationship so that a bivariate equation appears sufficient for estimating federal welfare assistance at $t + 1$ from welfare spending by state and local governments at t.

Although the problem of trend is eliminated, a second problem is evident on returning to Table 5-1—a discontinuity in the relationship between federal welfare assistance and AFDC caseloads between 1964 and 1965. This abrupt change in the relationship coincides with implementation of 1965 amendments to the Social Security Act discussed above and, therefore, presents no conceptual difficulties. If the disruption is significantly large, however, it will represent a source of error in the estimating equation.

Since the coefficients appear relatively stable before and after the discontinuity, it is feasible to test its significance by analyzing differences in means of the relationship before and after 1965. Table 5-4 shows that differences in the coefficients of pretest and posttest series are significant at the 0.02 level and therefore likely to become a source of error in the estimating equations. Examination of other sets of relationships in the model reveal no similar discontinuities.

Impacts of these changes in federal welfare policy can be observed in other linkages of the model as discontinuities in the intercepts (Table 5-2 and 5-3). These discontinuities are interpretable as *lagged* effects of the changes that took place in federal welfare policy since 1965. Although these effects are consistent with intuitive perceptions of the impacts of federal welfare legislation, they do pose probable sources of error for equations specifying linkages of the welfare spending model.

Exploitation of dummy variable techniques are helpful for coping with this type of data situation. The basic strategy is to include a binary variable in the estimating equations to account for discontinuities in the data.[1] In this

---

[1]Gordon Hilton of Northwestern University and Jong Lee of Virginia Polytechnic Institute and State University have made helpful suggestions regarding use of dummy variables in this context.

Table 5-2
Multivariate Analysis of AFDC Caseloads and Federal Welfare Assistance as Predictors of Welfare Spending by State and Local Governments, 1960-70

	Bivariate Coefficients of Regression of Welfare Spending on AFDC Caseloads	Intercepts of Multivariate Estimation Equations	Multivariate Coefficients of Regression of Welfare Spending on AFDC Caseloads	Multivariate Coefficients of Regression of Welfare Spending on Federal Welfare Assistance	Multiple R
1960	1.24547	−5,895.36608	0.39489	1.37194	0.97
1961	1.13170	−10,408.05281	0.40224	1.47461	.97
1962	1.12629	−13,502.70408	0.19376	1.78362	.97
1963	1.18623	−11,966.85302	0.22451	1.60536	.98
1964	1.22566	−15,269.47124	0.40842	1.38971	.99
1965	1.47069	−13,153.46615	0.59946	1.36646	.99
1966	1.75588	−29,641.95748	0.71629	1.51285	.99
1967	2.06782	−40,541.27257	1.39907	0.85533	.99
1968	2.29574	−42,468.45369	0.60049	1.77998	.99
1969	2.30067	−39,939.62666	0.30550	2.04011	.99
1970	1.84913	−32,937.88233	0.41590	1.62863	.99
Slope of Series =	0.12269		0.03268	0.01963	
Series Mean =		−23,239.55510	0.51459	1.52789	

Source: U.S. Department of Commerce, Statistical Abstract of the United States (Washington, D.C.: U.S. Government Printing Office, 1961-74 editions).

case the dummy variable signifies independent effects of the federal welfare policy intervention. Prior to implementation of 1965 amendments to the Social Security Act the value of the variable is set at zero; when the amendments become effective, value of the dummy variable is set at unity. The variable thus becomes unity in the equation determining AFDC caseloads in 1965, coinciding with observed step-level change in federal welfare assistance coefficients (Table 5-1). Unity is assigned to the variable in the equation determining state and local welfare spending beginning in 1966 when independent effects of the amendments are noted as an increase in the level of intercepts (Table 5-2). Although the discontinuity in Table 5-3 is less a step-level change than it is a change from stable intercepts to increasing intercepts, the dummy variable attains unity in 1967, coincident with lagged effects of increases in welfare spending by state and local governments of the previous year. These lagged values of the dummy variable signifying independent effects of changes in the welfare policy mechanism correspond to observed discontinuities in the data and intuitive perceptions of dynamic interactions of variables included in the model.

When these adjustments have been made, relationships of variables in the welfare spending model are specified by estimating parameters from the data for the period under consideration, 1960-70. The model is defined as a set of equations:

$$A_t = -10,863.64945 + 10.73707(P_t) + 0.84450(F_t)$$
$$+ 5,248.51592(S_t) \tag{5.1}$$

$$W_t = -28,543.17428 + 0.40702(A_t) + 1.78125(F_t)$$
$$+ 2,015.36034(S_{t-1})^* \tag{5.2}$$

$$F_t = 8,833.03278 + 0.51156(W_{t-1})^*$$
$$+ 5,908.09829(S_{t-2})^* \tag{5.3}$$

* signifies lagged effects.

where A = AFDC caseloads

W = Welfare spending by state and local governments

F = Federal welfare assistance

P = Population size

S = Social Security Act Amendments of 1965

In a recursive system simultaneous equations pose a problem for identifying unique values of coefficients when parameters are estimated by least-square methods. Specifically, the problem arises in models that contain more endogenous (variables determined within the model) than

Table 5-3

Relationship of Welfare Spending By State and Local Governments with Federal Welfare Assistance, 1960-70[a]

	Intercepts of Estimation Equations	Coefficients of Regression of Federal Welfare Assistance on Welfare Spending	Pearson's r
1960-61	5,252.52559	0.51951	0.97
1961-62	5,974.58789	.53126	.97
1962-63	6,138.26150	.55702	.98
1963-64	6,770.88010	.56128	.98
1964-65	5,018.90509	.56621	.99
1965-66	6,604.16485	.52126	.98
1966-67	8,078.61326	.53340	.99
1967-68	11,393.39425	.54307	.99
1968-69	16,812.79176	.49679	.99
1969-70	22,489.16924	0.49148	0.98
Series Mean =	8,593.93578	0.53213	
	Slope of Series =	−0.00477	

Source: U.S. Department of Commerce, Statistical Abstract of the United States (Washington, D.C.: U.S. Government Printing Office, 1961-74 editions).

[a]Relationship is lagged, that is, Federal Welfare Assistance at t is conceived as a function of welfare spending at $t - 1$.

exogenous (independently determined) variables. If the model is "under-identified" a unique set of parameters cannot be obtained since an indefinite number of combinations of coefficients will produce the same result. When a variable is lagged, however, it is treated as an independently determined or exogenous variable for purposes of estimating parameters. Because the feedback relationship is lagged, federal welfare assistance is exogenous for identification purposes. The dummy variable is also exogenous, insuring that all parameters of the model are at least fully identified.[8]

The welfare spending model may now be precisely specified by applying estimated parameters of the above equations as statements of interactions among variables. In this form, the model is subject to manipulation by the computer and may be tested in a simulation.

Operation of the Simulation

Simulation tests a model's ability to represent actual social dynamics by

Table 5-4

Test for Discontinuity in a Series of Regression Coefficients Representing Relationship Between Federal Welfare Assistance and AFDC Caseloads: Difference of Means Test[a]

Pretest Slope	Posttest Slope			
0.00671	−0.01983			

Pretest Mean	Posttest Mean	df	t-Value	Level of Significance (One-tailed Test)
0.42854	0.78735	9	2.80715	0.02

[a]Discontinuity occurs in the transition from 1964 to 1965.

generating values of variables that correspond to those of historical events. If the model performs this task successfully, the simulation lends confidence that the model captures essential relationships of the system under examination.

In order for the simulation to operate, data on population size for each of the 50 states is input into the system. All other variable values are generated by the model with the single exception of federal welfare assistance values for 1960. In all other years values of this variable are generated solely from values and parameters of the model.

When equations of the model are manipulated to simulate behavior of the welfare spending system, 1960-70, the operation results in highly accurate projections of system values throughout the period. Table 5-5 indicates the degree of accuracy in these projections—over 92 percent accuracy in all estimates of total welfare spending by state and local governments and, in at least five cases accuracy exceeds 98 percent. Similarly high levels of success are maintained in projecting AFDC caseloads and federal welfare assistance.

An additional test of a model's reliability or consistency is its ability to project variable values beyond the time period of the data on which its parameters are based. When values of the model are generated to simulate the period 1971-73, projections of welfare spending by state and local governments continue to be highly accurate (Table 5-5). Values of AFDC caseloads and federal welfare assistance prove to be less accurate than in previous iterations. The simulation underestimates both caseloads and welfare spending for 1971 and 1972.

These errors are most likely a result of two extraneous factors. The first is the economic recession that began in 1969 and continued until 1972. Most states reported abnormally high increases in caseloads during these years

Table 5-5
Accuracy of Prediction By the Welfare Spending Model: 1960-73

	AFDC Caseloads		Welfare Spending		Federal Welfare Assistance	
	Accuracy of Prediction %	Direction of Error	Accuracy of Prediction %	Direction of Error	Accuracy of Prediction %	Direction of Error
1960	90.4	+	95.8	−	a	
1961	99.1	−	97.1	−	90.5	+
1962	97.5	−	99.5	−	87.4	+
1963	98.6	−	96.1	+	97.3	−
1964	97.0	−	92.6	+	98.9	−
1965	94.7	+	99.4	−	96.5	+
1966	99.0	+	98.7	−	97.9	+
1967	94.5	+	98.1	−	96.8	+
1968	95.2	+	94.9	−	96.4	−
1969	98.0	−	94.7	−	96.4	−
1970	83.4	−	99.5	−	94.6	−
1971	81.4	−	99.0	+	82.9	−
1972	87.4	−	98.5	−	69.9	−
1973	99.4	−	99.6	−	87.2	−

aValues for Federal Welfare Assistance are not generated for 1960.

so that, without an additional variable in the equations representing caseload pressures generated as a result of these conditions, the model tends to underestimate caseloads for these years. The low estimation of federal welfare assistance is probably a result of several holdout states simultaneously adopting medicaid programs at the 1970 deadline. While adoption of the program need not have increased state welfare spending for medical assistance, it would substantially increase the amount of reimbursement paid to the state the following year. Because the simulation largely recovers its ability to predict variable levels for 1973, it is reasonable to assume that inaccuracies are the result of these temporary, extraneous factors that have only short-term effects on operation of the system.

Results of the Welfare Spending Simulation

Development and testing of the welfare spending model by computer simulation represents an effort in theory-building that attempts to avoid what Harold Lasswell has called "distortions that come from mistaking cross-contextual correlations or formal beauty for satisfactory results."[9] Although the model incorporates insights from "theories" of welfare spending, it comprises theory on a limited scale—not a general model of public policy. Nevertheless, the model provides insights into operations of welfare policy structures and is a valuable tool for analyzing policy decisions as well as for projecting future developments in the welfare policy area.

The four-variable model posited here explains welfare spending by state and local governments with a high degree of accuracy. All variables included in the model are of considerable interest to policy makers, especially AFDC caseloads, welfare spending by state and local governments, and federal welfare assistance to states. By identifying these major determinants of welfare spending systems, the model points to areas where policy decisions will substantially change outcomes of the welfare process.

What are the advantages of simulations of this type over other forms of policy analysis? One of the most important advantages is the ability to incorporate into an analysis the profound effects of longitudinal factors on the course of welfare policy. Although population size of states is highly correlated with AFDC caseloads, dynamics of the welfare spending model show that it is a poor predictor of welfare caseloads because of a pronounced trend in the relationship (Table 5-1). In order to stabilize the relationship, federal welfare assistance factors must be included in the prediction equation. When this variable is added, coefficients that represent the relationship between AFDC caseloads and population size become stable over time.

A major development in policy analysis has been a growing interest in nonincremental change occurring in policy systems. Table 5-1 provides an operational definition of nonincremental change as a radical (statistically significant) discontinuity in the relationship between federal welfare assistance and AFDC caseloads—a result of federal legislation adopted in 1965 that modifies structures of federal-state arrangements for providing assistance to the needy. In this case the binary dummy variable (representing independent effects of amendments to the Social Security Act adopted in 1965) must be included in the equations to improve accuracy in estimating crucial variables. The multivariate form of these equations provides evidence of the complex nature of transactions in the welfare system—both longitudinal and cross-sectional—that are captured by this form of analysis.

The importance of federal welfare assistance as a determinant of state and local welfare spending lends considerable support to the "marble-cake" concept of public policy activity. While not all policies at state and local levels are stimulated by massive inputs of federal funds, a model that purports to explain welfare policy at state levels is clearly deficient unless it includes existing components of federal activity in this area. Where a state or local policy involves considerable amounts of federal funds, importance of federal involvement for determining policy at lower levels of government can be evaluated by techniques of simulation suggested here.

Measurement of independent effects of the Social Security amendments of 1965 on dynamics of the welfare spending system (coefficients of the dummy variables) should be persuasive evidence that "political" factors do exert significant impacts on policy at state and local levels. Both variables needed to correct for longitudinal variance in the relationship between population size and AFDC caseloads—federal welfare assistance and federal legislative innovations—are distinctly *political* variables that contribute substantially to an explanation of welfare spending. In fact, all variables crucial to the conversion process are "political" variables (or at least variables identified with government administration of welfare policy), indicating that very important aspects of state welfare policies are explained without reference to socioeconomic values apart from population size. Efforts to develop similar models for investigating linkages between legislative outputs and policy outcomes should be encouraged by this analysis.

Uses of the Simulation

Simulation techniques permit evaluations of alternate structures of federal welfare policy. By substituting values for the federal welfare assistance variable or the feedback parameter, the simulation of welfare spending may be repeated to test effects of federal policy modifications on welfare policies at state and local levels. For example, instead of the complex formula for reimbursement based upon grants to individuals, one might determine values of federal assistance to each state based upon reimbursement of a fixed percentage of all funds spent for welfare assistance by state and local governments.[j] Substitution of these values for the federal welfare assistance variable in an operation of the simulation will indicate effects of this policy change on state policy—either increasing or decreasing AFDC caseloads and/or state and local welfare spending.

---

[j]Effective in 1966, the federal formula provided reimbursement to states providing AFDC assistance on the basis of $15 of the first $18 per recipient plus a fraction of the remainder up to a maximum of $32. This feature has stimulated an emphasis in caseload increases as opposed to grants increases since any increase in grants above the $32 maximum is provided solely from state revenues. Increases in caseload size, however, permits reimbursement of some portion of the increased spending at state and local levels and generation of a flow of federal dollars into a state that would not otherwise be available.

What is suggested here is the substitution for actual federal welfare assistance values of a value that is computed on the basis of a fixed proportion of *total* welfare spending by state and local governments. Impacts of this policy change can then be predicted from the simulation.

Further use of the simulation requires reestimation of the model's parameters from data for which the time series is extended as far as possible into the future. In other words, parameters should be redetermined from data that includes federal welfare assistance and AFDC caseloads for 1971-73. Unless step-level changes in relationships of the model occur (which can also be accommodated by addition of other dummy variables) this procedure will keep the model current for predicting future welfare spending.

When simulation models are supplied in this fashion, the model satisfies one of the most crucial criteria of policy research. By identifying variables subject to manipulation by policy makers, for example, federal reimbursement structures, the model indicates areas in which the system is amenable to modification of its outcomes. Computer simulation techniques thus offer models and methods that promise more precise knowledge of government policy actions and more effective controls. It is important to note that this knowledge does not necessarily imply development of more effective or even more desirable welfare policies. How this knowledge is utilized is subject to the aims of decision makers and the arts of politics. Without such knowledge of the dynamics that shape public policy, however, more effective policies are beyond human reach. With such knowledge, development of policy is at least subject to the directions in which mankind chooses to live.

Notes

1. Jay Forrester, *Urban Dynamics* (Cambridge, Massachusetts: M.I.T. Press, 1969). See also his *World Dynamics* (Cambridge, Mass.: Wright-Allen Press, 1971).

2. For an effective use of these factors in explaining poverty see A. Dale Tussing, *Poverty In A Dual Economy* (New York: St. Martin's Press, 1975), pp. 69-113.

3. Seymour Sachs and Robert Harris, "The Determinants of State and Local Government Expenditures and Intergovernmental Flows of Funds," *National Tax Journal* (March, 1964), pp. 75-85.

4. Jack Osman, "On the Use of Intergovernmental Aid as an Expenditure Determinant," *National Tax Journal* (December, 1968), pp. 437-447.

5. This analogy was developed by Morton Grodzins, "The Federal System," in The President's Commission on National Goals, *Goals For Americans* (Englewood Cliffs, N.J.: Prentice-Hall, 1960).

6. Forrester, *Urban Dynamics,* pp. 13-14.

7. For a discussion of these techniques see Hubert M. Blalock, Jr., *Theory Construction* (Englewood Cliffs, N.J.: Prentice-Hall, 1969), pp. 88-94.

8. Problems of identification, assumptions associated with use of simultaneous equations in recursive systems, and use of lagged variables are treated in Blalock, *Theory Construction*, pp. 59-71, 78-84. Problems associated with auto-correlated error from lagged endogenous variables also pose a threat to reliability of regression coefficients generated by ordinary least squares methods but are too complex to be treated here.

9. In a Preface to Ronald D. Brunner and Garry D. Brewer, *Organized Complexity* (New York: The Free Press, 1971), p. xii.

Part II
Inadequate Coordination

Administrative Politics and the War on Poverty

James E. Anderson

This is a case study in administrative politics. Its focus is the Office of Economic Opportunity (OEO), which was established in 1964 to handle the implementation of a major socioeconomic program, the Johnson administration's War on Poverty. It is primarily concerned with three aspects of the political life of OEO: first, the creation of OEO and some of the issues involved therein; second, the role of OEO as coordinator of the War on Poverty at the national level, which especially involves the relationships of OEO with the national bureaucracy; and third, the political viability of OEO, which concerns its external relationships with the general political environment. Little is said about substantive programs or the administrative process within OEO, except as such commentary may be useful to the understanding and explanation of OEO's political life (and demise). Notwithstanding these limitations, this chapter should convey useful insight into administration of the War on Poverty and its substantive thrust.

The Genesis of OEO

In his State of the Union Message on January 8, 1964, President Johnson announced to the Congress that his administration had declared "unconditional war on poverty" and spoke generally of the means for combating it. Two months later he sent a special message on poverty to Congress, along with a draft bill embodying his recommendations for dealing with the problem of poverty. As passed by Congress in August, 1964, the Economic Opportunity Act provided for ten different substantive programs to combat poverty: the Community Action program, Job Corps, Neighborhood Youth Corps, work experience program, adult basic education program, college work study program, aid to migratory workers, rural loan program, small business loan program, and Volunteers in Service to America (VISTA). The Office of Economic Opportunity was created with authority to administer directly some of the new programs and to provide overall coordination of the War on Poverty.

In the course of the development of the War on Poverty proposal within the Executive branch, especially during the period from November 1963 to March 1964, a number of important issues for the future administration of the war on poverty arose and were at least temporarily resolved. What

75

substantive programs should be included in the new poverty program? What kind of administrative apparatus should be established to administer the new program—a new agency, a coordinating council, or what? If a new agency was to be set up, where should it be located in the executive branch? Should a new agency have only coordinating responsibilities, or should it operate programs as well? Which agencies should administer which programs? The answers to these questions were provided through a process of bargaining among various executive officials and agencies.[1]

A brief review of the development of the poverty proposal is necessary to deal adequately with the first question concerning the program's substantive content. Following President Kennedy's decision in the fall of 1963 that he wanted "a comprehensive, coordinated attack on poverty" to be included in his 1964 legislative program, Chairman Walter Heller of the Council of Economic Advisers called on the executive departments and agencies to submit their ideas on how to combat poverty. A large number of suggestions were received, with each agency's proposals generally falling within its particular policy area. The task of developing a specific antipoverty proposal was given to the Council of Economic Advisers and the Bureau of the Budget (now the Office of Management and Budget). Initially, a limited community demonstration program was decided upon by the Council-Budget planners. It was to take the form of federal grants to several selected communities to help them develop their own broad antipoverty proposals and was to be administered by a council consisting of a chairman appointed by the President and the heads of the involved departments and agencies. This alternative appeared attractive for several reasons. It was a way to deal with the poverty problem with limited funds, $500 million having been earmarked for poverty in the President's proposed budget for 1965. Also, it utilized grass-roots initiative and appeared to be a means for getting the various agencies to focus on poverty rather than their jurisdictional boundaries.

However, many of the old-line departments and agencies were not pleased with this proposal. The Department of Agriculture wanted more attention on rural poverty, the Department of Commerce thought the role of local business leadership was not adequately emphasized, and so on. At a White House meeting on January 23, 1964, called to discuss a draft bill of the proposal prepared by the Department of Health, Education, and Welfare, Secretary of Labor Wirtz sharply attacked the community program proposal and contended that the poverty program should take the form of an expansion and redirection of activities currently being administered by existing agencies. He succeeded in winning support for this position from some of the other officials present.

To end the threatened stalemate, President Johnson announced on February 1st that he was appointing Sargent Shriver to head a special task force to draft the antipoverty legislation. At a meeting of departmental representatives and others called by Shriver a few days later, it became apparent that substantial support existed for a broad assault on poverty and consequently the limited Community Action pilot program was abandoned in favor of a package of several legislative proposals. It "was simply not compatible with the President's rhetoric to fight an 'unconditional war' on a pilot basis."[2] In its final form the administration's proposal included something for everyone among the poor and was essentially an amalgam of distinct proposals favored by a number of agencies, for example, work training by Labor, rural loans by Agriculture, work experience for those on relief by HEW, adult basic education by the Office of Education. The community action idea, which was retained, was the one really new element in the draft bill sent to Congress.

A second issue concerned the type of administrative apparatus to be utilized to administer the new program. Two basic positions emerged. Some wanted a separate new agency with its own director, arguing that independence was necessary to insure innovation in the poverty program and to prevent its capture by an existing agency. It was further said that an independent agency would help dramatize the poverty issue and facilitate coordination of the overall effort. A second group favored administration of the new program by the existing departments, contending that they had the expertise and could get the new activities quickly underway. Some sort of general coordinating mechanism (a special assistant to the president, a committee or council in the Executive Office were possibilities) would be established to conduct studies, set guidelines, and exercise general supervisory power. This alternative was favored by the Departments of Labor and HEW and other operating agencies. The President decided in favor of the new independent agency alternative. "The best way to kill a new idea," he remarked at one point, "is to put it in an old line agency."[3]

Another issue requiring resolution was whether the new agency should have program operating responsibilities, be limited to coordinating existing agencies, or be assigned a combination of these duties. The selection of Shriver to direct the drafting of the legislation, and presumably to head the new poverty agency, in effect settled the issue as he apparently had no desire to spend his time simply trying to coordinate his other agencies. This did not fit his "administrative style." Thus, the new agency was to have both operating and coordinating duties.

This in turn gave rise to yet another question: Which programs should be assigned to the new agency and which to existing agencies. A major controversy here involved the Department of Labor. Secretary Wirtz, at the least, wanted work experience programs for his department. Apparently, under a "gentleman's agreement" made at one point during deliberations on the poverty bill, the Job Corps and the Neighborhood Youth

Corps were to be assigned to Labor in return for Labor's withdrawal of its Youth Employment Bill then before Congress. However, Shriver decided he wanted the Job Corps for OEO, apparently anticipating that it would yield quick results and bring favorable publicity to the new agency. At the same time HEW contended that work training for those on relief was properly within its jurisdiction. The President finally resolved this controversy, with the Job Corps going to OEO, the Neighborhood Youth Corps to Labor, and work experience to HEW. (A Department of Labor official cited this dispute as one cause of the ongoing conflict between Labor and OEO.) The community action, migrant assistance, and VISTA programs were also given to OEO to operate. Informal agreements provided that the other programs (rural loans, small business loans, the work study program) would be delegated to the relevant agencies for operation, subject to OEO supervision.

A final issue concerned the location of OEO in the executive branch. Shriver wanted it put in the Executive Office of the President so as to give it the leverage needed to coordinate the poverty activities of the other departments and agencies. This was opposed by the Bureau of the Budget, which, as a matter of principle, opposed the location of agencies with operating responsibilities in the Executive Office. Given the Budget Bureau's "institutional vested interest" in coordination, OEO was probably also viewed as a potential competitor. The President again decided in Shriver's favor, although it was agreed that a provision in the law should provide for review of OEO's status after one year (which has never been done).

Thus, the OEO was the product of a variety of conflicts and compromises. Some of these conflicts were only temporarily resolved and soon reemerged, once the poverty bill was passed by Congress and OEO began operations.

The Way of the Coordinator Is Not Easy

While coordination is a procedural task, it has clear implications for the substance and impact of public policy. Coordination involves the common direction of policies or programs to eliminate conflicts and divergencies, and to insure their focus on a common goal for its better attainment. A working definition provided by an OEO official states: "Coordination is action taken by persons responsible for a variety of programs to mesh their programs with other related programs so that the total needs of individuals and families can be met with maximum effectiveness and . . . conveniences to the client."[4] When policy is viewed as a course of action, as what is actually done in dealing with a problem, then coordination helps determine policy content and impact.

President Johnson, in his March 1964 message to Congress on poverty cautioned lest it ''[should] become a series of uncoordinated and unrelated efforts—that it perish for lack of leadership and direction.'' To prevent this he recommended creation of the Office of Economic Opportunity, whose director, as his ''personal Chief of Staff for the war on poverty,'' would be ''directly responsible'' for the new program and would ''work with and through existing agencies of the government.''

As enacted by Congress, several sections of the Economic Opportunity Act (EOA) (especially Sections 610-613) provided OEO with a statutory base to act as coordinator of the overall war on poverty, not just the programs started by the act, such as Community Action, Neighborhood Youth Corps, and rural loans. This was a large task as in fiscal 1967, which was around the peak of the war on poverty, federal spending on behalf of the poor totalled $21.1 billion, including $1.6 billion by OEO. About $9 billion of the total went for programs limited to the needy, such as EOA and public assistance. The remainder was accounted for by programs providing some aid to the poor as part of their broader purpose. *The Catalog of Federal Programs for Individual and Community Improvement,* compiled in 1965 by OEO, listed some 250 programs administered by 15 agencies as being related to the antipoverty effort. We turn now to a look at some of OEO's efforts and accomplishments as coordinator of the war on poverty.[5]

1. Several programs authorized by EOA were delegated to other agencies for operation. These included the Neighborhood Youth Corps and some other employment programs to the Department of Labor, the rural loan program to the Farmers Home Administration, and the work experience program to the Department of Health, Education, and Welfare. Delegation agreements negotiated by OEO and the delegate agencies specified conditions under which the programs would be administered and took the final form of executive orders signed by the President. OEO sought to maintain continuing influence over delegated programs through its Office of Governmental Relations. Concerning this relationship, it was stated that:

Some departments desire as free a rein in program operations as possible under a delegation of authority, while others prefer to work closely with OEO on program matters. Sometimes conflicts occur. Nevertheless, the coordination of activities is much greater than would be the case were the programs being operated by separate organizations without the common legislative authority.[6]

2. Checkpoint agreements, a procedure developed by OEO, were negotiated with several agencies. Under these agreements, for example, federal agencies having responsibilities for programs related to community action, such as the Department of Housing and Urban Development, required local applicants to include with their applications a check sheet indicating community action agency comments on the proposed projects.

This neither involved a veto nor insured close coordination; it did insure that projects inconsistent with other local projects or plans were not *knowingly* funded.

3. Formal agreements ("memoranda of understanding") were negotiated with individual departments and agencies under which they and OEO agreed to cooperate toward common goals. Most related to programs directly operated by OEO. Thus, an agreement with the Departments of Agriculture and Interior concerned the operation of Job Corps camps on land under their control. An agreement with HEW in 1965 led to "operation medicare alert," whereby the two agencies cooperated in signing up eligible old people for medicare.

4. OEO developed a national antipoverty plan that set fund allocations for OEO programs and proposed funding levels for all antipoverty programs for a five-year period, annually updated. This five-year plan, developed in cooperation with other agencies, was submitted to the Bureau of the Budget, which reserved final decisions on funding for itself with OEO acting as an "occasional commentator" on other programs.[7] The 1967 Economic Opportunity Amendments provided that OEO should submit an annually updated national antipoverty plan to Congress. These plans appear not to have had much impact on actual budget decisions.

5. The Economic Opportunity Council, comprised of a number of agency heads, was intended to be a top-level coordinating body and adjunct of OEO. In actuality, its accomplishments were modest. It did set up a Federal Information System with county-by-county data on 160 federal grant programs and helped organize multiagency projects to deal with the problems of displaced farm workers in the Mississippi Delta and Indians on reservations, and with some consumer programs. Yet, as the Senate Manpower Subcommittee concluded, while the council "has been a useful forum for communications among federal agencies and for discussion of some relatively minor problems of coordination on an *ad hoc* basis, . . . it has not served as an effective tool for concerted action with coordinated followthrough."[8]

6. Through its activities and the exhortations and urgings of some of its officials, OEO undoubtedly did keep the attention of other agencies more focused on poverty than would have been the case in its absence. It is, of course, not really possible to measure such accomplishments.

In all, OEO accomplished little in coordinating the overall war on poverty. Most of its efforts were confined to activities required by its own operating programs and delegated EOA programs. Following an extensive examination of the war on poverty in 1967, the sympathetic Senate Manpower Subcommittee observed that "One of the major unresolved problems of the poverty program . . . is the lack of sufficient coordination among the wide variety of programs which serve the poor."[9] In retrospect, it was perhaps too much to expect otherwise, notwithstanding the brave words spoken about coordination, given the conditions and problems that OEO confronted.

By assigning both broad coordinating and operating duties to OEO, the Economic Opportunity Act gave the agency tasks that were essentially incompatible. James Sundquist suggests that "It is the 'Gresham's Law' of administration that operations tend to drive out staff work."[10] Most of OEO's energies were absorbed by the demands of its operating programs. The focus on operations was strengthened by the preference of Sargent Shriver, its first director, for an operating rather than coordinating role for OEO and by his desire and that of President Johnson to get the poverty program rapidly underway and quickly to show some concrete results. Coordination, by its nature, is often both slow and unspectacular, however important its ultimate payoffs may be.

The statutory coordinating authority given OEO was, as an OEO official put it, primarily paper authority. Political power, direct responsibility, and money generate action in the government establishment and OEO had too little of these. OEO's experience clearly demonstrates Norton Long's proposition that legal authority is a "politically insufficient" basis for effective administration.[11] President Johnson never clearly designated and fully supported OEO as his agent in directing the war on poverty. As time went on his interest and enthusiasm for the agency clearly diminished. Nor could OEO use its underprivileged clientele, the poor, as an effective power base.

Even with respect to its delegated programs OEO's coordinating power was limited. Once delegated, a program would have been difficult to reacquire because of the disruption this would cause in its administration and the predictable opposition of the delegate agency. Budget controls over delegated programs did give OEO some "clout," which it lacked elsewhere. Still, for example, there was not much OEO could do to keep the Department of Labor from running the Neighborhood Youth Corps "its" way.[12]

As an operating agency, OEO competed with other agencies for operating authority and funds. They looked upon OEO as an equal, at best, and resisted coordination by an equal. The formal location of OEO in the Executive Office of the President did not provide it with status that could be converted into coordinating authority. Agencies did not view it in the same light as the Council of Economic Advisers or the Budget Bureau. Indeed, OEO itself was subject to coordination by the Budget Bureau.

The agencies and programs that OEO was supposed to coordinate were not only many and diverse, they were also based on their own laws, traditions, and institutions, which made them resistant to change. Agency rivalries, personality conflicts, and political support can reinforce such separation. Thus, Labor was reluctant to coordinate its manpower training activities with OEO, believing that manpower training belonged in "its bailiwick." Personal antagonism between Shriver and Secretary of Labor Wirtz was another complicating factor.[13] On the other hand OEO had generally good working relations with Agriculture and Interior on job corps conservation camps. Conflict is a tendency but not a "law" of interagency relations.

OEO officials often referred to their agency as the representative of the poor in the government and perceived its task as goading other agencies into more responsiveness to the poor. Another "self-conception" was that OEO was an innovator, seeking new means to effectively combat poverty. In practice, OEO did act as a gadfly, helped "stir up" the poor, and criticized the existing order. Other agencies consequently tended to resent OEO. Moreover, in the first year or two some attitudes and actions of OEO officials caused ill-will or strained relations with other agencies. A well known example was lack of regard for social workers expressed by Shriver in 1965, a position from which he later had to retreat.

Finally, it is not uncommon for interdepartmental committees like the Economic Opportunity Council to be meagre in their accomplishment. In its case, other coordinating committees had overlapping jurisdiction; agencies viewed it as a part of OEO and were reluctant to submit problems to it; and it had no independent staff and no means to see that its decisions were implemented. An attempt was made to revive the council by legislative action in 1967 but President Johnson never appointed the members to the reconstituted council.

The Struggle for Existence

A well-known quotation in the literature of public administration states that "organizations are in a continual process of adjustment to the political environment that surrounds them—an adjustment that seeks to keep a favorable balance of political support over political opposition."[14] This statement encapsulates an important proposition about the political life of administrative agencies. The political support that brings an agency into existence is not a static phenomenon. Some agencies, over time, lose their support, or incur so much opposition, as the case may be, and subsequently disappear. Notable examples include the Farm Security Administration, the National Resources Planning Board, and the Area Redevelopment Administration. Other agencies suffering an unfavorable change in their balance of political support may survive but have some of their programs transferred to other agencies or they may be restricted in their operations by budget reductions and statutory limitations. It is not simply a "will to survive" that enables agencies to continue in existence; they need, and usually must seek, political support.

OEO was probably one of the most controversial agencies created in recent decades. Much criticism and comment was directed at the agency, its programs and personnel, and it was the subject of a variety of political conflicts. In part this was undoubtedly due to the highly visible nature of the agency. Following its well-publicized birth, its wide range of programs affected many hundreds of communities (for example, there were over a thousand community action programs at one point) and the press, both local and national, gave much attention to its activities, especially to its administrative difficulties and operating errors. In its early years OEO appears to have been the "victim" of what Harold Wilensky calls "crisis journalism," whose "dominant feature . . . is the failure to distinguish the trivial from the significant."[15] Relatively minor problems and imbroglios (in terms of actual seriousness, amount of money involved, number of people affected) were seized upon and publicized along with such accusations against OEO as that it was variously a "bureaucratic boondoggle" characterized by "giant fiestas of political patronage" and paying "wildly excessive salaries." One found comparatively little in the press about OEO's accomplishments. This undoubtedly cost OEO some public support.

Too, the position of OEO was not aided by the overenthusiastic and exaggerated claims initially made in behalf of the agency and its programs by the president, Sargent Shriver, and others. The antipoverty activities that developed after 1964 did not assume the magnitude of an "unconditional war on poverty." Claims were made concerning the goals and results of programs that have turned out to be inaccurate or overly optimistic. Disillusionment and cynicism may follow from a program's failure to meet created expectations, and that seems to have been the case here. On the other hand, in spite of all of the publicity received by OEO, the public did not appear to be very well-informed about its programs, which were confusing in their variety and operations. One top OEO official remarked that the agency's programs were not popular because its ways of doing things were different. "People don't understand what we are up to," he opined.

Civil rights problems also contributed to the problems of OEO. Because most of its programs benefitted urban blacks, OEO became identified to many as a "black agency." Southerners viewed OEO as a force for integration, and consequently opposed it. Riots in black ghettos in the summers of 1966 and 1967 produced notions in Congress and elsewhere that OEO's assistance to blacks had been useless or even "counterproductive." Conversely, as one observer noted, many blacks suspected that the basic purpose of the program was to dampen the black drive for equal rights. Others thought that the program was designed simply to "cool" tempers in the black community, particularly during the summer, rather than promote real change and genuine opportunity.[16] OEO was thus caught in a squeeze.

With the increasing expenditures required for the Vietnamese War as it expanded after 1964, directives from the White House and the Budget Bureau called for "holding the line" on domestic spending. OEO's request for $3.4 billion for fiscal 1967 was reduced to $1.75 billion by the Budget Bureau and Congress actually appropriated $1.612 billion, as against $1.5 billion for fiscal 1966. It was at this point that the escalation of the war on poverty levelled off. The Vietnamese War also enabled opponents of OEO to argue against the antipoverty program, or for a reduction therein, on the ground that the nation could not afford both "guns and butter." Moreover, as the President's attention turned to the war in Vietnam, he devoted less time and attention to the war on poverty.

Because the adoption of the Economic Opportunity Act was primarily the result of executive initiative, lobbying, and support, the poverty program came into being lacking the broad support and understanding that usually produces legislation of such magnitude. An observation by James Sundquist is pertinent here.

Nobody in either house of Congress, nor any leadership group outside the government felt a sense of paternity toward the Economic Opportunity Act or the Office of Economic Opportunity; and accordingly the program had no organized and vigorous defense in its early years when it came under fire. Republicans in Congress felt free to make the war on poverty a partisan issue since it had been presented as one. But the Democrats in Congress felt little responsibility to defend it.[17]

In Congress OEO early became a partisan symbol and voting on major issues concerning OEO was rather sharply divided along partisan lines. Northern Democrats and some southern Democrats supported the agency while most Republicans have opposed it. The agency had more support in the Senate than in the House, and in the House it did better in 1965 and 1966 when the northern Democrats were stronger. However, both supporters and opponents of the antipoverty program expressed criticism of it. Frequent complaints included lack of coordination in the War on Poverty, its lack of results, poor administration with OEO, loose handling of funds, and OEO's poor congressional relationship. The result was that Congress in 1966 tightened administrative controls over OEO and transferred some of its programs (see below) to other agencies while continuing it in existence and making relatively small cuts in its budget requests. Most of the restrictions and budget cuts originated in the House.

In 1967, as criticism of OEO continued and intensified, it appeared for a time that there were not enough votes in the House to pass the antipoverty extension legislation. A major source of difficulty for OEO was that some antipoverty officials saw the antipoverty programs, especially community action, as means for warring on local political establishments, which were viewed as unresponsive to the poor. Mayors in many cities found themselves hard-pressed politically and complained to Washington. Because of doubt concerning the outcome, House Democratic leaders delayed action on the extension legislation until late in the year. Then, to win southern votes and to break a conservative coalition against the bill, the northern Democrats, with White House support, amended the bill to permit local governments to take control of community action programs (the "Green Amendment"). This strategy worked as intended and, along with increased local support for the program stimulated by a temporary cutback in poverty funds and a strong lobbying effort mobilized by OEO, helped get the bill through the House. It had no difficulty in the Senate and thus the life of OEO was extended for another two years. By this time, however, it was clear that the Johnson administration had lost much of its enthusiasm for the antipoverty program and that OEO could not count on strong executive support to help sustain it.

The prospects for OEO again appeared dim in 1969 with the advent of the Nixon administration, which felt no obligation to OEO and the War on Poverty as symbols of the Great Society. Somewhat surprisingly, though, the President recommended a two-year extension for OEO while favoring its conversion from an operating to a "research and development arm" of the effort to eliminate poverty. By 1969 considerable support had developed in Congress and elsewhere for OEO and the poverty programs, particularly the latter, as they became more established and domesticated. Local officials and clientele groups acquired a stake in the continuation of the programs. Many city officials viewed them as vital sources of funds, for example. Moreover, it was difficult to oppose the programs directly as this made opponents appear in favor of poverty, which was not a very viable political stance. Republicans in Congress began to provide more support as, through the legislative process, they had an opportunity to affect the content of the programs. Liberally oriented groups, of course, continued to support OEO programs. Suffice it to state that the life of OEO was extended through fiscal 1975 by legislation enacted in 1969 and 1972. Appropriations for OEO reached a peak of $2.08 billion in fiscal 1971.

In early 1973, following his landslide reelection, and in line with his intention to cut back on domestic programs, President Nixon announced that no funds would be requested for fiscal 1974 and that the agency would be dismantled by July 1973. Howard Phillips was appointed director of OEO and was to be in charge of the dismantling. He started proceedings. The administration's action was quickly challenged as illegal in lawsuits filed by unions representing OEO employees and by local community action agencies. In April a federal district judge ruled that the administration's actions were illegal because they violated the Economic Opportunity Act, which authorized funding through fiscal 1972, and because under the Reorganization Act an agency could be abolished only under a plan submitted to Congress for its action. Subsequently the judge also ruled that Phillips could not continue as director of OEO because he had not been approved by the Senate. Once again, OEO stayed alive.

While OEO managed to survive for a decade, by the end of 1974 the only major program it had left was Community Action. Many others had been transferred to other agencies by either legislative or executive action. (See Table 6-1.) Various factors contributed to this piecemeal dismantlement of OEO. Old line departments and agencies sought control of programs that fell within the areas of their "traditional" jurisdictions. Conservatives and opponents of the war on poverty believed that transfers would result in the "domestication" of particular programs. As its political support lessened, OEO was less and less able to fend off such actions. Although top-level OEO officials had frequently stated that a purpose of OEO was to "innovate" new programs, get them well underway, and then "spin them off" to existing agencies, the agency usually opposed such transfers.

In late 1974 Congress enacted the Head Start, Economic Opportunity, and Community Partnership Act, which abolished the Office of Economic Opportunity and transferred the Community Action program to a newly created Community Services Administration. Ironically, the Nixon administration's assault on OEO had helped stir up much support for the community program. Most governors and scores of local officials indicated to Congress their support for the program. However, there was sufficient opposition to OEO as a symbol of controversy, especially in the House, that support for its continuation was inadequate. As Congressman Hawkins said during floor consideration of the bill: "Discussions with (Education and Labor) committee members disclosed that opposition to continuation of OEO was with the symbolism of the agency itself, and not with the community action program."[18]

Concluding Comments

The issue of poverty no longer occupies the place on the policy agenda that it did during the middle and later 1960s. The Office of Economic Opportunity as a symbol and focal point of the War on Poverty is now gone. The War on Poverty as a readily identifiable and distinct set of programs has disappeared, although most of the poverty programs remain in old line departments and agencies. Poverty, of course, is still with us.

The experience of OEO and that of an earlier antipoverty agency, the Farm Security Administration, raise some interesting questions concerning the American political and administrative processes. Can an agency whose focus is poverty survive over the long run? Are the centrifugal pressures in the administrative system such that the notion of a coordinated

Table 6-1
Dismantling OEO, 1965-74

Program	Transfer Date	Recipient Agency
Work study	1965	HEW
Adult basic education	1966	HEW
Small business loans	1966	Small Business Administration
Neighborhood youth corps	1968	Labor
Foster grandparents	1969	HEW
Headstart	1969	HEW
Upward bound	1969	HEW
Job corps	1969	Labor
VISTA	1971	ACTION
Rural loans	1971	Discontinued
Comprehensive health care	1973	HEW
Migrant labor aid	1973	HEW
Alcoholism and drugs	1973	HEW
Aid to Indians	1973	HEW
Legal services	1974	Legal Services Corporation
Community economic development	1974	Commerce
Community action	1974	Community Services Administration

attack on a major public problem, such as poverty, is illusory? Why is it seemingly impossible to mobilize the political support necessary for a sustained, integrated effort to eliminate poverty. Finally, how does one measure the impact, or "success," of an agency such as OEO. Would it have been more successful had it acted less as a "free-swinging troublemaker" and more as a conventional agency, particularly in its earlier years? Limitations of space prevent me from attempting to provide answers, but this is no reason for the reader to avoid the challenge.

Notes

1. There are a number of good treatments of the development of the Economic Opportunity Act, including: John Bibby and Roger Davidson, *On Capitol Hill* (Hinsdale, Ill.: Dryden Press, 2nd ed., 1972), pp. 225-249; James L. Sundquist, *Politics and Policy* (Washington: Brookings Institution, 1968), pp. 134-154; Sar A. Levitan, *The Great Society's Poor Law* (Baltimore: John Hopkins Press, 1969), esp. chs. 1, 2; and John C. Donovan, *The Politics of Poverty* (Indianapolis: Pegasus, 2nd. ed., 1973).

2. Sundquist, *Politics and Policy,* p. 142.

3. Rowland Evans and Robert Novak, *Lyndon B. Johnson: The Exercise of Power* (New York: New American Library, 1966), p. 430.

4. Robert C. Crawford, "Coordination: A Long, Long Trail A-Winding," paper presented at the Southeastern Regional Community Action Conference, Orlando, Florida (November 15, 1968), p. 2.

5. A very useful source for this paper has been James L. Sundquist, "Issues of Organization and Coordination," in Senate Committee on Labor and Public Welfare, *Examination of the War on Poverty: Staff and Consultants Reports,* 90th Cong., 1st Sess. (1967), III, pp. 787-792.

6. "OEO and Coordination" (Washington: Office of Economic Opportunity, mimeo., 1966), p. 5.

7. Robert A. Levine, "Program Budgeting for an Interagency Program," paper presented at the Thirty-sixth Conference of the Southern Economic Association, November 11, 1966, pp. 9-11.

8. Senate Report 563, 90th Cong., 1st Sess. (1967), p. 6.

9. Ibid., p. 2.

10. Sundquist, "Issues of Organization and Coordination," p. 788.

11. Norton Long, "Power and Administration," *Public Administration Review,* Vol. IX (Autumn, 1964), p. 257.

12. Robert A. Levine, *The Poor Ye Need Not Have With You* (Cambridge: M.I.T. Press, 1970), pp. 59-60.

13. Jonathan Spivack, "Antipoverty Flaw: The Aim of Coordinating Federal Efforts Hasn't Been Achieved," *Wall Street Journal,* (March 1, 1966), p. 16.

14. Herbert A. Simon, Donald W. Smithburg, and Victor A. Thompson, *Public Administration* (New York: Alfred A. Knopf, 1960), p. 389.

15. Harold L. Wilensky, *Organizational Intelligence* (New York: Basic Books, 1967), pp. 149-150.

16. Carl McCall, "Negro Voices: Antipoverty Programs Can Work," *The New York Times* (November 18, 1967), p. 36.

17. Sundquist, *Politics and Policy,* p. 494.

18. *Congressional Record,* Vol. 120 (May 28, 1974), p. H4409.

7

State Legislative Oversight and Social Welfare Policy

William J. Hagens

Introduction

Historically, the indigent community has had limited access to the legislative process. This is especially true in the formation of social welfare policy—public assistance, medical care, and other programs that affect the poor directly. This chapter discusses the current disabling effects that legislative oversight, or the lack thereof, has upon state welfare systems. Included are comments on the diminishing role of "war on poverty" programs on the social welfare system, abuses of administrative rule-making powers, and the role of professional staff in policy development.

The bulk of this material is based on a study of the Washington State Legislature. However, the research generally applies to most part-time legislatures.

Legislative Oversight

Legislative oversight can be defined as the "watchdog" function of legislatures that monitors the implementation and administration of laws and policies by state agencies. The goal is to guarantee that these operations comply with legislative intent.[1] In legislatures where oversight is effective, such as California, New York, and the United States Congress, a great deal of time and effort is allocated to this function.

In oversight activities legislatures are concerned with three major policy areas: (1) the amount of funds expended, (2) the policy developed, and (3) the structure through which the policy is implemented and administered. For example, if a legislative body were to create a new program of child care services for persons receiving public assistance, it would monitor the Executive branch of the government by considering the following questions: What type of program was developed? Who was eligible? What types of care were available? Who administered the program? And, how much was it costing? The overall concern would be whether the answers complied with the intent of the legislature. In the purest sense oversight would guarantee that such intent was adhered to in the formulation of the above three policy areas.

In the eyes of most citizens this "watchdog" function is accomplished through highly visible methods such as controversial investigatory hearings, à la "Watergate." There are also extensive audits of the executive agencies by the General Accounting Office—the ubiquitous auditing arm of Congress. Though these oversight approaches are by far the most visible, they are less extensive than one would think.

Oversight is accomplished not so much through formal investigatory hearings as through an informal understanding between the agency and the legislature. Knowing that the solons have at their disposal the ultimate weapon—the power of the purse—the agency is usually reluctant to violate their intentions. Defiance may result in a reduced appropriation in the future. For a legislature to engage effectively in oversight, several important components must exist. The most crucial of these are: (1) a full-time commitment, (2) adequate staffing, and (3) mutual respect between agency and legislature. First, lawmakers must dedicate a considerable amount of time to legislating and approach their roles with more than casual interest. It must be, if not a full-time job, a full-time responsibility. Second, there must be adequate professional staffing available. Staff members play a key role in oversight. This is true because usually only they possess the expertise and technology needed for data gathering and analysis. One must remember that part-time lawmakers frequently earn their living from nonlegislative wages. Therefore, there is less incentive to acquire complete expertise. Third, and interrelated to the other two points, there must be a mutual respect and understanding between the Executive and Legislative branches. It is this relationship that comprises the matrix of oversight.

The Part-time Legislature—Its Shortcomings

One of the major controversies today among students of state government is whether state legislatures should maintain a citizen part-time status or evolve into professional ongoing bodies. A recent (1971) study of state assemblies labeled the part-time variety "sometime governments."[2]

A citizen legislature is one that meets usually in abbreviated session and whose members make their livings by some other means, as juxtaposed with the body that meets for regular extended periods and whose members usually make their livings from their legislative salaries. Some believe that by maintaining a citizen part-time legislature the political process stays closer to the people. Others feel, as does the author, that a full-time legislature is necessary to meet the growing demands of governmental operations.

In the early years the role of the legislature was rather limited. It would meet once every two years, approve the governor's budget, adopt a few pieces of legislation, and return home to families, farms, and businesses. This concept was prevalent up to the years following World War II. As a matter of fact, some state assemblies, such as Arkansas', still adhere to this concept.

Under this format the governor and the executive agencies had most of the responsibility and authority to run the government. There seldom appeared a need for the solons to meet for more than 60 days every two years—a common state constitutional guideline.[a]

However, during the decade following World War II, the responsibility of state governments expanded immensely. This is the result of a myriad of new programs, mostly federally created, dealing with welfare, housing, transportation, and other contemporary issues. In addition to the diversity of the expanded responsibility of government, the policy decisions involved became more complex and technical. This included not only the substantive policy issues, but also the funding processes, such as federal categorical grants, or matching formulas.

In response to this expanded function, most state executive branches followed the lead of the federal government and began to build a state bureaucracy by creating new agencies and expanding existing ones. Over the past two decades the number of state employees in this country has almost tripled, from 1,103,441 in 1954[3] to 1,938,211 in 1972.[4] Reflected in this increase is not only manpower but also technical expertise.

To this growing demand upon state government, most legislatures made a feeble response. Instead of following their executive counterpart by bolstering and revamping their operations, they attempted to approach a full-time commitment with a part-time modality. Most expanded into the extended session concept, but without adequate staff or technical assistance.

In an examination of all the state legislatures, the author has listed only nine in the full-time category.[b] The remainder fall into the "sometime government" classification. This is where the problem lies. It is impossible to approach an adequate level of oversight with such a disparity in capability. The mutual understanding mentioned above will not thrive in this political environment. Agencies, realizing that the legislature is unable to monitor their programs, will find a lessening need to adhere strictly to the intent of law.

---

[a] A prominent lieutenant governor of Washington was reported to have said, when asked what he thought of limiting sessions to 60 days every two years: "It's wrong! It should be limited to two days every 60 years."

[b] California, Massachusetts, Michigan, New Jersey, New York, Ohio, Pennsylvania, Maryland, and Florida. This determination was made basically on three considerations: (1) adequate pay, equal to full-time employment; (2) adequate length of legislative sessions; and (3) adequate staffing. It should be noted that in the *Sometime Governments* study (see note 2) Massachusetts, New Jersey, and Maryland were found lacking in staff.

92

The Lack of Oversight in Social Welfare Policy

Though inadequate oversight was not specifically mentioned in the sometime government survey, it was generally contributory to many of the shortcomings cited.[c] Further, it is the author's conclusion that inadequate oversight is most prevalent in social welfare policy. Though the part-time status of the lawmaker is significant—they come, pass laws, go home—the absence of permanent professional staff appears to be the crux of the problem.

Until recently, most often the only staff allocated to a legislator was a secretary. This person was often a relative or friend who typed constituency mail and knew little about public policy. Of course, the committees had some professional staff, such as attorneys, budget and program analysts; however, since these were usually temporary positions, the more competent members often left for permanent jobs. Therefore, only those who stayed in the few full-time positions acquired the expertise necessary for proper monitoring of agencies.

Generally speaking, lawmakers make decisions based on data acquired from three sources: staff, agencies, and lobbyists. When staffing is inadequate, sources are limited to the remaining two. This, at least, allows for minimal input variance.

Under this input structure, well organized interest groups, such as labor, business, and the professions, greatly benefit. With one less source, there is generally less dispute over the merits of policies. These groups also benefit because of a growing phenomenon in governmental relations. This is the development of close relationships between agencies and interest groups for the purpose of affecting policy. Often these two sources work together in lobbying efforts. For example, in the state of Washington, the highway construction lobby's strongest ally is the State Department of Highways. They often collaborate in the procurement of funds for highway projects.

With this agency-lobbyist relationship, oversight is not essential from the lobbyist's viewpoint, because the two factions are usually in accord. When conflicts infrequently arise, these lobbyists can enlist the aid of financially dependent representatives to help with impacting the executive agency.

However, when the lobbyist input is rather limited, as is frequently the case with indigents, the legislature acts almost solely on the advice and counsel of the agencies. This usually occurs with social welfare legislation. The solons turn to the very agency that will administer the policy for data and analysis. This subrogates the legislative function to the Executive

[c] Burns, *Sometime Governments,* p. 101. ff. One of the main categories surveyed was how well the lawmakers were informed. This is directly related to the oversight function.

branch of the government and leaves the political system somewhat less than wholesome.

For example, until recently Washington State granted $5 per day for child care to needy families requesting such services.[d] In reaching this amount the legislature did not consult with the families or even the child care centers that provided the services. Rather, the legislative committee considered the appropriation and requested a cost analysis from the administering agency. The nicely rounded figure of $5 was chosen in an arbitrary manner and in no way reflected the actual cost of child care.

For years legislatures have been placating the poor by appropriating welfare funds. These funds were frequently allocated without input regarding need levels and types of services. The needy, due to diversity in background and ideology, and to the lack of resources, were unable to organize to the degree necessary to protest this disfranchisement. Therefore, the representatives were under no pressure to acquire expertise about the needs of the impoverished as they were concerning business, professional, and organized labor matters. Usurpation resulted.

Delegating the design and operation of social welfare policies to the administrative agency has created a system insensitive to recipients, for it has been removed from the realm of responsible government. No community, no matter how indignant, has the direct recourse to remove a civil service bureaucrat.

Community Organizing and Legal Services

In the past decade there have been concerted attempts to organize the poor around policy issues for the purpose of providing input from the program population. The best example is the National Welfare Rights Organization (NWRO). The NWRO was created to develop grassroots advocacy groups to work in local communities while maintaining national political prominence.[5] However, organizations like the NWRO were most effective during the era of the "War on Poverty," when social welfare programs held some priority in the White House. Since that era (1964-69) many of the programs have been drastically reduced or eliminated.

Two components of this era that impacted social welfare policy were legal services and the community organizing component of the Office of Economic Opportunity (OEO). This office, which was created during the Johnson administration, was designed to supply the poverty community with the skills and expertise that would eventually provide an avenue into the political arena.

The Legal Services program, which until recently was a part of OEO,

---

[d] The current rate is $5.31 per day.

was created to provide legal assistance to those who were unable to afford a lawyer. In addition to direct client services, the program has been actively involved in legislative law reform. Throughout the nation, legal services lawyers have lobbyed in state houses on behalf of the poor to bring about increased assistance grants and medical care, establish the rights of tenants and minorities, etc.

To complement the legal services lobbying effort, community organizers contributed the community grassroot support. The vehicle most often used to organize was the Community Action program (CAP). CAPs were funded primarily by OEO and were established on a county or multicounty basis. These programs provided the funds, personnel, and technical assistance necessary to organize. It was because of these local efforts that the legal services lobbyists could rely on demonstrations by recipients in state capitols to protest welfare services cutbacks and demand better programs.

From a cursory view of the legal services-community organizing lobbying structure, one might conclude that the poor people's lobby is on par with others. However, a closer examination reveals that it is not so.

Here, unlike the friendly lobbyist-agency relationships, legal services lobbyists are seldom in accord with the state welfare agency. It is in these cases, when an agency administers a policy that it initially opposed, that oversight is most crucially needed. A question arises: Who is available to oversee, when the legislature is unable to do so and the agency cannot be expected to police itself? The burden most often falls upon the lobbyists themselves—legal services and indigent groups.

The lobbyist oversight capability is limited, remembering that the ultimate tool—the power of the purse—is absent. This limitation notwithstanding, the legal services lobbyist does have some recourse. He can bring the issue to the attention of sympathetic legislators or muster grassroots support to express indignation through rallies and demonstrations. However, the most effective method has been litigation or the threat thereof. Though sometimes successful, this method is costly and time consuming.

For example, during the 1971 session, in an effort to comply with the Twenty-sixth Amendment to the United States Constitution, the Washington State Legislature adopted a statute that made the age of majority 18.[6] However, soon after, using this law as a basis, the state welfare agency (Department of Social and Health Services) promulgated administrative rules rendering those between the ages of 18 and 20 ineligible for Aid to Families with Dependent Children (AFDC). Twenty-one had been the previous age limit. There are indications that such interpretation went beyond the intent of the law.[e] This ineligibility created considerable hardship upon recipients. This was especially true concerning those

---

[e] In a survey of the important legislators involved in the adoption of this measure, less than 5 percent projected it would have any effect upon AFDC eligibility.

families with children of that age bracket who were still in high school but could not receive assistance.

Legal services responded by filing a class action lawsuit against the department, *Welfare Rights Organization* v. *Smith,*[7] citing among other arguments, a violation of legislative intent. Though the suit was initially lost, the decision was reversed in the State Supreme Court two years later. During the interim, many needy families' assistance was reduced or terminated. This case is an example of the use of litigation as an oversight tool; but the deprivation caused by the case's pendency made the victory a Pyrrhic one.

Though legal services lobbyists have been somewhat successful in the past, their future role in legislative law reform and oversight is dubious. Their accomplishments have incurred the wrath of citizens and government officials who feel that such activities should be precluded. Congress has recently (1974) adopted legislation that limits legal services personnel in lobbying activities.[8] Further, a 1974 court decision has restricted the use of litigation as an oversight tool. In *Eisen* v. *Carlisle and Jacquelin,*[9] the court limited the scope of the class action suit by requiring that notice be given to all members of the class. This type of litigation has been useful because it permits the inclusion of all those aggrieved as plaintiffs without listing their names. The requirement of notice will result in a reduced class size.

There has also been a marked decline in the community organizing activities. This is true for several reasons: First is the drastic reduction of OEO funding. Both the Nixon and Ford administrations have looked unfavorably on these programs. The cuts have affected both the amount of funds available and the technical manpower. The second is a continual resistance of local governmental bodies (usually counties and cities) to the active political role CAPs have taken in the past. The third is inherent problems of organizing the poor[10] and a general disenchantment about the utility of grassroots political activity. Victories and incentives to continue the effort are infrequent; the basic struggle to survive requires a great deal of the energies of the poor.

The Power of Administrative Rule Making

No chapter on oversight and social welfare policy would be adequate without comments on administrative agencies' rule-making authority. This power can be simply described as an extension of the legislative prerogative to executive agencies. Laws passed by the legislatures are usually broad and general in nature. This is especially true when creating program policy. However, to implement these programs, it is necessary to go into some detail. To assist the agencies, legislatures have granted them the power to promulgate rules and regulations. The rules have the same clout as the law; they, also of course, must fall within the purview of the law's intent.

Abuse of this power arises when agencies construe this prerogative too loosely and overstep the statutory guidelines. This can occur blatantly, as when an agency delays or outright refuses to publish rules, or in more subtle fashions, as in the minute and intricate details of such complex programs as social security or supplemental security income.

To govern the adoption of rules and regulations, most legislatures have created a body of law called the Administrative Procedures Act (APA). As a model, states have used the federal APA,[11] which governs the adoption of federal rules promulgated as the Code of Federal Regulations (CFR).

Lobbyist's Role

The Administrative Procedures Act provided the lobbyist with three oversight tools. First, prior to the adoption of rules and regulations, agencies must publish them and provide interested persons with an opportunity to comment and propose alternatives. A lobbyist can use this opportunity to bring improprieties to the attention of both agency and the legislature.

Second, if the lobbyist feels that the rules and regulations adopted are beyond the intent of the law, the APA provides for an administrative review or hearing where the aggrieved can voice his complaints. If the case is lost at that level, a petition for judicial review can be filed and that review can be appealed all the way to the United States Supreme Court. *Welfare Rights Organization* v. *Smith,* supra, was initiated in this fashion.

Finally, one may also file a petition directly with the agency if it is felt that the rules are not in compliance. However, this approach is usually only successful when the petitioner has the support of some other governmental body (federal or local) that also desires the rule changed.

As with most oversight tools, there is a caveat. It should be noted when using either the first or third of the above methods that the agencies are usually under no obligation to consider the proposals. It can summarily dismiss them after complying with the law's requirement to publish. Thus, it is most often necessary to exert collateral pressure or voice realistic threats of litigation to be successful.

Legislature's Role

Recently legislatures have begun to take interest in overseeing administrative rule adoption. This concern has been expressed by the formation of special committees to review proposed rules. Currently there are eight state legislatures that have such committees: Alaska, Connecticut, Iowa, Kansas, Michigan, Nebraska, Virginia, and Wisconsin. Several of these committees have the power to declare these rules null and void but use restraint in doing so.

The reason for this restraint is that there is inherent in this authority a question of constitutionality. The critics of such review say that the powers of the Legislative branch of the government are quite explicit and do not include such power; and, further, that once legislation is law, any review of its application is clearly the prerogative of the courts.[12] It should be noted that the court is most likely the place where the issue will be resolved.

The Emerging Professional Staff

The merits of professional staff have been clearly elaborated above. In the past few years a number of part-time legislatures have initiated the permanent professional staff concept. It is too early to evaluate this change; however, it can be safely said that it will bring the lawmakers closer to par with the Executive branch.

The reasons for this change are twofold: The first is that legislative leaders are finally facing up to the vast disparity between their professional capability and that of the governor's; and the second is the revitalization of interest in the role of state governments. This has been a slow but growing phenomenon that has culminated in state governments demanding a reversion of power from Washington, D.C. back to state capitols. To prepare, legislatures in states like Washington and Louisiana have begun to bolster professional staff.[13]

The underlying importance of this change is that staff will be available throughout the year, even when members are not in session. This allows for long-term research and evaluation, and eventually oversight.

Conclusion

Just as the child care example shows the insensitivity of the legislative process, *Welfare Rights Organization* v. *Smith,* supra, exposes the incredible vacuum created by the absence of legislative oversight.

A proper conclusion is difficult to pen. The problems continue to exist, but the changes that are occurring in state legislatures make a final word inappropriate. It is prudent to wait to observe what evolves from these impending changes.

Legislatures face not only conflict from the Executive branch, but also from their constituencies. At the onset of this chapter it was suggested that the optimal remedy would include the full-time status of the legislature. In many states the decision to do so would be politically precarious. The citizenry often becomes irate whenever legislatures attempt to expand, while state agencies continue to grow incrementally in a less visible fashion. The result is that solons are hesitant to incur the anger of their constituents by enlarging their salaries,[f] staff, and status, while continuing to increase the allotment of professional employees to the state agencies. However, failure to make those hardline decisions may turn the legislature into an extinct political species.

Notes

1. For a thorough discussion of oversight, see: Dale Vinyard, *Congress* (New York, Charles Scribner's Sons, 1968), pp. 25-29; and William J. Keefe and Morris S. Ogul, *The American Legislative Process, Congress and the States* (Englewood Cliffs, N.J., Prentice Hall, 1973), pp. 405-34.

2. John Burns, *Sometime Governments* (New York, Bantam Books, 1971).

3. *The Book of the States, 1954-1955* (Chicago, Council of State Governments, 1954), p. 189.

4. *The Book of the States, 1974-1975* (Chicago, Council of State Governments, 1974), p. 192.

5. For a discussion of the development of NWRO, see: Lawrence N. Bailis, *Bread or Justice: Grassroots Organizing in the Welfare Rights Movement* (Lexington, Mass.: Lexington Books, D.C. Heath and Co., 1974).

6. Chapter 292, Laws of Wash., 1st Ex. Sess., 1971 (May 21, 1971).

7. 82 Wn 2nd 437 (1973).

8. "Legal Services Corporation Act of 1974," Pub L. No. 93-355 (July 25, 1974), 42 USC 2996.

9. 40 L. Ed 2d 732 (1974).

10. Lawrence N. Bailis, "Organizing the Poor: Some Lessons of the 1960's," *Policy Studies Journal,* Vol. 2, No. 3 (Spring, 1974), pp. 210-13.

11. 5 USC 501-576.

---

[f] In the 1973 session, the Washington State Legislature approved a salary increase for itself. This was quickly negated by a citizens' initiative (Int. 282, Wn. St. Nov. 73 Election). The vote was 3 to 1 against the increase.

12. "Legislative Agencies Reviewing Administrative Rules," Illinois Legislative Council, Springfield, Illinois, File 8-138 (September 28, 1972).

13. Carolyn L. Kenton, "Modern Legislative Staffing," *State Government,* Vol. XLVII, No. 3 (Summer, 1974), pp. 165-69.

8 Revenue Sharing and the Poor

Joseph A. Cepuran

In the United States low-income citizens have become increasingly dependent on the federal government for aid of all kinds. Today the involvement of the federal government in such domestic programs is changing. This change started with general revenue sharing and is continuing with the adoption and discussion of special revenue sharing programs. Given the dependence of the poor on existing programs, it is appropriate to question what the impact of these changes might be for the poor.

The Poor Will Be Hurt

This chapter argues that revenue sharing programs will hurt the poor and other minorities. It is symptomatic of the arguments used here that few commentators have raised this question. To some revenue sharing will result in little or no change in policy.[1] To others the freeing of state and local programs from federal interference will result in better local policy and, presumably, improvement of the situation of all citizens.[2] There are few arguing that revenue sharing will help the poor. The literature largely has ignored the poor.[3] Perhaps the loudest complaint against revenue sharing has been raised on behalf of blacks.[4] There are several examples of such discrimination charges, for example, Michigan's revenue sharing portion has been challenged because a portion of the funds indirectly aid an alleged segregated system. Apart from this, however, there has been little concern for the detrimental effects of revenue sharing.

Revenue sharing will hurt the poor for a variety of reasons. The reasons of concern in this chapter can be grouped into four general headings. First, more power will be shifted to citizens who are less interested in programs to aid the poor. Second, more power will be shifted to local bureaucracies and bureaucrats who are restrictive in their view of poverty programs. Third, more power will be shifted to local government where various bodies representing the poor and other minorities are experiencing a reduced role in policy. Fourth, more power will be shifted to an arena that is used to dealing with problems and away from an arena that is used to dealing with more programmatic concerns.

Before discussing the reasons and their impact it is necessary briefly to discuss the grants-in-aid system and the growth of revenue sharing.

The Grant-in-Aid System

Prior to 1935 the poor in the United States were dependent on state and local government and private agencies. They depended on almshouses, the dole, and mother's aid. With the passage of the Social Security Act, Congress and the federal bureaucracy became involved in welfare programs. After 1935 and well into the sixties the role of the national government in welfare and other domestic programs has been large.

The role of Congress in these grants-in-aid has been to draw general policy guidelines and to use federal dollars to buy compliance. The federal bureaucracy, in turn, prepares rules and regulations to reflect the guidelines. Finally the states and localities, within the federal parameters, implement the programs.

To many observers of government programs, as well as participants, Congress assumed the role of state legislature and city council.[5] Particularly in the area of welfare it was hoped that the federal involvement would end when the unemployment crisis ended.[6] The problem, however, with removing the national government from social and other programs is that the national government is the level of government with the funds necessary to implement the programs. The rhetoric about the national interest in domestic programs often implied or camouflaged a need for federal revenues.[a]

As a result of the grant-in-aid programs, states and localities were able to offer greatly expanded programs. In the case of welfare in at least one state this meant that the state and its localities could provide aid for a larger number of recipients with virtually the same portion of available income as was true prior to 1935.

Revenue Sharing

The adoption of revenue sharing as one of the solutions to the problems mentioned earlier can be attributed to the coincidence of the election of Richard Nixon and the so-called taxpayers' revolt. Richard Nixon wanted to reduce the federal influence in domestic programs. His refusal to establish an agency with responsibility for his wage and price control program indicates the depth of his concern. Early in his administration he talked of a new federalism that would return power to the states and localities. During this same period there was the feeling among state and local politicians and commentators that the state and local taxpayer had reached a limit. The

[a]The reports of President Eisenhower's Commission that studied the grants-in-aid system appear to have concluded this. See: *Federal Aid to Welfare, A Study Committee Report* (Washington, D.C.: Commission on Intergovernmental Relations, June, 1955).

fact that tax increases were generally voted down, and the general outcry against the few tax increases that were adopted was offered as proof of this revolt.

Revenue sharing offered the hope of dealing with both of these concerns as well as being above partisan politics (it had been discussed by the earlier Democratic administration). Revenue sharing would provide states and localities with set amounts of funds on the basis of population and tax effort. It would remove federal interference in state and local policies while retaining federal dollars. Further, the general idea could be expanded into those areas presently funded under the grants-in-aid system. This was done with the adoption of specific revenue sharing for community development in 1974. This was the background that led to the adoption of general revenue sharing in 1973. What could the poor expect from revenue sharing? Very little!

Different Drummers

Revenue sharing not only increased the role of states and localities in determining how these federal monies would be spent, it also increased the importance of those citizens who are most active in dealing with state and local government. This constituency is least likely to support programs to aid the poor.

The community study literature has grouped citizen participation according to the participant's interests. Robert Merton discussed the difference between locals and cosmopolitans. Edward Banfield and James Q. Wilson divided behavior between a public- and a private-regarding ethic.[7] Of more specific concern here is the finding that people can be divided according to the level of government in which they are interested.[8] Although it is unclear that the locals and private-regarding citizens are the major constituency of local government, it is clear that they would be likely to oppose programs at the local level that would aid the poor. More pertinent, citizens for whom state government is the most salient have attitudes (distrust of fellow-man, dislike of federal activities, and opposition to integration activities) that would make them likely to oppose aid for the poor.[9] Some corroboration of these attitudes was provided in personal interviews in the state of Virginia. They indicated that many welfare board members believed their restrictive attitude toward welfare represented the wishes of local taxpayers.[10]

It is probable that even people who are more oriented to the national government or who may be more supportive of aid for the poor simply do not see the role of local government as providing this aid. To many citizens, local government is more concerned with providing physical services, education, and law enforcement.[11] Given this view, a citizen could support congressional actions such as the Economic Opportunity Act while being uninvolved or even opposed to the expenditure of local funds to expand such programs at the local level.

Beyond political questions, people's life-style affects government behavior. People appear to select homes that fit their own economic character. As a result, metropolitan areas are composed of communities of widely differing wealth with the problems accompanying varying tax bases.[12] Furthermore, in urban communities when the higher income individual is faced with problems, he is as likely to move as he is to try to solve the problem.[13] In such situations there is likely to be a premium on keeping higher income individuals. Therefore, there tends to be an emphasis on the services these people want (e.g., education and recreation) rather than the competing needs of the poor. Indeed, studies have found differences in the services provided in richer and poorer neighborhoods.[14]

Combined, these factors mean that there will be slight support for the needs of the poor where they constitute a minority. Where they constitute a majority, there will be insufficient funds to meet normal local services, let alone special needs of the poor. At the national level the poor are a large enough group to have some power.[b] At the national level the public can act altruistically and the local administration can blame someone else for unpopular programs. There are numerous anecdotes that indicate this "blaming" phenomenon. For example, during Congressional hearings on public housing, a councilman commented that making the council the one to approve the location of public housing would mean no public housing. Similarly, a mayor of a southern city, when informed that any future relocation costs would have to be paid directly from the community development funds rather than by HUD, made it clear that he was not going to pay any black family $10,000 (the average relocation payment).

Who Benefits?

The traditional grants-in-aid programs with their associated books of rules and regulations have contributed to the growth of local bureaucracies to operate the programs.[15] Therefore, it could be expected that the reduction of such programs would hurt the local bureaucracy. It, however, will give the local bureaucracy more flexibility to do its job. There is evidence to suggest that the local agencies may use this freedom to limit the amount of services they will provide the poor.[16]

[b] E.E. Schattschneider argues that minorities attempt to expand the political arena to the level at which they are a large enough group to have power. *The Semi-Sovereign People* (New York: Holt, Rinehart and Winston, 1960), pp. 38-43.

Perhaps the total agency behavior is reflective of the situation faced by local bureaucrats. Unlike most of his federal brethren, the local bureaucrat must deal directly with clients and is likely to receive criticism on a personal level. Michael Lipsky has argued that the street level bureaucrats find it difficult to admit their impact on clients.[17] Rather, they use bureaucratic devices to cope with the pressure. A case study has shown the general disorder associated with attempts to treat clients as peers rather than objects of action.[18] Finally, other authors have argued that the bureaucrat (at all levels) is middle-class oriented and virtually unable to deal with the poor.[19]

Under the traditional grants-in-aid system the federal bureaucracy, in splendid isolation, can require the local bureaucrats to do things that the federal bureaucrats would be unwilling to do. Removing these remote actors may result in programs never being tried because they are difficult or "won't work." We are likely to see programs that control the "voluntary poor."[20]

Local Centralization

Given the generally low level of participation by the poor,[21] they need to organize to have an impact on policy. Some initial efforts in this direction were made with community action commissions, model city boards, and various neighborhood bodies. At the present time, however, these actors are either being phased out or otherwise being rendered powerless. The harbinger of this erosion was the Green Amendment to the Economic Opportunity Act.[22] In response to the demands of local administrations the law was amended to insure participation by the local governing bodies. In part this contraction of power is reflective of political realities. Existing administrations are not anxious to see possible competitors being given a platform and money to use with a constituency. This is as true for the older white administrations as for the new black administrations. There also is a realization that the administration will be blamed for most failures in their communities. As a result they see a need to control all programs.

A final element contributing to this centralization is the pressure associated with increased unionization at the local level. There is pressure from the unions to remove the interference of the various outside bodies. Additionally, the more formal employee relations associated with unionization have led to a pulling in of a variety of loose ends.[c]

Hoping that the poor will be aided in their fights for adequate repre-

---

[c] Although there are no works that have focused on this question, the issues in the citizen board fights in New York City were of this type. See: David Rogers, *110 Livingston Street* (New York: Random House, Inc., 1968).

sentation in the deliberations over spending the new funds is questionable at best. Rather they will have to depend on a local administration whose constituency is not likely to support the poor.

Narrow Concerns

Changing the major arena of policy making will mean that the poor will compete with specific problems rather than as part of general principles. State and local administrations are faced with specific problems, whereas the national government often deals with more general, almost programmatic concerns. As a result state and local units are more likely to deal with those problems that are the most pressing. The federal government designs programs that deal with principles, programs that allow flexibility when specific situations are faced by states and localities.[23]

While there is consideration of political constraints at the congressional level (particularly in pork barrel bills), often these represent outside parameters within which abstract principles are constrained.[24] At the local level the first concern is likely to be who is helped and hurt. As was indicated above this will harm the poor.

Under the more programmatic view, Congress and HEW can afford to operate a pilot program of guaranteed incomes for the poor in selected areas of the country.[25] It would be an unusual state or locality that would be willing to implement such experimental programs on a large scale.

The Record

While the argument thus far is based on what is already known about grants-in-aid and other domestic programs in general, the record on general and special revenue sharing tends to support these arguments. The poor have received little benefit from the general revenue sharing program. Likewise, preliminary evidence indicates that while the specific grant-in-aid programs of model cities, urban renewal, and public housing were aimed at the poor, their replacement, the Community Development revenue sharing program, will be aimed more at middle class concerns rather than those of the poor.

One of the early concerns of revenue sharing has been a consideration of the impact of the fund distribution formula for the poor. Charles Brown and James Medoff, in a consideration of the formula for revenue sharing, conclude that the poor will receive a small portion of the benefits associated with general revenue sharing.[26] The low gain for the poor is even more pronounced if the funds are used to reduce taxes.[27] If these funds result in a general reduction in grants-in-aid programs, they expect a general decrease in the benefits to the poor.[28]

The Brookings Institution report *Setting National Priorities* considered the impact of the various proposed formulas for distributing the community development funds. When comparing these funds to the patterns in the programs which community development was intended to replace (housing and urban renewal), they found that many large cities, particularly those in the Northeast, would receive less and that many communities that had virtually no expenditures in the past would experience large increases.[29] While there can be no direct proof that such a result would hurt the poor on a one-for-one basis, it is reasonable to expect that the poor in these large cities will have less money available for their needs. Similarly, there can be little expectation that communities that have shown little interest in these programs in the past will suddenly create programs for the poor.

The Brookings study of revenue sharing provides the first set of data and analysis of the operation of general revenue sharing. The report indicates that the bulk of revenue sharing has been used for capital expenditures, tax reduction and stabilization, and avoidance of borrowing. At the local level these accounted for about 75 percent of the expenditures.[30] In terms of the reports of all local governments, the GAO and Treasury reports indicate that expenditures for health and social services, which could be expected to be of most direct aid to the poor, constituted from 5.7 to 7.5 percent of the total local revenue sharing expenditures.[31]

Formal reports are not available for the Community Development program. Rather, conclusions are limited to a review of the action of individual communities. Discussions with people associated with HUD's community development structures indicate a lack of a clear understanding of what they will accept as meeting the citizen participation element of the program. Initially everyone presumes that the simple holding of public meetings will meet the requirement, regardless of what did or did not transpire at the meetings. Some preliminary investigation of the meetings in the western Detroit metropolitan area by one of my students indicates that few people attend the meetings (the highest total was about 300 for a community of 80,000). The emphasis in the meetings appears to be on recreation programs. Finally, the elderly have appeared with some strength in numbers. Apart from the role of the elderly, the initial reports are not encouraging. The communities are putting an emphasis on recreation and other devices that are more middle than lower class oriented.[32] The exception is some emphasis on housing rehabilitation. Furthermore, there are allegations that the communities are avoiding any actions that might aid the bringing of lower income and nonwhite families into the community.[33]

108

Conclusions

This chapter has raised questions about the impact of the revenue sharing program on the poor. The alteration in the federal system that revenue sharing represents will harm the interests of the poor and other minorities. It is not the intention of this chapter to present the existing grants-in-aid programs or the pluralist system as providing adequate or satisfactory concern for the poor. Indeed, several authors have effectively criticized them.[34] The question must be—is the new system superior to the old? It is not.

Perhaps over time the citizens could readjust their behavior within the system, local bureaucracies could be made more responsive to the poor, more meaningful representation of the poor could be achieved, and local arenas could concern themselves with principles as well as the principals. Can the poor wait?

Revenue sharing results in a priority on local participation. The author's own work in Iowa indicates that where there is opposition to an individual's wants added to a relatively low income level in the community, participation by poorer individuals is below average.[35] This situation holds for many poor.

William H. Riker ended his book on federalism by saying that segregationists were beneficiaries of federalism.[36] It is my view that the poor are the victims of revenue sharing.

Notes

1. For example, see: Phillip Monypenny, "Federal Funds and Illinois State Finance, 1958-1972," *Illinois Government,* 36 (February, 1973).

2. See: *State Government,* 46 (Winter, 1973); and *The New Federalism; Possibilities and Problems in Restructuring American Government* (Washington, D.C.: Woodrow Wilson International Center for Scholars, 1973).

3. A notable exception is: Michael D. Reagan, *The New Federalism* (New York: Oxford University Press, 1972).

4. For an example, see: Morton H. Skler, "Revenue Sharing: What Share for Minorities?" *Focus,* 3 (March, 1975), pp. 4-5.

5. See: Monypenny, "Federal Funds," pp. 6-7.

6. For a general presentation of the withering away fallacy see: Gilbert V. Steiner, *Social Insecurity: The Politics of Welfare* (Chicago: Rand McNally and Co., 1966), pp. 18-47.

7. See the general discussions in: Edward C. Banfield and James Q. Wilson, *City Politics* (New York: Vintage Books, 1966), Chapters 3 and 16.

8. M. Kent Jennings and Harmon Ziegler, "The Salience of American State Politics," *American Political Science Review,* 64 (June, 1970), pp. 523-535.

9. Ibid., pp. 528-529.

10. In connection with research for: *Public Assistance and Child Welfare: The Virginia Pattern, 1646 to 1964* (Charlottesville, Va.: University of Virginia, Institute of Government, 1968).

11. See: Everett F. Cataldo, "Orientations Toward State and Local Government," in James A. Reidel, ed., *New Perspectives in State and Local Politics* (Waltham, Mass.: Xerox College Publishing, 1971), p. 115.

12. Richard Child Hill, "Separate and Unequal ," *American Political Science Review,* 68 (December, 1974), pp. 1557-1568.

13. John M. Orbell and Toru Uno, "A Theory of Neighborhood Problem Solving," *American Political Science Review,* 66 (June, 1972), pp. 478-479.

14. Herbert Jacob, "Contact with Governmental Agencies," *Midwest Journal of Political Science,* 16 (February, 1972), pp. 132-134. Charles S. Benson and Peter Lund, *Neighborhood Distribution of Local Public Services* (Berkeley: University of California, Institute of Governmental Affairs, 1969), pp. 94-96. Blanche D. Blank, Rita J. Immerman, and C. Peter Rydell, "A Comparative Study of an Urban Bureaucracy," *Urban Affairs Quarterly,* 4 (March, 1969), pp. 348-350.

15. See: Richard Cloward and Frances Fox Piven, "The Professional Bureaucracies," in Murray Silberman, ed., *The Role of Government in Promoting Social Change* (New York: Columbia University School of Social Work, November, 1965), reprinted in Cloward and Piven, *The Politics of Turmoil* (New York: Vintage Books, 1975), pp. 7-17.

16. Advisory Committee to HUD, Subcommittee on the Planning Process and Urban Development, *Revenue Sharing and the Planning Process* (Washington, D.C.: National Academy of Science, 1974), pp. 89-91.

17. "Street-Level Bureaucracy and the Analysis of Urban Reform," *Urban Affairs Quarterly,* 6 (June, 1971), p. 406.

18. Orion F. White, Jr., "The Dialectical Organization: An Alternative to Bureaucracy," *Public Administration Review,* 29 (January/February, 1969), pp. 32-42.

19. Gideon Sjoberg, Richard A. Brymer, and Buford Farris, "Bureaucracy and the Lower Class," *Sociology and Social Research,* 50 (1966), pp. 325-337, reprinted in Elihu Katz and Brenda Danet, eds., *Bureaucracy and the Public* (New York: Basic Books, Inc., 1973), pp. 61-72. For a more

specific reference to the local level see: Frances Fox Piven, "Militant Civil Servants in New York City," *TRANS-action,* 8 (November, 1969), pp. 24-28.

20. The distinction between attitudes toward the voluntary and involuntary poor is made in: Joel F. Handler, "Federal-State Interests in Welfare Administration," in U.S. Congress, Joint Economic Committee, Subcommittee on Fiscal Policy, *Studies in Public Welfare, Paper #5, Pt. 2, Issues in Welfare Administration* (Washington, D.C.: U.S. Government Printing Office, March 12, 1973), pp. 2 and 32.

21. See: Sidney Verba and Norman Nie, *Participation in America* (New York: Harper & Row, Publishers, 1972).

22. For discussions of this issue see: J. David Greenstone and Paul E. Peterson, "Reformers, Machines, and the War on Poverty," in James Q. Wilson, ed., *City Politics and Public Policy* (New York: John Wiley & Sons, Inc., 1968), pp. 267-292. For the amendment see: *Organizing Communities for Action* (Washington, D.C.: Office of Economic Opportunity, February, 1968).

23. There is a broad literature on the flexibility allowed (or assumed) by local administrators. See: Martha Derthick, "Intercity Differences in Administration of the Public Assistance Program: The Case of Massachusetts," in Derthick, *City Politics and Public Policy,* pp. 243-266. Frances Fox Piven and Richard A. Cloward, *Regulating the Poor: The Functions of Public Welfare* (New York: Pantheon Books, 1971). U.S. Congress, *Studies in Public Welfare.*

24. A sense of the use of more abstract principles (even given political infighting) can be seen in: Harold Wolman, *Politics of Federal Housing* (New York: Dodd, Mead & Co., 1971).

25. See: Alice Rivlin, *Systematic Thinking for Social Action* (Washington, D.C.: The Brookings Institution, 1971), pp. 94-106.

26. Charles Brown and James Medoff, "Revenue Sharing: The Share of the Poor," *Public Policy,* 22 (Spring, 1974), p. 178.

27. Ibid., p. 177.

28. Ibid., p. 178.

29. Edward Freid et al., *Setting National Priorities* (Washington, D.C.: The Brookings Institution, 1973), pp. 210 and 211.

30. Richard P. Nathan et al., *Monitoring Revenue Sharing* (Washington, D.C.: The Brookings Institution, 1975), p. 193.

31. Ibid., p. 247.

32. For some general figures see: Don Tschirhart, "Bids in for U.S. Money," *The Detroit News* (March 10, 1975), p. B1.

33. See: Dave Anderson, "Cities Face Probe on Federal Funds," *Detroit Free Press* (February 20, 1975), pp. 3A and 11A.

34. An effective presentation on this is contained in: Theodore Lowi, *The End of Liberalism* (New York: Norton, 1969).

35. Joseph Cepuran, "Government as a Problem-Solver: Which Citizens Use Government with What Effect?" Ph.D. dissertation, University of Iowa, 1973, pp. 141-144.

36. William H. Riker, *Federalism: Origin, Operation, Significance* (Boston: Little, Brown and Co., 1964), p. 155.

**Part III
The Impact of Community
Action Agencies**

9

Organizing the Poor: The Persistence of Unanswered Questions

Lawrence Neil Bailis

The 1960s were marked by widespread efforts to create community organizations to help poor people achieve a wide variety of goals: civil rights, tenants rights, welfare rights, better conditions for farmworkers, "black power," "brown power," "red power," and "gold power." But in spite of the wealth of experience in organizing poor people, and the numerous books and articles that have been written on this topic, many of the basic "how to do it" questions remain unanswered. In particular, there is only limited knowledge of what makes some poor people's organizations more effective than others, what tactics and strategies are most appropriate for particular situations, and the policy implications of effective community organizing.

In this chapter an effort is made, first of all, to explain why this has occurred. This is followed by a brief description of some of the lessons that have been learned from the 1960s, and a concluding section that discusses the need and prospects for further research.

Why Have We Learned So Little?

In the physical sciences it is relatively simple to devise an experiment that helps us to understand the effect of force "A" upon object "B". All one needs to do is to set up a "controlled experiment" in which the force is applied a number of times, and the results compared with a situation in which no force is applied while *everything else remains the same*.

In theory we could conduct this same kind of experiment in which the "force" of a community protest organization was either present or not in efforts to bring about changes in the "object" called local government. In fact, however, we can never conduct such experiments because "everything else" is never the same in any two political protests: no two situations in different cities are ever the same; no two situations involving the same poor people's organization at different times are ever the same. The success of any poor people's organization in any given effort to affect public policy appears to be dependent upon such difficult to generalize factors as:

1. The strength of the organization in ability to mobilize large numbers of people on a given occasion to take a given set of activities
2. The strength of the organization in terms of its ability to mobilize active support from the more influential elements in the community
3. The nature of the target of the protest (is it strong enough to ignore the protest activities and is there sympathy for the causes espoused by the poor people's organization?)
4. The personal characteristics and organizing philosophies of the community organizers
5. The personal characteristics of the leaders of the organizations that have the power to grant the requests of the poor people's organization
6. The structure of the political system in which the poor people's organization is operating (who has the authority to make the desired concessions and what is the likelihood of arrest for illegal disruptive activities?)

The most sophisticated efforts at analysis of protest activities by poor people's organizations on an *aggregate* basis have been those of Peter Eisinger. Eisinger's studies of 120 protest incidents in 43 cities have provided a wide range of quantitative results linking the incidence and results of protest activities with a large number of political variables. But he has concluded that there are a broad range of factors that give rise to protest activities by poor people's organizations and the "structure of political opportunities" as measurable by aggregate indicators "plays only one small part."[1] In other words, studies such as Eisinger's can only analyze the last of the above-listed six factors, those variables that are directly related to the political system in which the protest activity takes place.

If we are to understand the effect of factors other than those directly related to the political system, it is necessary to get closer to the actual poor people's organizations than any aggregate approach will allow. In short, we need a wide range of detailed and objective case studies.

Very few such case studies have ever been written, however. In part, this is the result of the fact that most community organizers are activists who devote every waking hour to their jobs and thus have neither the time nor the inclination to keep detailed notes and to analyze them at some later point. Outsiders, on the other hand, may have these interests, but have faced a number of barriers that have precluded the development of accurate accounts. In the first place, many leaders of poor people's organizations have preferred not to reveal the inner workings of their groups to nonmembers. Thus, for example, there is a saying that is widely attributed to the Black Panthers: "Those who know don't tell; and those who tell don't know." Beyond this, there is a second problem resulting from the fact that many of the outside observers who have gained access to the inner workings of such organizations have been deeply sympathetic to the goals of these groups and have, therefore, decided to present their accounts in a manner that puts organizational activities in the best possible light rather than striving for accurate portrayals of the groups and their leaders.

Finally, there is a problem that is endemic to case studies: there is usually little or no effort to relate such studies to each other. Case studies are often conducted without reference to *any* analytic framework or upon frameworks unique to the author of the study.

But in spite of these shortcomings it is possible to review the literature on political protest and the activities of poor people's organizations in the 1960s and draw some theoretical lessons from them. The most important of these lessons relate to the dynamics of community organizing and to the ultimate impact of these protest activities by poor people's organizations. The highlights of these lessons are presented below.

What We Have Learned: The Lessons of the 1960s

Perhaps the most important of these lessons of the 1960s relate to the *internal dynamics* of poor people's organizations and the relationship between these dynamics and the protest activities they undertake. In particular, it has become evident that the "incentive theory" of organizational behavior propounded by Peter B. Clark and James Q. Wilson to explain the dynamics of *all* voluntary associations provides an excellent framework to analyze poor people's organizations.

According to Clark and Wilson, the most fruitful avenue for the analysis of formal organizations lies in the study of their maintenance needs and the "incentives" offered by the leadership of groups in order to induce the participation and continued contribution of members and supporters. In their theory, Clark and Wilson assert that these incentives can generally be divided into three categories: *material incentives,* tangible rewards that can be easily translated into monetary value; *solidary incentives*, intangible inducements that derive in the main from the act of associating (such as a sense of fellowship); and *purposive incentives*, intangible inducements that derive from the goals of the association. Clark and Wilson further assert that understanding the nature of these incentives and their roles in organizations can offer the "rudiments of a predictive theory of organizational behavior."[2]

Incentive theory therefore suggests that we look beyond the formal goals of poor people's organizations and pay considerable attention to the inducements offered to members. Doing so provides a number of insights. Most importantly, it appears that the majority of successful efforts at community organizing occurred in those cases in which organizers offered poor people tangible benefits. Most movements that were successful in mobilizing large numbers of poor people for at least some period shared an ability credibly to promise changes that would have a tangible impact upon the lives of potential members of the groups. Effectiveness of poor people's organizations was further increased to the extent that these tangible changes could be promised in the immediate future.

The clearest example of this is the National Welfare Rights Organization (NWRO), founded by the late Dr. George Wiley. The NWRO was perhaps the largest grassroots organization of poor people in the past decade. The NWRO organizers were able to sign up dues paying members in such great numbers primarily because they were able to offer welfare recipients who were potential members of the organization a virtual guarantee of supplementary cash benefits, food, clothing, or furniture, courtesy of the Welfare Department, if and only if they joined. (They were able to make this offer because of a "loophole" in the welfare regulations that provided for such benefits but that had been largely unknown at the time.)[3] Tenants rights organizations promised clear-cut improvements in housing conditions, and antiurban renewal groups promised maintenance of the status quo as opposed to large-scale dislocation. This theory about the importance of tangible benefits is further strengthened by the observation that organizers have usually had great difficulty in mobilizing communities against urban renewal until just before the house-taking was to begin, that is, until the impact upon people's lives became tangible, clear, and imminent.

In some cases it is difficult to disentangle the types of incentives offered by particular poor people's organizations. Cesar Chavez's United Farmworkers Organizing Committee offered the tangible promise of better wages and working conditions along with the religious/racial/mystical appeal wrapped up in the term "La Causa." Mixed incentives were also offered by such groups as the Black Panthers and Young Lords. While both of these groups developed purposive ideologies, much of their appeal was derived from solidary and tangible incentives, a sense of togetherness, release from fear of police brutality, and the provision of free breakfasts to the wider community.[4]

But in spite of this intermingling of incentives, it can still be said that the most successful poor people's organizations in terms of size, continuity, and achievement of goals, were those that attracted their members primarily by offering tangible, quickly realizable benefits in return for their participation.

As is also clearest in the case of the welfare rights movement, these organizations have generally been able to maintain their mass followings only so long as they have been able credibly to offer new tangible benefits. Regardless of past performance, once future rewards could no longer be promised, active membership began to decline severely. Some people could be counted upon to continue coming to meetings for the pleasures of social interaction or for mystical/religious reasons, but mass membership could be maintained only when there were benefits to pass out.

This analytical framework suggests an explanation for the widely differing records of many civil rights organizations that had similar formal goals. Thus, for example, many such groups in the 1960s experienced difficulties in building mass followings among inner city blacks. In many cases, however, the achievement of the goals of these groups, such as integration of some schools, either would have had little direct impact upon the lives of these inner city residents, or could be hoped for only years in the future, or both. These demonstrations for "school integration" and "quality education" can be sharply contrasted with the objectives of some of the activities instigated by Saul Alinsky to improve the school system; one of Alinsky's goals was better toilet paper in school lavatories.

Even though tangible incentives have been shown to be the most powerful, there have been many cases in which there were no such incentives available. In these cases organizers have had to rely on purposive, issue-oriented incentives that have rarely proven sufficient to mobilize large numbers of poor people on a continuing basis. Seen in this regard, the weakness of the issue-oriented civil rights organizations directly parallel the difficulties faced by political reformers in the first half of the twentieth century who found inner city residents indifferent to discussions of the "issues of the day" while remaining responsive to the tangible promises of jobs, or even Thanksgiving turkeys, offered by political "bosses" and the "big city political machines."

As is suggested by the above example, the incentive framework is also useful in relating the activities of poor people's organizations to those of other politically oriented groups. The similarities between the welfare rights movement and the urban political "machine" extend far beyond their dependence upon tangible incentives. The leadership of the welfare rights groups and the political bosses both avoided any discussion of issues when they could offer direct benefits instead. Abstract ideological questions, be they welfare reform or structural reform of city government, were discussed only in those instances in which the organization was not strong enough to offer concrete benefits in the immediate future.

The second important lesson from the history of the 1960s relates to the variety of available *protest tactics* that can be used by poor people's organizations and their interrelationship. James Q. Wilson wrote that the paradigm case for protest activity consists of direct *confrontation* between a protest group and its target, that is, the person or organization that is the potential source of the benefits which the members seek. Since poor people's organizations generally have nothing positive to offer these targets in negotiations, they generally seek to gain concessions through threats of harm, annoyance, or behavior that will embarass the target. Wilson calls these threats "negative inducements" that rely on a credible threat of mass action for their fulfillment.[5]

Michael Lipsky has introduced an entirely different protest paradigm. According to Lipsky, the essence of protest involves *showmanship* whereby a poor people's organization stages a demonstration not so much to threaten its target, but instead to attract the mass media that in turn can carry the protest message to influential elements in the community. These elements, it is hoped, will then become active allies of the protesters and will use their political influence to persuade the target to take the action favored by the poor people's group. According to Lipsky, the essence of protest thus lies in "activiting third parties to participate in the controversy" in a way that will help to achieve the protest goals.[6]

In reviewing the history of poor people's organizations in the 1960s, it becomes apparent that (Wilson's) confrontation model and (Lipsky's) showmanship model are in fact *tactical options* facing the protest group leader/organizer at a given point in time. To the extent that a protest group leader/organizer were fully rational, he or she would employ whichever of these tactics held the promise of being the most successful in a given context, that is, given the strength of the poor people's organization, the vulnerability of its target, the attitudes of the general public toward the group, the norms of the mass media, and so forth. In fact, the same poor people's organizations did employ different tactics at different times, but there is little documented evidence concerning how the leaders and organizers reached their tactical decisions.

In retrospect there appears to have been a relationship between the incentives utilized in poor people's groups and their tactics at given points in time. Organizers seeking to build mass-based groups were successful only when they were able to find a target that had the authority to disburse tangible benefits, and when they were able to devise tactics suitable to win concessions from these targets. If the target appeared to be unable (or unwilling) to stand firm in the face of confrontation tactics, such tactics were employed. If not, they were generally ruled out. Similarly, if there were no influential groups in the city that might be sympathetic to the protesters, there was little or no point to seeking to employ the showmanship-oriented kind of protest.

Based upon the experience of the 1960s, it appears that the showmanship-oriented protest requires significantly fewer participants than does confrontation. A handful of protesters might be enough to attract the media in spite of the fact that they would not be enough to create a real disturbance or even annoyance to a given target. If this relationship is indeed true, and the number of poor people that can be mobilized is a function of the kind of incentives used by the organizer/leaders, it would then follow that there is a direct relationship between the kind of incentives necessary for successful confrontation and the kind necessary for successful showmanship.

The final lesson of the 1960s relates to the *policy implications* of the first two lessons. To the extent that incentives play a key role in determining the nature and success of given protest activities, it should be possible to associate many proposed reforms in social policy and governmental institutions with a positive or negative impact upon future efforts to build poor people's organizations. Thus, for example, the welfare rights movement throve upon a welfare system that gave individual social workers a good deal of discretion over the disbursement of supplementary cash benefits to meet the "special needs" of their clients. The possibility of arranging welfare office confrontations to win such discretionary benefits offered an unrivaled opportunity for organizers to utilize tangible incentives. Shortly after the rise of the welfare rights movement in the late 1960s, many state welfare departments began a series of "reforms" that had the effect of limiting this discretion allowed to social workers. The reforms were justified on the grounds that giving some recipients benefits that were not offered to others was both inequitable and administratively complex. But whatever their advantages with respect to equity and simplicity, the reforms served to eliminate an extremely effective organizing tool. This same argument would hold true of most administrative reforms that serve to decrease the discretion to disburse benefits.

On the other hand, the advent of decentralization and community control in many of our large urban centers may well promote protest based upon confrontation. Devolution of authority to smaller units of government, geographically closer to the neighborhoods they serve, may well increase the vulnerability of such units as targets of protest. If the constituencies of some of these smaller units are more sympathetic to the demands of demonstrators than is the public in the city at large, then protest and community organization based upon showmanship may be furthered as well.

How Can We Learn More?

The lessons of the 1960s provide us only with a starting point in the effort to develop comprehensive theories concerning the most effective ways to create and utilize poor people's organizations as part of a broader strategy to help the poor to achieve their aspirations. As indicated above, comparative studies of protest behavior such as Eisinger's hold some promise in further specifying those aspects of protest activity that can be correlated with the political structure of governmental units in which they occur. But in order to conduct such studies across large numbers of cities without a huge research budget it is necessary to sacrifice the kind of fine detail that is essential in understanding protest behavior. If this detail is to be achieved on a reasonable budget, it is therefore necessary to sacrifice the large numbers of sites that are necessary to yield statistically valid findings in favor of more intensive study of a far smaller number of sites. Yet, case studies have their drawbacks as well.

The research dilemma, then, is a difficult one: there are shortcomings related to quantitative studies and there are shortcomings related to isolated case studies. The way out of this dilemma would appear to be the development of additional case study material that does not have the disadvantages normally associated with individually designed and executed case studies such as those that generally describe the protests of the 1960s.

This, in turn, could be accomplished through a two-fold process: first, development of explicit hypotheses concerning the dynamics of protest activities and their impact; then, continual reassessment of these hypotheses through the evidence provided in new, detailed, and realistic case studies designed and executed with these hypotheses in mind.

This chapter presents an analytic framework for the study of poor people's organizations. Implicit or explicit hypotheses can be found in many of the popular and scholarly case studies that are already in print.[7] But the work of putting the pieces together and "testing" the hypotheses in the light of the evidence of the protests of the 1970s remains largely undone. Until this is accomplished community organizers will have to proceed pretty much as they have in the past, relying upon word of mouth lessons from their peers and upon political instinct.

Notes

1. See, for example, Peter Eisinger, "The Conditions of Protest," Vol. 64, No. 1, *The American Political Science Review* (March, 1973), pp. 11-28.

2. The "incentive theory of organizations" was first described in Peter B. Clark and James Q. Wilson, "Incentive Systems: A Theory of Organizations," Vol. 6, *Administrative Science Quarterly* (September, 1961), pp. 129-166. Its most recent exposition can be found in James Q. Wilson, *Political Organizations* (New York: Basic Books, 1974).

3. See, for example, Lawrence N. Bailis, *Bread or Justice: Grassroots Organizing in the Welfare Rights Movement* (Lexington, Mass: Lexington Books, D.C. Heath, 1974).

4. See, for example, Gene Marine, *The Black Panthers* (New York: New American Library, 1969); and in particular Eldrige Cleaver's statement that "since I've been in this movement and working with all these cats, I've found people who really dig me, people I really dig. People care about me, people like me. I've . . . got friends for the first time in my life," quoted on pp. 195-196.

5. This paradigm is fully explained in James Q. Wilson, "The Strategy of Protest," Vol. 5, No. 3, *Journal of Conflict Resolution* (September, 1961), pp/ 291-303.

6. This paradigm is fully explained in Michael Lipsky, "Protest as a Political Resource," Vol. 62, No. 4, *The American Political Science Review* (December, 1968), pp. 1144-1158.

7. One set of hypotheses can be found in Bailis, *Bread or Justice*, pp. 133-134.

10 Problems of Policy Evaluation: The Case of Community Action

Richard D. Shingles

In the mid-1960s a new strategy was developed to assist the poor. The strategy, community action, was to be the primary weapon of the War on Poverty. It involved the establishment of a network of federally sponsored agencies at the local level for the purpose of channeling federal assistance and overseeing federally supported programs. A principal feature of community action was, and continues to be, the effort to involve the poor in the control and implementation of the programs by requiring their participation in both the umbrella community action agencies and in a number of the single-purpose programs set up under their auspices.[a] It was felt by those originally sponsoring the policy that by including the recipients in the effort to fight poverty, community action would serve to organize and mobilize the poor to represent and articulate their collective interests effectively and, by so doing, give the poor a greater stake in the American way of life.

The basis for that goal and the expectation that it could be realized was well founded. It lay in the belief—largely supported by scholarly theory and research at the time[b]—that a major cause of poverty is the utter powerless-

---

[a] The nature and meaning of this participation, never very clear from the start, has changed considerably since the program's first enactment. The concept of "community action" originated from dissatisfaction with traditional approaches to poverty that treat it solely as the product of economic or psychological maladies. It was felt that the usual practice of assisting the poor on an individual basis through compensatory services, administered by middle class professionals, was insufficient if not harmful. The advocates of community action argued that the causes of poverty lie in widespread social inequalities and cultural maladies and that therefore the only way to deal with poverty is with a coordinated attack on the institutional causes of it under the auspices of a single agency in which the poor are given a central and influential role. Title II, section 202 (a)(3) of the Economic Opportunity Act of 1964 declares that the community action programs are intended to coordinate local antipoverty activities "with the maximum feasible participation of the residents of the areas and the members of the groups served." Over the years, however, local officials, congressional committees, and executive departments have reestablished firm control over antipoverty programs, the "maximum feasible participation" clause has been deleted and representation of the poor has officially been set at one-third of CAA boards. The remaining two-thirds is comprised equally of local politicians and community influentials who have a professional interest in the program.

[b] The lot of the American poor may be likened to what is called a "mass society": weak primary group ties, dependence on a large (welfare) bureaucracy, a relative absence of associational membership of a political or social nature, and a general state of isolation and powerlessness against forces over which the individual has very little or no control. Such conditions have been found to be associated with feelings of insecurity, purposelessness, powerlessness, self degradation, and a sense of aloofness from, and hostility towards, government and other social institutions.

Membership in autonomous secondary associations, particularly when accompanied by

ness of the poor to do anything about it and their knowledge and subsequent acceptance of that fact. It was believed that by having the poor participate in self help programs at the local level, they would acquire a collective strength that would provide both the ability and the motivation to seek their own social, economic, and political betterment.

Problems of Evaluation

Unfortunately, as is so often the case, it is extremely difficult to estimate the success with which these goals have been obtained. The history of community action has been accompanied by sharp polemics, claims, and counterclaims by supporters and opponents alike, as well as by supposedly more "neutral" academic observers. Evaluations have varied in temperament from those who condemn community action as the source of irresponsible acts of dissent and protest, to apologists who claim that it has stimulated a new awareness and bred a new leadership among the disadvantaged, to critics who argue that community action agencies (CAAs) have actually impeded efforts to mobilize the poor, to those who deny that they had any significant impact at all.[1]

Several factors account for the controversy. First, the early years of community action were characterized by such intense partisan debates that it was difficult to evaluate the program objectively solely on the basis of its merit. In fact, there was little agreement as to how merit should be defined. Verbal duels occurred between liberal advocates of the Great Society and their conservative opponents, between Democrats and Republicans, be-

---

grassroots participation in organizational decisions, is said by mass society theorists to reduce or prohibit forms of personal and political alienation and to counteract the concurrent mass apathy and political extremism likely to result from them. The ability of people to join such organizations allegedly leads to a desirable state of affairs in which people are mobilized and politicized in such a way as to play a necessary and creative role in the political process. By leading to a greater awareness and interest in politics, by providing an effective voice in the political process, and by creating a stake in the existing social order, associational membership is said to be vital for creating and sustaining a democratic process and a democratic citizenry.

It would be naive to accredit the behavior of the poor solely to their lack of affiliation with autonomous, voluntary, secondary associations. The absence of such ties is much more a consequence than a cause of poverty. Nevertheless the organization of the poor in semi-independent, self-help community agencies promised to serve as a device that could provide the poor with some control over governmental activities affecting their lives, reduce dependency, and stimulate their involvement. For a statement of the Mass Society thesis and its critique, see: William Kornhauser, *The Politics of Mass Society* (Glencoe, Ill.: The Free Press, 1959); Scott Greer and Peter Orleans, "The Mass Society and Parapolitical Structures," *American Sociological Review,* XXVII (October, 1962), 634-46; Joseph R. Gusfield, "Mass Society and Extremist Politics," *American Sociological Review,* XXVII (February, 1962), 19-30; Maurice Pinard, "Mass Society and Political Movements: A New Formulation," *American Journal of Sociology,* LXXIII (May, 1968), 682-90.

tween the then newly founded Organization for Economic Opportunity (OEO), on the one hand, and a coalition of big city mayors and the existing welfare establishment on the other, and between liberal reformers and critics further to the left who condemned community action as a thinly concealed effort to dupe the lower class into quiescence.

Second, the concepts, "community action" and "maximum feasible participation," were not fully discussed, debated, or defined by federal or local elites prior to their enactment into law.[2] The reformers in Washington who originally formulated the idea presented it in broad, loose language in order to conceal differences among themselves and to present a palatable package to the administration and Congress. They also desired to keep the program flexible so as to allow for later adjustments. The OEO package was hastily reviewed and ratified by Congress with little knowledge or examination of the bill or discussion of its key concepts by either congressmen, members of relevant administrative departments, or the mayors of the communities in which the CAAs were to be located. As a result there never existed more than a superficial concensus, concealing deep divisions as to the purpose of the program and the basis upon which it should be judged.

Third, the image of community action has varied because community action itself has varied both over time and from one locality to another. It was the original intent of OEO officials to execute the war on poverty largely as an instrument of social change and agent of mobilization; but the realities of local and national politics soon forced the OEO to make repeated adjustments in an effort to blunt the criticisms from local establishments and to maintain the waning support of both Congress and the President. The diversity at the local level stemmed from emphasis of the OEO on community autonomy and local initiative and from the fact that different elites, of varying sympathy with community action and having different impressions of poverty and what to do about it, ultimately gained control of the CAAs in their communities and shaped them to their own desires.

Finally, disagreement over the effectiveness of community action reflects the quality of the evidence upon which conclusions have had to be made. Much of it is partisan, emotionally laden, and based on unsubstantiated assertions. Administrators who have a vested interest in the continuation of the program are prone to self-advocacy.[3] Critics are equally obliged to pick and choose among CAAs to buttress their arguments. Documentation has been haphazard, superficial, and rarely systematic. Much of the reporting is journalistic in nature. Where rigorous empirical investigations have been made, they are typically burdened by crude measuring devices and inadequate procedures for determining the impact of policy.

Problems of Analysis

Scholarly research on the topic is insufficient in two principal ways: (1) a lack of comparability, and (2) an inability to separate the consequences of community action from its causes.

The Problem of Comparability

Three distinct types of community action agencies have been depicted:[4] (1) *unorganized service CAAs* that provide welfare as usual, serving solely to coordinate established welfare and educational institutions in the administration of traditional services on an individual, deviant case basis; (2) *organized service CAAs* that also emphasize traditional, individual oriented services, but that do so with the organized assistance and participation of the poor as either employees, elected representatives of advisory boards, or participants in self help programs; and (3) *organized social action CAAs* that seek primarily institutional (as opposed to individual) change and that actively strive to mobilize the poor into a political force for bringing it about.

Of the three types, unorganized service CAAs are not intended to mobilize or politicize the poor, nor have they appeared to have done so. In fact, existing research suggests that they may actually impede such processes.[5] At the other extreme, organized social action agencies that have deliberately sought to organize the poor for a confrontation with established interests and that have taken a leading role in the education and training of the poor in the art of politics appear to have had at least some success. Most of the evidence indicating an association between the political involvement of the poor and the presence of community action agencies stems from studies of these organizations.[6] Government funded programs of this nature, however, were few in number and now are all but extinct. They throve only during the first few years of the War on Poverty. Since then the abolition of the "maximum feasible participation" clause, the tightening of statutory control, and the requirement that all federal funding be made through local government has led to the successful curtailment of CAAs used for the encouragement of direct confrontation.

The CAAs that appear to have prospered most over the years are those with an organized, service orientation. While the organized social action CAAs were being abolished or forced to retreat to less aggressive policies, others were encouraged to organize the poor for self help on a much more contained basis. Though the mandate for "maximum feasible participation" was amended by Congress in 1967, participation of at least one-third of the poor or their representatives was made a statutory requirement.

Once in firm control, local elites could afford to be much more sympathetic and supportive of participation from the poor. In such agencies today the poor play the role of junior partners, having insufficient numbers, skill, or experience to single handedly direct CAA policy, but able to represent their clientele's interest and, in that limited sense, exert influence within the programs.[7]

Whether such CAAs are capable of stimulating community involvement is uncertain. Little systematic evidence exists as to whether participation within the organization carries over into involvement in the community. What evidence there is generally fails to distinguish between organized service agencies and organized social action agencies. Furthermore, it is difficult to generalize from the success or failure of any of the CAAs during the 1960s, when most of the research referred to here was conducted.

The Difficulty of Differentiating Cause from Effect

Even more difficult is the question of causality. Sufficient evidence exists to support the conclusions that (1) localities with community action agencies are more likely to be characterized by institutional change and active involvement among the poor than localities without such agencies (even though we do not know the extent that this is equally true for all *kinds* of agencies), and (2) participants in the programs are generally more socially and politically active than nonmembers.[8] The crucial question, however, is whether this means that the CAAs have induced the observed institutional and behavioral differences. Does the presence of CAAs modify behavior or does it simply reflect one aspect of a broader change stimulated by some other factor or factors in the community? Do CAAs with mobilization goals stimulate mobilization of the poor, or is their occurrence in some cities (while not others) a result of mobilizing forces within those communities that mold CAAs to their image? Do we conclude that community action has helped to breed a new generation of activists in poverty neighborhoods, or is it that active residents, who are already mobilized, join and participate in the programs as they would any other organization that appears to benefit their interests?

Certainly the fact that CAA participants are generally more active than nonparticipants may just as well reflect the propensity of interested and involved citizens to voluntarily join CAAs as the ability of CAAs to stimulate their involvement. What needs greater clarification, however, is the equal and very real possibility that the co-occurrence of social action CAAs and an involved citizenry is coincidental, reflecting the direct impact of neither one upon the other. The predominance of several significant events in the 1960s strongly suggests that the association between social action CAAs and political activism may be the result of the unique history of the period and not the act of membership in the organization per se.

The first two events were the civil rights movement and the worsening economic plight of American blacks during a period of otherwise national prosperity.[9] It has been claimed that participation in community action agencies in the 1960s led to black militancy and to a refinement of Black Power ideology.[10] It may well be, however, that the preexisting state of militancy in a community determines the likelihood of social action, and that the militancy in turn is a result of both the strength of the civil rights movement in the area as well as changes in the relative economic status of blacks. The finding that organization and mobilizing goal-oriented CAAs are more likely in cities with large black populations suggests that this may indeed be the case.[11] If true, social action CAAs are more appropriately described as the *products* of political mobilization rather than their cause.

The other event that may be responsible for the association between CAA involvement and political dissent is the manner in which the entire war on poverty was handled. It began with a great deal of fanfare and excessive promises that could not possibly be fulfilled, at least not in the short run, and ended with the withdrawal of active federal support, budget cuts, and co-optation by local institutions. The poor were made aware of their relative plight. They were told that they were entitled to something better and that their condition was not entirely their own responsibility. Many were encouraged to engage in self help with the promise of massive federal support for the eradication of poverty. Yet, the support was not forthcoming and the goals never realized.

The result is likely to have caused a great deal of frustration on the part of those who, after becoming cognizant of the possibility of and the "right" to a better life, had adjusted to the idea psychologically and in many cases invested their time and effort in their local CAA. The intense sense of deprivation of the type resulting from the reversals of the War on Poverty, and the frustration and hostility that often accompany it, have been cited by theorists as the principal cause of most forms of violent dissent.[12]

The federal government's War on Poverty is somewhat analogous to Alexis de Tocqueville's analysis of the causes of the French Revolution. He suggests that in legitimizing discontent with their attack on existing inequalities, followed by their failure to act on their word, the French authorities had "provided less relief for the poor than fuel for their passions. . . . It was indiscreet enough to utter such words, but positively dangerous to utter them in vain."[13] If the comparison is valid, then the protests of those poor involved in CAAs during the 1960s are less explainable in terms of the organizations themselves than the federal government's refusal to support the organization. Since most of the research on community action was conducted during the period in which the government reversed itself on community action (1964-69), it may be that their results reflect a reaction to *policy,* not to an organization.

A Case Study

The problems of policy impact analysis and accurate causal inference are well illustrated by a study of 113 low-income mothers in St. Paul, Minnesota who were interviewed during the Autumn of 1970 and again in the Spring of 1971. Eighty-two are mothers of children who were enrolled in 5 of 11 neighborhood centers. Forty-eight had enrolled their children in the program for the first time that fall. The remaining 31 subjects in the sample were randomly selected from a matched sample of AFDC (Aid to Families with Dependent Children) mothers who lived in the same neighborhoods as the Head Start parents.[14]

Head Start was chosen as the subject of analysis because it is a principal example of organized service agencies.[c] Not only is Head Start easily the most predominant and best financed of all antipoverty programs, it is the one area today where government sponsored participation by the poor has probably reached about as effective a level as will be permitted by local community influentials. Its narrow focus does not present the threat associated with private, multipurpose agencies. It is hardly a "dangerous" area to leave entrusted to an organized group of indigenous poor.

Though a single-purpose program originally operating under the umbrella of CAA, Head Start has probably allowed more opportunity for participation than the overseeing agency.[d] Whereas most target neighborhood residents can participate only rarely in the politics of their local CAA (typically by voting in CAA elections—and few do that), and whereas only a handful can actually serve on the CAA board at any one time, many more parents of preschoolers can and do become politically active within Head Start. The Office of Child Development insists upon a minimum level of parental involvement in both the planning and implementation of the program as a requirement for funding. There *must* be a Policy Advisory Committee (PAC) at the administrative, communitywide level where most decisions are made, which is composed of at least 50 percent parent or parent representatives, each of whom is elected as delegates from local

---

[c] In 1966-67 Head Start alone received more funds than allotted for unrestrictive use in all other fields, $352 to $323 million, respectively. John G. Wofford, "The Politics of Local Responsibility: Administration of Community Action Programs 1964-1966," in *On Fighting Poverty,* ed. by James L. Sundquist (New York: Basic Books, Inc., 1969), 70-102.

[d] On April 9, 1969 Head Start was transferred out of the Organization for Economic Opportunity to the Office of Child Development in the Department of Health, Education, and Welfare.

target neighborhoods. It is also recommended, and usually enacted, that smaller parent organizations (Target Neighborhood Committees) function in each neighborhood on a year-round basis. The parents are free to organize the TNCs any way they choose. Finally, there is a great deal of emphasis on parent "volunteers" at the individual centers to help in the care and education of the children. To encourage all of this a parent coordinator is required for each program to stimulate involvement and to help organize the participants in program activities.

A principal purpose of the St. Paul study is to determine whether membership in Head Start, and particularly active participation in PAC/ TNC activities, in any way alters the political behavior of the poor. To this end, during both the fall and spring interviews, a battery of questions were asked of the respondents relating to the nature and level of their political involvement in the community.

Answers to the questions contained in the survey are collapsed into eight indexes measuring various types of political involvement. Three of the indexes are indicative of *psychological involvement:* interest in politics, self-exposure to the news media, and level of information about political parties and public officials. Two others measure more overt or *active involvement:* a political activity index (indicating frequency of effort to keep informed, inform others, send messages of a critical or supportive nature to public officials, take public and critical stands on political issues, and play a leading role in discussions involving politics); and civic involvement index (compiled from open-ended questions inquiring as to the respondents' membership and level of participation in political and semipolitical clubs, community centers, and local PTAs). The last two indexes measure respondents' perceived obligation or duty to take an active role in the politics of their community. One indicates obligation to take an active, supportive role in the community by keeping informed, informing others, voting, working in the campaigns, and writing messages of support to public officials. The other indicates the respondents' felt obligation to dissent by either publicly pointing out and criticizing improper government behavior, sending messages of protest, joining in peaceful as well as nonpeaceful protests, and refusing to blindly love their country whether it is right or wrong. All of the indexes (except for the political information and civic organizations, which are not amenable to scalegram analysis, and political interest, which consisted of only two questions) are satisfactorily internally consistent in terms of standard Guttman criteria ($CR \geq 0.90$).

The number of PAC/TNC meetings attended by Head Start mothers have been recorded from the minutes of the meetings and serves as an indicator of the level of parental involvement within the program. This information is supplemented with records as to the number of hours per month parents volunteered their services at the neighborhood Head Start centers.

Table 10-1
Involvement in Community Politics (Means)

Community Involvement (T_2)	Nonmembers (31)	New Members (48)	t
Psychological involvement			
Interest in politics	2.26	2.08	N.S.
Media exposure	7.81	8.66	N.S.
Level of information	7.36	8.90	N.S.
Active involvement			
Civic organizations	1.71	2.06	N.S.
Political activity	6.13	7.64	N.S.
Perceived civil duty			
Support	18.97	17.71	N.S.
Protest	5.61	5.36	N.S.

Political Mobilization vs. Self-selection

Are Head Start members politically more involved than the comparable group of nonmembers? And, if so, is the greater involvement due to their membership in the organization? The answer to the first question is affirmative. The answer to the second is generally negative. A comparison of the new members and nonmembers in the spring of 1971 (Table 10-1) concurs with numerous other findings that participants in voluntary associations are more likely to be well informed and politically active than nonparticipants.[15] Though the differences are neither large nor significant, the new Head Start mothers are for the most part more psychologically and actively involved in politics—in spite of the fact that they feel less of an obligation to participate than do the nonmembers.

Without further information such findings could well be used to support the proposition that secondary associations, and community action agencies in particular, are at least moderately capable of mobilizing the poor. This may seem a particularly sound conclusion given the apparent lack of motivation among Head Start mothers to engage in politics. Certainly their lower sense of obligation to participate does not support the rival hypothesis that the reason organizational members are more active generally is because they are activists who find the program an outlet for their interests in politics and the community.

At least in this case, however, such reasoning is invalid. An analysis of the same respondents' answers to the same questions six to eight months earlier (depending upon when they joined) and at least two weeks prior to their children beginning classes at the neighborhood centers, indicates that the new members are more involved in community politics *before* they entered Head Start. For every type of behavior—psychological involvement, active participation, and the respondent's perceived civic duty—members are more involved at the time of the first interview than nonmembers.

When the data are broken down by level of participation within Head Start (Table 10-2) some interesting differences emerge. First, those most active in the community are also most likely to join and become the most active participants in the organization. This supports the suspicion that the relationship between political activity and organizational membership reflects the propensity of some people to be socially concerned, outward going, and generally active, rather than the ability of organizational membership to alter behavior. Even the nonactive Head Start mothers (those people for whom there is no record of any participation in Head Start) are consistently, if only slightly, more involved in the community than the nonmembers.

The second finding of interest centers on the semiactive members—mothers who only attend one or two PAC/TNC meetings and who "volunteer" at the centers, but only reluctantly and well below the minimum eight hours per month urged by Head Start officials. With the exception of a very small reversal for membership in other kinds of civic organizations, they are consistently the most apathetic, isolated, and least well informed group in the St. Paul sample. They represent a number of low-income, primarily AFDC mothers who are coaxed (often by their caseworkers) into enrolling their children into Head Start and participating in the program, but who do not have the interest, energy, or the time to sustain their involvement. Their participation is largely token, the minimum they believe necessary to remain in the program. These same mothers are also the least sophisticated subjects of the sample. When asked to answer questions dealing with their ability to cope with their environment or participate effectively in the political process, they express a level of optimism that, to this researcher, appears terribly naive and inconsistent with their actual condition.

Perhaps the most interesting group among the Head Start mothers are the members who never participate in the organization's activities. It will be shown that the inactive members are the most likely Head Start mothers to alter their level of involvement in the community as a result of their experience in the program. Contrary to expectations, however, the change is for the worst, towards demobilization, *not* mobilization.

Political Mobilization vs. Political Withdrawal

A more select group is employed in the analysis of changes in respondents' behavior between the two surveys. A major problem of trend studies

Table 10-2

Level of Community Involvement Before Entering Head Start by Level of Involvement Within the Program (Means)

Prior Community Involvement (T_1)	Nonmembers	New Members[a]			F
		Inactive	Semiactive	Very Active	
Psychological involvement					
Interest in politics	2.32	2.63	2.08	2.82	N.S.
Media exposure	7.68	7.92	6.39	9.09	N.S.
Political information	4.48	5.67	2.54	9.36	N.S.
Active involvement					
Civic organization	0.90	1.54	1.00	2.00	N.S.
Political activity	6.00	8.08	5.21	10.09	$p < 0.05$
Perceived civic duty					
Support	16.63	17.91	16.29	18.73	N.S.
Protest	5.03	5.54	4.77	5.30	N.S.

[a]*Nonactive members* ($N = 23$) are those newcomers to Head Start who are members in name only, there being no record of them ever having attended PAC/TNC meetings or having volunteered their services. *Semiactive members* ($N = 14$) are those who come to only one or two PAC/TNC meetings or who volunteer only occasionally. *Active members* ($N = 11$) are the newcomers who participate regularly at both PAC/TNC meetings and neighborhood centers.

relying upon successive measurements in time is that of separating the impact of seasonal fluctuations in the variables of interest (such as behavior) from the impact of the independent or experimental variable (in this case membership in an organization). In the St. Paul study respondents were initially interviewed over approximately a two-month period as they entered the Head Start program. Much of the interviewing occurred during the height of the 1970 congressional campaigns. Therefore, a decrease in participation might be expected simply on the basis of the surge and decline normally associated with the periodic occurrence of political campaigns.[16] Much of the American public and particularly the poor are not consistently active nor interested in the political process. Many are not involved at all, living largely apolitical lives. Most of those who do participate do so on a periodic basis. Every two to four years, for a period of a few months, their political consciousness is aroused by election campaigns for state and national office. Occasionally, between elections, particularly intense local or national events may also stimulate their concern. In the absence of such short-term forces, however, political involvement dwindles and attention turns to more salient concerns such as one's family, job, or other social pursuits.

To guard against having this type of extraneous influence confuse the analysis, change scores are evaluated only for those respondents who were initially interviewed during a two-week period two months before the election and just prior to the traditional Labor Day kick-off to political campaigns. The more select group includes 23 nonmembers and 45 members (composed of 18 newcomers to Head Start and 27 individuals who had been members prior to the beginning of the school year in September).

The results may be found in Table 10-3. Head Start activists and semiactivists (which are combined in the table under the label ''Active Members'') do change during the course of the study, particularly in their level of information and to a lesser extent in their sense of civic duty. However, such changes are not significantly different from similar changes recorded for the nonmembers. In fact, for five out of the seven indicators of political involvement, nonmembers record a greater increase in political involvement than active members. This is particularly noticeable in the case of the respondents' felt obligation to engage in traditional or supportive activities (which accounts for the greater sense of obligation expressed by the nonmembers during the spring interview noted in Table 10-1). The finding suggests that, if anything, participation in Head Start impedes changes that would have occurred had the mothers never entered the organization.

Even more startling is the behavior of the inactive mothers. In every case, except one (membership in other civic organizations), they either increase less than the active members and nonmembers, or they decrease in involvement. The differences are not so much large as they are impressive considering the expectations encouraged by the scholarly literature and the advocates of community action. It would appear that the impact of Head Start is either weak or else so subtle that it cannot be measured over a period of eight months. What little effect it does have is the opposite of that either intended by strategists or predicted by theorists.

The Varied Impact Among Individual Members

The analysis thus far has been limited to the study of mean changes between a control group and members in Head Start and between subgroups among the members themselves. Such comparisons average out and therefore conceal a considerable amount of individual variation within each of the groups. The effect of community action on Head Start mothers is examined from a different perspective in Table 10-4. The data is presented for the full sample of 82 members who have been interviewed both times. The purpose of the analysis is to discover whether the individual variation in level of involvement over time is random or whether it is systematically associated with the respondents' level of participation

Table 10-3
Mean Changes Over Time in Level of Community Involvement by Level of Activity in Head Start

Community Involvement	Nonmembers (23)			Inactive Members (20)			Active Members (25)			
	Original Score	Change Score	t	Original Score	Change Score	t	Original Score	Change Score	t	F
Psychological involvement										
Interest in politics	(2.39)	0.13	(N.S.)	(2.25)	−0.50	($p < 0.05$)	(2.46)	0.29	(N.S.)	N.S.
Media exposure	(7.13)	1.17	(N.S.)	(8.85)	−1.50	(N.S.)	(8.17)	0.92	(N.S.)	N.S.
Level of information	(4.30)	3.30	($p < 0.01$)	(3.00)	2.90	($p < 0.05$)	(6.29)	3.18	($p < 0.01$)	N.S.
Active involvement										
Civic organizations	(.78)	1.00	($p < 0.10$)	(0.95)	1.25	($p < 0.10$)	(1.08)	0.46	(N.S.)	N.S.
Political activity	(5.86)	0.59	(N.S.)	(5.05)	0.00	(N.S.)	(7.96)	0.17	(N.S.)	N.S.
Perceived civic duty										
Support	(15.73)	3.54	($p < 0.01$)	(13.83)	0.83	(N.S.)	(17.71)	1.26	(N.S.)	N.S.
Protest	(5.23)	0.86	(N.S.)	(5.11)	−0.83	(N.S.)	(5.04)	1.38	($p < 0.05$)	N.S.

138

Table 10-4
Correlations (T_b) Between Change in Levels of Community Involvement and Participation in Head Start for Both Active and Passive Citizens

| | Association Between Community and Head Start Involvement | | | |
| | Passive Citizens Who Increased in Involvement | | Active Citizens Who Decreased in Involvement | |
Community Involvement	T_b	(N)	T_b	(N)
Psychological involvement				
Interest in politics	0.40[a]	(31)	0.10	(38)
Media exposure	.06	(31)	− .03	(24)
Level of information	.05	(17)	− .18	(23)
Active involvement				
Civic organizations	− .15[b]	(55)	− .13	(18)
Political activity	.08	(25)	.26[b]	(35)
Perceived civic duty				
Support	− .05	(32)	.25[b]	(27)
Protest	0.11	(54)	0.43[c]	(16)

[a]$p < 0.001$
[b]$p < 0.05$
[c]$p < 0.01$

within the organization. Two questions are asked: First, to what extent is community action able to mobilize formerly passive citizens? Second, to what extent does it serve as a basis for sustaining political involvement among community activists.

Former Apolitical Types. Perhaps the crucial question for community action is whether involvement in grassroots politics can encourage heretofore politically apathetic individuals to take an active interest in their community. The ability of grassroots antipoverty programs to accomplish this for the poor is severely limited. The most apathetic and withdrawn of them refuse to join CAAs. Many who do join remain members in little more than name only. In the St. Paul case only 50 percent ever attend a PAC/TNC meeting and of those only half can be said to have done so with any frequency. Thus, only a very few apolitical types come into close enough contact with community action agencies to be positively affected by them.

Nevertheless, those members who, though politically apathetic, are enticed into active participation in the politics of Head Start do experience a very limited change in their political orientations. There is a clear and significant tendency for such activity to lead to a greater interest in politics. Forty-three percent of the PAC/TNC activists who express little interest in politics during the fall reveal a high level of interest by spring. This compared with 27 percent of the semiactivists and only 9 percent of the nonactivists.

However, during the same period, participation in PAC/TNC meetings demonstrates absolutely no ability to otherwise mobilize formerly apathetic people. In fact, there is a tendency for greater levels of participation in Head Start to lead to a withdrawal from other sorts of *organized* activities. The more active an individual becomes in any Head Start activity (whether it is political or nonpolitical in nature) the less likely she is to join any new organizations over the period and the greater is her propensity to quit those few organizations of which she is already a member.

Thus, while Head Start has contributed narrowly to the psychological involvement in politics of those members who do become organizationally active, it reveals no ability to create activists, as is so commonly assumed. There is no evidence of formerly apathetic, isolated residents of poverty neighborhoods being drawn up by the organization and cast into the political arena. It is more often the case that their limited time and energy allows them little opportunity for further involvement other than the CAA—at least of an organized nature. To the extent that they participate in a program like Head Start, they are less able to afford active membership in other organizations. Hence, if they choose to continue in the program they find it necessary to withdraw from other activities that compete for their time or else to refrain from undertaking any new commitments.[e]

Former Community Activists. Though a number of individuals who are active during the fall decline in political involvement after the election, those community activists who become active participants in the St. Paul Head Start are the *least* likely to do so. The greater one's level of participation in the decision-making process of the program, the greater is the likelihood that one will remain active in community politics during the year. Those individuals who are politically active in the fall, but who do *not* participate in the internal politics of Head Start, are the most likely to return to a state of relative political apathy.

The type of overt activity that is most likely to persist is of a protest nature. The Head Start activists who are prone to dissent in fall are just as critical in spring. Of all those who originally indicate a high propensity to

[e] Sixty percent of the Head Start members who indicate that they have little spare time at the time of the first interviews never attend a PAC/TNC meeting, compared with 44 percent who say they usually have part or most of their day free. Thirty-five percent of those who have little spare time never show up at the neighborhood center to donate their services, whereas only 22 percent of those with more leisure fail to do so. The practical problems and competing responsibilities confronting many people at this level (and probably any level) are such that any commitment on their part to CAA requires that they give up other activities. In some cases—particularly among those lower strata where people have few resources for activity—membership in a new organization leads to a withdrawal from other social pursuits that rival for one's time, rather than immediate increases in community involvement.

speak critically of government officials and write protest letters, 93 percent of the activists persist in such activity during the spring compared with 67 percent of the semiactive members and 50 percent of the inactive members. The relatively greater stability of dissentive as opposed to supportive behavior is also indicated by respondents' answers concerning their civic obligations. Though there is an association between PAC/TNC attendance and both types of responsibilities, the obligation to dissent is the more persistent of the two.

When the changes in the types of political behavior discussed here are correlated with the number of hours parents volunteer at the neighborhood centers (rather than PAC/TNC meetings) these relationships largely disappear. In fact, among those who never attend PAC/TNC meetings, but who do volunteer with the children, there is a slight tendency for a withdrawal from community involvement similar to that found for the inactive members in Table 10-3.

In short, participation in the *politics* of Head Start (PAC/TNC) appears to help preserve an active level of community involvement where it *already* exists, but simple membership alone or participation of a nonpolitical nature provides no such stimulus to political behavior, and instead detracts from it. Among the activists, the type of behavior that is most likely to be preserved is of a dissenting nature.

It is not at all surprising that participation in the internal decision making process of a CAA contributes to a continuing involvement in community politics. Nor is it surprising that the involvement tends to emphasize dissent. The people who join Head Start and become most active in it are the most alienated and dissatisfied in the first survey. By creating a forum where potential political activists can meet, discuss the fate and the merits of OEO/HEW, as well as exchange opinions and information about other government policies, PAC/TNC meetings provide a year-round stimulus for political involvement and organized dissent (though in St. Paul the dissent takes a very mild form). Those actively involved in an organized setting—particularly one in which politics is a salient topic—are more alert to events that transpire in government and conscious of how they may be personally affected. On the other hand, those community activists who do not participate in CAA or similar organizations are generally only reached once every two to four years through election campaigns, or occasionally in between elections by politically salient events. Most of the time their attention and activity turn elsewhere.

Conclusion

Three principal findings emerge from the St. Paul study concerning the impact of community action as a tool for mobilizing the poor. First, in the St. Paul Head Start, community action demonstrates very limited capacity for stimulating political involvement. What is most often lost sight of in discussions of the role of secondary associations in mobilizing individuals is that only a small percentage of the membership of any one association becomes sufficiently involved to be in any way affected by it. For those who do become regularly active, there is a clear limit as to how much their existing behavioral patterns can be altered. Most participants in the organization are activists to begin with. The organization simply provides an ongoing stimulus and a platform for their continuing involvement in community politics. It fails to mobilize the truly apathetic members. This is particularly true for the nonactive members, but is largely true for those who do participate in organizational politics as well. The experience does little more than stimulate an active interest in politics, having no noticeable effect on overt behavior or the level of sophistication of the participants.

It may be that, given their new concern for politics and their continued presence in CAA, over a longer period those citizens who were formerly apathetic may become politically active in their community. Coming elections may witness their participation. Local administrators may at some time experience their demands. Evidence of that possibility, however, is not provided in the interval from the early fall of 1970 to the spring of 1971. Neither is it clear whether such people retain their newly found involvement once they leave an organization like Head Start. After the stimulus of organized behavior is withdrawn, do they continue their interest? Do they join other organizations and thereby sustain or increase their level of involvement? Or, like their children in the Head Start program, do they rapidly return to the molds of behavior they shared before ever hearing of "community action?"[f]

Second, a number of the members, particularly those who are only marginally involved or involved in nonpolitical activities within the organization, actually display a slight *decrease* in community activity. The occurrence of such withdrawal cannot be completely accounted for by concurrent or known historical events. The only conclusion possible is that there is something about the St. Paul Head Start, and perhaps Organized Service CAAs in general, that turns some people away from politics. Part of their withdrawal is no doubt due to a lack of free time available to people of this income level for much other than subsistence activities. The participation in Head Start, which is demanded of most parents, forces them to sacrifice

---

[f]A common finding as to the ability of Head Start to accelerate the cognitive development of disadvantaged children is that there is an improvement, but that it is temporary. Within several years after leaving the program most traces of its effect are gone. See The Westinghouse Learning Corporation, Ohio University, *The Impact of Head Start–An Evaluation of the Effect of Head Start on Childrens' Cognitive and Evaluative Development* (Springfield, Va: Clearing House, U.S. Dept. of Commerce, 1969).

142

other activities and organizational pursuits. However, the reasons for their withdrawal are not limited entirely to a lack of available resources for effective participation.

Additional research on the St. Paul sample has demonstrated that the same individuals who are most likely to withdraw from politics are also the most likely to alter their attitudes towards both th emselves and the political system. The attitudinal change is toward greater alienation, suggesting that the withdrawal from community involvement may be the result of a dissatisfaction with politics stemming from their experience in Head Start.[17] It should be noted, however, that the number of respondents who report such dissatisfaction are a minority of the membership. Most of the mothers seem very pleased with the program, but nevertheless unaffected by it.

Finally, how common these findings are to other community action programs or similar organizations is not clear. The answer will have to wait more rigorous research than has been done to date. To those who would do such research, however, the St. Paul case offers a basis for caution. Impact analysis based on data collected at one point in time may be highly misleading. What may be taken as proof of a successful policy may mean something quite the opposite—or nothing at all. As a study of an isolated program, the data presented here cannot say anything conclusive about the success or failure of community action. However, it does raise serious questions about the problems of policy evaluation and the limitations of existing research.

Notes

1. For a taste of these polemics, see: Charles E. Silberman, "The Mixed-Up War on Poverty," in *Poverty: Power and Politics,* ed. by Chaim Isaac Waxman (New York: Grosset and Dunlap, 1968), 81-100; Daniel P. Moynihan, *Maximum Feasible Misunderstanding: Community Action and the War on Poverty* (New York: The Free Press, 1969), 128ff; Kenneth B. Clark and Jeannette Hopkins, *A Relevant War Against Poverty: A Study of Community Action Programs and Observable Social Change* (New York: Harper and Row, 1969), 107-8; Stephen M. Rose, *The Betrayal of the Poor: The Transformation of Community Action* (Cambridge: Schenkman Publishing Co., 1972); Saul D. Alinsky, "The War on Poverty—Political Pornography," in Waxman, *Poverty: Power and Politics,* 171-97.

2. For a history of community action, see: Richard Blumenthal, "The Bureaucracy: Anti-poverty and Community Action," in *American Political Institutions and Public Policy,* ed. by Allan P. Sindler (Boston: Little Brown and Co., 1969), 128-79, 171-72; Stephen M. David, "Leadership of

the Poor in Poverty Programs," *Academy of Political Science Proceedings*, XXIX (1968), 87-102; John C. Donovan, *The Politics of Poverty*, 2nd ed. (Indianapolis: The Bobbs-Merrill Co., Inc., 1973).

3. John W. Evans, "Evaluating Social Action Programs," *Social Science Quarterly*, L. (December, 1969), 568-81.

4. Clark and Hopkins, *A Relevant War Against Poverty*, 19ff; Rose, *The Betrayal of the Poor*, 123ff.

5. James J. Vanecko, "Community Mobilization and Institutional Change: The Influence of the Community Action Program in Large Cities," *Social Science Quarterly*, L (December, 1969).

6. Ibid., and Clark and Hopkins, *A Relevant War Against Poverty*, 78ff.

7. Dale Rogers Marshall, *The Politics of Participation in Poverty* (Berkeley: University of California Press, 1971), 51-78.

8. Vanecko, "Community Mobilization and Institutional Change"; Clark and Hopkins, *A Relevant War Against Poverty*, 78ff, 88, 98, 106-8; Kirschiner Association, Inc., *A National Survey of the Impact of Head Start Centers on Community Institutions*, prepared for Project Head Start, The Office of Child Development (Washington, D.C.: U.S. Government Printing Office, May, 1970); Walter Gove and Herbert Costner, "Organizing the Poor: An Evaluation of a Strategy," *Social Science Quarterly*, L (December, 1969), 648.

9. Nathan Cohen, ed., *The Los Angeles Riots: A Socio-Psychological Study* (New York: Praeger, 1970), 5-6.

10. J. Kenneth Benson, "Militant Ideologies and Organizational Contexts: The War on Poverty and the Ideology of Black Power," *The Sociological Quarterly*, XII (Summer, 1971), 328-39.

11. Vanecko, "Community Mobilization and Institutional Change."

12. Ted Robert Gurr, *Why Men Rebel* (Princeton: Princeton University Press, 1970); James C. Davies, "Toward a Theory of Revolution," in *When Men Revolt and Why*, ed. by James Chowning Davies (New York: The Free Press, 1971).

13. Alexis De Tocqueville, *The Old Regime and The French Revolution*, trans. by Stuart Gilbert (New York: Doubleday and Co., Inc., 1955), 180-82.

14. For an extended discussion of the methodology employed in this study, see R.D. Shingles, "Organizational Membership and Attitude Change," in *Quasi-Experimental Approaches*, ed. by James A. Caporaso and Leslie L. Roos, Jr. (Evanston: Northwestern University Press, 1973), 226-70.

15. V.O. Key, *Public Opinion and American Democracy* (New York: Alfred A. Knopf, 1964), 504ff; Gabriel Almond and Sidney Verba, *The Civic Culture* (Princeton: Princeton University Press, 1963).

144

16. Angus Campbell, "Surge and Decline: A Study of Electoral Change," in *Elections and the Political Order,* ed. by Angus Campbell, Philip E. Converse, Warren Miller, and Donald E. Stokes (New York: John Wiley and Sons, Inc., 1966). The ability of election campaigns to produce temporary increases in political involvement has been reported in other panel studies. See Bernard R. Berelson, Paul F. Lazarsfeld, and William N. McPhee, *Voting* (Chicago: University of Chicago Press, 1954), 24-33.

17. Richard D. Shingles, "Community Action and Attitude Change: A Case of Adult Political Socialization," *Experimental Study of Politics*, 4 (December, 1975).

11

The Urban Bias of the Poverty Program

Terry L. Christensen

The Economic Opportunity Program and its offshoots were never intended or designed to treat all types of poverty. Their most apparent bias was in favor of racial and ethnic minorities; poor whites were seldom an important "target" for the War on Poverty. A less apparent and rarely noticed bias of the poverty program was its focus on urban poverty. Created in response to or anticipation of the demands of the urban, inner city poor, the program was designed to meet the needs of this segment of America's poverty population and was never fairly or broadly extended to the white or rural poor. Most social scientists who have studied the problem of poverty have shared this urban bias and have paid little attention to the phenomenon and treatment of rural poverty.

The Genesis of the Poverty Program

The forces that are generally agreed to have produced the War on Poverty help explain the urban bias of the program.[1] Among these forces were: the growing assertiveness of urban minority populations; President Johnson's hope to emulate Franklin Roosevelt's "New Deal" with his own "Great Society"; the interests of the Democratic party in the continued allegiance of urban and black voters; and a group of ambitious, liberal, academic reformers recently involved in government by the Kennedy administration. These reformers came to believe that meaningful change in government policy toward the poor was impossible within traditional governmental structures. They feared that significant reforms would be resisted by reactionary local power structures or by rigid, self-serving welfare bureaucracies. The reformers also believed that existing welfare, unemployment, education, and other programs designed to combat poverty were weakened by the fact that they were administered in a fragmented and uncoordinated way by various agencies of city, county, state, and federal governments.

The Johnson administration thus proposed the Economic Opportunity Act, which was approved by the Congress in 1964. The poverty program they proposed was based on the concept of the "independent" community action agency (CAA). Each CAA operated within a specified city or county but was independent from local government. The CAAs were funded by the federal government and assigned to perform a plethora of difficult tasks. Among these were the coordination of programs for the poor; cooperation with traditional social service agencies such as welfare departments and schools; development and administration of innovative programs to fight poverty; community organization and the participation of poor people in the development and administration of local programs.

Attention Means Money

The urban poor and minorities were the most assertive clientele group for the newly created poverty agency and they were also of greatest concern to the Johnson administration. The ghetto riots had begun by 1964 and the urban black poor constituted a serious threat to the political tranquility of the period. Consequently, they received the greatest attention from the Office of Economic Opportunity. Ultimately, with the Model Cities program, the Johnson administration gave up all pretense of attempting to treat the problem of poverty generally and focused only on selected neighborhoods of selected large cities.

Attention means money, and most of the poverty program funds went to the urban community action agencies. These CAAs received a far greater share of dollars per poor person than did rural CAAs. As Frances Fox Piven and Richard A. Cloward pointed out in their excellent analysis of federal poverty policy, *Regulating the Poor*, "urban areas got more . . . ; only about one quarter of CAA funds went to rural areas."[2] Table 11-1, also extracted from Piven and Cloward, illustrates this distribution as well as the distribution of poverty funds by region. Approximately half of the nation's poor lived in rural areas during the 1960s; yet, these areas received only 24 percent of the funds of the nation's poverty program. This distribution of funds clearly demonstrates the urban bias of the program.

A further look reveals that most of the money that did go to rural areas went to southern and Appalachian CAAs. The southern CAAs had larger black populations and blacks were a prime target of the poverty program. As the civil rights movement and voter registration progressed in the rural South, the Johnson administration had an obvious interest in the establishment of local programs to serve new voters. Appalachian poverty was primarily white, not black, and this appears to have been the rare case of genuine attention and substantial money being devoted to white, rural poverty. Appalachian poverty had evidently been sufficiently publicized and romanticized to permit these predominantly white communities to receive a fair share of funds.

In sum, the poverty program made only a token commitment of funds to rural areas. It was enough, however, to make the program appear to be a

Table 11-1

Total Dollar Effort for Community Action Agencies by OEO and Localities, Fiscal 1968

	Millions of Dollars	%	% Urban Dollar Effort	% Rural Dollar Effort
National	1,120	100		
Urban	851	76	100	
Rural	269	24		100
Northeast	249	21		
Urban	220	20	26	
Rural	19	2		7
North Central	241	22		
Urban	196	18	23	
Rural	45	4		17
West	213	19		
Urban	189	17	22	
Rural	35	2		9
South	426	38		
Urban	246	22	29	
Rural	180	16		67
Deep South	156	14		
Urban	73	7	9	
Rural	83	7		31
Other South	270	24		
Urban	172	15	20	
Rural	98	9		36

Source: OEO, Community Action Agency Analysis Report as of 11/22/69. [Table extracted from Frances Fox Piven and Richard A Cloward, *Regulating the Poor: The Functions of Public Welfare*, (New York: Vintage edition published by arrangement with Pantheon Books, a Division of Random House, Inc., 1971), p. 305. Reprinted by permission.]

Notes: Coterminous United States, columns may not total properly because of rounding; dollar effort includes a small proportion of money appropriated by localities as a condition of receiving OEO funds. In this table, we follow OEO's definition of urban: counties with a subdividion containing more than 10,000 persons.

national one treating all types of poverty everywhere, though such was clearly not the case.

The Treatment of Poverty

The urban bias in the conception, perceived target populations, and financing of the poverty program also extended to the types of programs for which funding was available. Although the original intent of the community action concept had been independent local agencies that could develop flexible programming to meet particular local variations in the problems of poverty, there was never sufficient financial and political support for the program to permit such flexibility. Instead, local agencies were permitted packaged programs and very little else.

Most of these packaged programs were not designed or adequately supported to work well in rural areas. Educational programs were handicapped by rural transportation problems and by the lack of adequate facilities and trained teachers. Job training was useless if there were no jobs. How do you train someone to be a field laborer? Some rural CAAs went so far as to train residents and then send them to cities where it was hoped jobs would be available. The problem of poverty in such areas was solved by exporting the poor people. It should be apparent from these two simple examples that there are aspects of rural poverty that make it different and more difficult to treat than urban poverty. The Office of Economic Opportunity gave this scant attention.

Perhaps the most complex, controversial, and urban aspect of the poverty program had to do with the "maximum feasible participation" clause of the Economic Opportunity Act. This required that poor persons participate on policy-making boards of community action agencies and through employment as CAA staff. In many cases the process went one step further, to community organizing. The idea was to organize the poor into viable interest groups that could take an active role in the poverty agencies, act in their own neighborhoods to develop and even administer programs, and most significantly, represent the poor in community politics beyond the poverty agency. In many communities the newly organized poor became politicized and assertive. Their actions as an interest group inevitably and intentionally extended beyond the scope of the poverty program to local politics. What followed was conflict and controversy as the organizations of the poor confronted antagonistic local power structures.

The citizen participation and community organization efforts of the poverty program caused political difficulty in large cities. They were, however, essentially urban aspects of the poverty program. They could not have been designed with rural poverty in mind. They had a very different and less dramatic impact in rural areas. The emphasis on neighborhood organization was obviated by the broad geographical dispersion of the rural poor. The entire structure of "community" was different for the rural poor and without discrete neighborhoods around which to organize, the more political aspects of the poverty program were made considerably more difficult to attain. Simple problems of communication and transportation became formidable barriers. Further, the poor lacked the education and previous experience, organization, and politicization that enhanced community organization and citizen participation in many urban areas. Almost all of the rural poor were novices at political activity, while many of the urban poor had the confidence and experience to attempt to manipulate or take over the new poverty agencies.

Thus was the Economic Opportunity Program biased in favor of urban areas. It was the inner city poor who were the primary concern of the instigators of the program. Proportionally, much more of the money went to the urban poor than to the rural poor. And the programs of the poverty agency were urban in conception, most particularly in their efforts at citizen participation and community organization.

The Rural Poor Are Different

Rural poverty is different from urban poverty and this was never recognized by the framers and administrators of the national poverty program with their pervasive urban biases. The rural poor are isolated. They live miles apart, not in densely populated ghettoes with high levels of interaction. This makes provision of services such as health care and education difficult. It may also minimize awareness of other poor people, common interests, and political potential. The rural poor may be less conscious of being poor and they are clearly less politicized. In political organization and assertiveness, the rural poor are decades behind the urban poor. The assertive rural poor leave. They move to cities in search of jobs. They become urban poor and start again.

There are other areas in which rural poverty lags behind urban poverty. The rural poor are unemployed because there are no jobs in their areas, not merely because they are not trained for available jobs. Economic development of entire communities may be necessary to improve employment among the poor. In urban areas the problem in the prosperous 1960s was to connect people to jobs through training and placement. Transportation is also a devastating problem for the rural poor. Urban dwellers may complain of expensive and inefficient bus systems that take them two hours to get to work or to a health clinic, but there are not even such inefficient systems in rural areas. Schools are poorer and worse in quality. Welfare systems are less extensive and stingier.

Political power in rural areas is also less broadly distributed. Simple, undiversified rural economies tend to be associated with monolithic power structures. The "tight little town" syndrome runs strong in rural towns and counties and the few men who run these communities run them as they have always been run, resisting change and unresponsive to the demands of newly organized groups. Poverty is not viewed as a social problem but as an accepted fact of life. The federal government is viewed as a meddling outsider and the poor are expected to stay in their place. Those who become "uppity" risk swift and powerful reprisals, for there is no urban mass of people into which to disappear and there are no alternative sources of credit, employment, or retail and other services.

Some might argue, however, that rural poverty is less oppressive than urban poverty. Clean air and water, trees and open space, gardens, and game, and the intimacy of community may make rural poverty less destructive than its urban counterpart. This is a romantic view of rural poverty and while it may have some validity, it overlooks the boredom, hunger, fear, frustration, and repression that usually accompany rural poverty. It is a grinding, dead-end experience for millions of Americans and the poverty program paid it scant attention.

Assessments of the Poverty Program

The popular image of urban community action is that of a fiasco. It has been said that the poor were bought off, permitted to play with power but not really to possess it. It has also been said that the poor or their spokespersons used the programs to further their personal gain by ripping off jobs and money or building a political base. Both circumstances occurred and in many cases the urban poor probably were diverted from long-range goals by fighting over jobs and money in community action agencies. The poverty program as a whole was not adequately funded and local agencies were not given sufficient flexibility in programming to lead to dramatic or significant change. And so the poor, instead of organizing politically for real change, found themselves fighting over crumbs—and dependent on the federal government as a crumb-tosser. The Economic Opportunity Program failed to provide more services or new and better services or substantial change.[3]

It is important to bear in mind that these generalizations are based almost exclusively on the study of urban poverty programs. The urban bias of the program extends to those who have studied it and little is known of the impact of the poverty program in those rural areas where CAAs were established. Quite unintentionally, things may have been different in rural areas. With so little to begin with—so little in terms of government services, political organization, jobs, education, resources—anything at all may have meant a great deal to the rural poor. How can people with nothing to sell be bought off? How can people with no political organization and no goals in mind be diverted? There were virtually no stirrings of discontent or political organizing in the rural areas before the CAAs moved in. Tom Wolfe may have been accurate about the mau-mauing of flak-catchers in

San Francisco,[4] but few of the rural poor were prepared to mau-mau anyone.

The Impact of the Poverty Program in Rural Areas

Both the popular and academic evaluations of the poverty program are based on analyses of urban, not rural, community action programs. There have been too few studies of the impact of the program in rural areas for comparison or generalization. Only speculation is possible. What follows is based on one study of rural community action agencies, which provides some insight as to the impact of the poverty program in rural communities.[5]

One of the most fundamental accomplishments of the rural CAAs was the provision of jobs on the CAA staff for people in rural communities—both poor and nonpoor. As an employer the CAAs provided a much needed stimulant to stagnant rural economies. In some areas they became the largest single employer.

The CAAs also acted to provide basic services not otherwise available to the poor. These included transportation in areas with no public transit facilities, health care and training, and assistance in development of rural sanitation facilities. In some areas new housing was built or assistance was provided in improving existing housing stock. In education the CAAs established head start programs in areas that had not previously had kindergartens and they also provided adult education including job training and household maintenance.

Some community organizing was done in rural CAAs, but its goals were economic rather than political. The thrust of these organizational efforts was self help through the establishment of various types of cooperatives. Agricultural producing and marketing cooperatives were organized to assist the rural poor in using available skills and resources in producing income for themselves. Handicraft co-ops made and sold the products of traditional rural arts such as quilting, pottery, woodcarving, and doll-making—again, earning a profit from existing skills and resources. One community established a credit union, providing the poor with new access to credit and a savings system. These are hardly revolutionary programs; yet, they had great significance in the lives of the rural poor and may have greater staying power than many of the urban organizational efforts. They would not have come about without the impetus of the poverty program.

The citizen participation requirements of the poverty program involved the rural poor in decision making in their communities for the first time. To be sure, most of the new representatives were diffident, overcome to be sitting at the same table with the mighty county commissioners, but many were activated and are still active. The boards of directors of the rural

CAAs tended to be dominated by traditional community leaders. The representatives of the poor went along with their decisions, either because they were too timid or fearful to oppose them or, more likely, because they agreed with them because they were all for needed programs.

Though they did not play a leading role in decision making, the representatives of the poor did learn to participate. They learned the rules of the game, political tactics, and greater self-confidence, and many continued to be active after the poverty program was phased out. Their activities in school, town, and county politics involve speaking for the interests of the poor in their communities. Such voices had not been heard before and, though they are now paid some attention, they are far from being accepted as a part of the local power structure. The change that has occurred is more one of opening communications than of redistributing power.

These new leaders and organizations, along with the new meeting grounds supplied by the community action agencies themselves, have improved relations among various segments of rural communities. The jobs available through CAAs introduced a new elite to rural communities and some poor people were included in this group. Another more general benefit of the poverty program was the setting of precedents for racially integrated hiring and services—and proving that integration could work.

In sum, the orientation of the rural CAAs toward the problem of poverty was a traditional and somewhat conservative service approach. Rather than trying to bring about substantial change through organization and citizen participation, the rural CAAs were satisfied to attempt to improve provision of needed basic services for the poor. Citizen participation and community organization were given a low priority. The poor in these areas were harder to organize and less experienced, as well as less committed to this way of resolving the problem of poverty. Rural CAAs were dominated by local elites who saw to it that the CAA staff was selected locally from "acceptable" candidates. Community organizers need not have applied.

This choice was acceptable to the rural poor, who wanted and needed basic services. The requests they made of their CAAs were more moderate than those of their urban counterparts. They did not seek innovative programing or funding of their own groups or an emphasis on community organizing. They wanted basic services in health care, sanitation, education, jobs and job training, housing, and the like.

This choice sat well with the local elites. Because of the service orientation of most rural CAAs, the men of influence in the rural communities generally supported (or dominated) the CAAs. Rural CAAs may have had an easier time of it with local political powers than urban CAAs because of this. The rural CAAs seemed safer to those in power because they never constituted a serious threat to the distribution of power, as their urban counterparts attempted to do. Though the rural poor were encouraged to be more active than before, there was no real political organization and there were few demonstrations. The CAAs were almost exclusively economic in the orientation, which made them less threatening to local elites because the communities themselves were so poor that the CAAs could be viewed by the nonpoor as community improvement agencies. As a consequence, local elites participated in the formation and continuation of the rural CAAs and were cooperative for the most part.

The approach adopted by the rural CAAs was not necessarily better than the more aggressive efforts of urban CAAs. The point is that it was a different approach, one that was adapted to the political realities of its environment. The service orientation was a safer, more conservative approach for which the rural poor and community leaders seemed ready. It is doubtful that more could have been done by other tactics. In fact, more aggressive techniques seem to have failed in urban areas due to the political controversy they produced and the gradual withdrawal of federal funding for such efforts. The urban programs may have been better in that they aimed at more substantial change, but in the final analysis it is doubtful that they can claim to have delivered more to the urban poor than rural CAAs produced for their constituencies.

Conclusions

These assessments of the impact of the poverty program in rural areas are speculation based on the study of half a dozen rural community action agencies. They must remain speculation because students of public policy have failed to study the phenomenon of rural poverty and the impact of the poverty program upon it.

The poverty program was subject to a strong urban bias that was apparent in the concerns of the political forces that created it, in the distribution of funds, and in the sorts of programs that were made available. It is unfortunate that social scientists have been victims of the same bias.

The urban bias runs deep and wide through the literature of the social sciences. Most social scientists reside, work, and do their research in urban areas. For the past decade we have been obsessed with the urban crisis. The crisis exists and must be studied, but it is unfortunate that the focus on the urban crisis has meant neglect of the rural crisis. For it is at least in part the rural crisis and the flight to the cities that have produced the crisis of urban poverty. We would have a better understanding of the urban crisis, urban poverty, and the poverty program as a whole if only our attention had been turned, at least in a small part, to what was happening outside the great cities.

Notes

1. See John C. Donovan, *The Politics of Poverty* (New York: Pegasus, 1968); Peter Marris and Martin Rein, *Dilemmas of Social Reform* (London: Routledge and Kegan Paul, 1967); Daniel Patrick Moynihan, *Maximum Feasible Misunderstanding* (New York: Free Press, 1969); or James L. Sundquist, ed., *On Fighting Poverty* (New York: Basic Books, 1969).

2. Frances Fox Piven and Richard A. Cloward, *Regulating the Poor: The Functions of Public Welfare* (New York: Vintage edition published by arrangement with Pantheon Books, a Division of Random House, Inc., 1971), p. 304. Reprinted by permission.

3. See Peter Bachrach and Morton S. Baratz, *Power and Poverty* (New York: Oxford, 1970); Kenneth B. Clark and Jeannette Hopkins, *A Relevant War against Poverty* (New York: Harper and Row, 1969); Ralph Kramer, *Participation of the Poor* (Englewood Cliffs, New Jersey: Prentice-Hall, 1969); Moynihan, *Maximum Feasible Misunderstanding*; Piven and Cloward, *Regulating the Poor: The Functions of Public Welfare*; or Tom Wolfe, *Radical Chic and Mau-Mauing the Flak-Catchers* (New York: Farrar, Strauss and Giroux, 1970).

4. Wolfe, *Radical Chic*.

5. The author's dissertation research involved a study of 11 North Carolina community action agencies, six of which were rural. "Citizen Participation and the Participation of the Poor in the Community Action Program," Ph.D. dissertation, University of North Carolina at Chapel Hill, 1972.

**Part IV
The Impact of Other OEO
Programs**

12 Native Americans and OEO—The Politics of Change

Elmer R. Rusco and
Mary K. Rusco

The War on Poverty was declared by the national government a decade ago. As part of an attempt to evaluate the results of the antipoverty effort, we want to examine the impact that programs of the Office of Economic Opportunity have had on American Indians. Aside from the obvious fact that there was and is much more poverty among American Indians than is to be found among the general population, there are only two generalizations that can be firmly supported. (Similar conclusions have been reached about OEO efforts affecting other groups, as several chapters in this book attest.)[1] First, no massive reduction of Indian poverty has occurred since the poverty program began, although there has been some progress. Second, we know surprisingly little about poverty among Indians and about the relation between governmental activities and poverty, in spite of the substantial national effort of the last decade. This neglect of American Indians is not new; Michael Harrington's remarkable book, *The Other America*, which may have played an important part in launching the national antipoverty efforts of the 1960s, surveyed many groups of the poor but did not discuss American Indians.[2]

Because the changes have been relatively limited and we lack adequate knowledge, the best that can be done now is to set out a framework by which to evaluate OEO's impact on Indian poverty, put forward some hypotheses, and bring together such evidence as we now have.

A major problem with evaluative research is that it necessarily is founded on assumptions about what would have happened in the absence of the effort whose effects are being studied. In other words, such research must presuppose a theory of social change or the absence of such change. We do not yet have such a theory of change, but believe that we can see a number of developments beginning among American Indians at about the same time as the Economic Opportunity Act (EOA) was passed. The Office of Economic Opportunity was created when a number of things were changing for American Indians, and we believe that a meaningful understanding of the effects of one government program is not possible without comprehension of the more general evolution of which it was a part.

157

Who Are Indians?

Substantial confusion exists over the definition of the term American Indian. While we do not have the space here to discuss the question adequately, it is essential to point out that popular and governmental definitions are based primarily on racial (physical-biological) criteria. The people called American Indians by Whites are some (but not all) of the descendants of native peoples present in what is now North and South America when Europeans arrived in the fifteenth and sixteenth centuries. We believe it is far more meaningful to look at how descendants of native peoples identify themselves and to be aware of the existence of cultural rather than racial elements in such self-perceptions.

Although a sense of being American Indian is undoubtedly growing among native Americans and although elements of a pan-Indian culture exist and are developing further,[3] tribal identifications are probably more important. Awareness of being Navajo (or one of the Diné, in their language) or Washo or Seneca may be most important, with awareness of being Indian or American of lesser importance (or perhaps of no importance at all.)[4]

Beyond tribal identifications, we think the attitude toward how to preserve native cultures is very important for understanding native American communities and what is happening in them today. To many White Americans accustomed to the notion that the melting pot has produced a society in which everyone has basically the same values and ways of looking at the world, the extent to which American Indians differ from most Americans can only be surprising. Several books by Sioux author and lawyer Vine Deloria, Jr. describe some basic elements found in many native cultures today as in the past, for example, a high value placed on survival of the tribe and its way of life, the attitude that man is part of nature and not antagonistic to it, an ethic of sharing at odds with competitive individualism, and the belief that land is crucial to tribal survival.[5]

We believe that most American Indians today have as a central objective the preservation and enhancement of tribal existence and culture. To them, saving their way of life is of first importance; poverty or other matters that Whites may think of as having first priority may come second. Understanding this fact is highly important for understanding poverty and government or other antipoverty programs among Indians. Indians differ, however, on how to preserve native cultures. Following anthropologist-historian Jack D. Forbes, we suggest that most American Indians today fall into one of four categories.[6]

White Indians

Some persons of native descent have accepted the general American culture and thus are no longer Indian except for census purposes or except to the degree that non-Indians react to them as Indians. Such people have been called Americans of Indian descent, assimilated (to White culture) Indians, or Apples (Red on the outside and White on the inside); we prefer to call them White Indians. At one time, such persons, racially of native stock, were politically important, because they concerned themselves with Indian politics and urged policies they believed would result in the eventual disappearance of Indians in a cultural sense. For example, early in this century a small group of White Indians (including doctors, scholars, and government officials) organized as the Society of American Indians and asked for an end to the reservation system and the Bureau of Indian Affairs as steps toward the full assimilation of Indians into American life.[7] It is highly significant that most of these individuals moved away from their assimilationist goals in the 1920s, that their organization died, and that, since the 1930s, there has been no national Indian organization advocating the abandonment of Indian culture and identity. Instead, Indians becoming White culturally since that time have largely done so as individuals; Indian organizations since the 1930s have agreed on the goal of resisting assimilation to White culture, although they have disagreed on the means to attain this goal.

Traditionalists

The most deeply committed to the culture of their tribe and the most concerned to preserve this culture in as pure a form as possible are the traditionalists. Undoubtedly, traditionalists were the most numerous segment in most tribes before the 1930s, although they were not the most visible to Whites because they resisted participation in White political structures, such as tribal councils established on a White pattern. Today, traditionalists may refuse to vote in tribal elections that they see as deviating from the traditions of their people.

Tribal Pragmatists

There were always individuals willing to make a partial accommodation to white culture, but a major change in the Indian policy of the national government in the 1930s, signified by the passage of the Indian Reorganization Act (IRA) of 1934, made tribal pragmatists the most important persons in Indian communities in terms of relations with the non-Indian world. Since the IRA became law, most tribes have organized tribal councils, with written constitutions or charters adapted to the needs of the particular tribe but basically reflecting a White conception of political organization. When the Bureau of Indian Affairs approves these constitutions or charters, tribal councils elected according to their provisions become recognized by the government as agents of the tribe. Some tribal pragmatists may be persons on their way to becoming White Indians, but we believe that most wish to preserve their people and its distinctive culture, and think that a partial accommodation to the ways of the dominant society is necessary to accomplish this end.

Urban Traditionalists

A fourth category is hardest to describe accurately. A number of Indians living in urban areas, able to function well in White society, and having lost some knowledge of their native culture, nevertheless identify strongly with the traditionalists. These persons have been called secular nationalists (because of the assumption that their knowledge of Indian religions is less than that of traditionalists); we prefer to call them urban traditionalists. This group has provided much of the leadership of militant Indian movements during the last few years, and we think its position is extremely important. If the assimilationist movement had attracted the majority of the urban Indians during the last few years, perhaps American Indians would be on their way to becoming "vanishing Americans," a fate predicted at many times in the past. Instead, the alliance of the politically involved urban Indians with the traditionalists (combined with the personal political passivity of those individuals who have left the Indian world culturally) means that all of the major Indian political groupings agree in wishing to preserve native peoples and their cultures. Thus, only those approaches to poverty that do not conflict with this goal are likely to be viable within Indian communities over the next few years.

The Legal Status of Indians

American Indians have a legal status that is unlike that of any other Americans.[8] The national government dealt with them almost entirely at one time as nation-states. Although there is confusion about the present legal status of tribes, there can be no doubt that the tribes retain some degree of their former sovereignty; as recently as 1959 a United States court declared that, in some respects, Indian tribes "have a status higher than that of states."[9] The most important aspects of this special legal status that need to be kept in mind in evaluating governmental activities affecting Indians are the following:

The Special Role of the National Government

Because the national government dealt exclusively with Indians while they were clearly separate societies, and because the treaties negotiated during this period still have some significance and as such are constitutionally part of the "supreme law of the land," the states can legislate for Indians only to the extent that Congress allows them to do so. For example, states may not assume civil and criminal jurisdiction over Indian reservations without the consent of Congress. While Congress, through Public Law 280, consented in 1953 to the assumption of such jurisdiction by some states, the movement since then has been back toward exclusive national jurisdiction. In 1968 Congress passed a law requiring that any future assumptions of state jurisdiction could only take place with the consent of the tribes involved, and also allowing states to give up jurisdiction they had assumed under Public Law 280; there is now a move to repeal the 1953 law and return to the earlier situation.[10] This is important because Congress has recognized tribal sovereignty to a much greater extent than the states. For example:

Tribal Councils as Governments

Since 1934, national law has recognized the authority of tribal councils over Indians on reservations and, to some degree, non-Indians on reservations. Most tribes have their own law and order code and tribal judges, although they are also subject to a national Major Crimes Act.

Indian Land and Resources

From the passage of the Indian Allotment Act of 1887 to the adoption of the IRA in 1934, the national government followed a policy of distributing formerly tribally held lands to individual Indians. Because this policy was disastrous and led to the loss of approximately two-thirds of the lands still in Indian hands in 1887, Congress repealed the policy in 1934. Since then Indian lands have theoretically been held in trust by the United States government for the tribes. Among other things, this means that tribal ownership is protected and that states may not tax such land. Similarly, national law protects Indian water rights; under the Winters Doctrine established by the United States Supreme Court in 1908, Indians are entitled to water for present and future needs, and this entitlement is superior to rights established under state water laws.

The Bureau of Indian Affairs and the Indian Health Service

While states provide some services to Indians, for the most part Indians deal with the national government. Moreover, two agencies, the Bureau of Indian Affairs (BIA) and Indian Health Service (IHS), provide most of the governmental services available to Indians. The programs of these two agencies are vital to Indian communities, especially where there are high rates of poverty. At the same time there is ambivalence toward the agencies because excessive paternalism has often accompanied their services.

It is abundantly clear that most Indians are unwilling to accept government policies, whether directed against poverty or not, that involve ending their special legal status. In the 1950s Congress stated a general policy of termination, ending the present legal status of the tribes with the goal of eliminating reservations and the BIA and IHS, so that Indians would become fully assimilated into White American life. While a few tribes were terminated during the 1950s, Indian opposition ot the policy was nearly unanimous. Since the statement by the Secretary of the Interior in 1958 that no tribes would be terminated without their consent, there have been no terminations, and the Menominees, who were terminated over their opposition, have recently succeeded after a long struggle in getting Congress to reverse the statute applying to them and restore their previous status.[11]

The Extent of Indian Poverty and Its Causes

There is no doubt that Indians are the poorest group in the United States, although the extent of Indian poverty is overestimated by the use of dollar income figures alone. Many traditionalists are able to live partially in ways similar to the ways of their ancestors, and are not poor; their lack of income in dollars reflects in part their lack of involvement with White culture. As some traditionalists view it, they are rich in a spiritual sense, while people who have let themselves be dominated by material possessions are poor. Also, their special legal status means that reservation Indians receive services, such as medical care, which have a substantial dollar value. Nevertheless, there is little doubt that Indians suffer more from poverty than any other group identified on racial grounds. A more specific look at statistics on Indian poverty will be presented later. Here, we want to discuss the reasons for Indian poverty. As with many other groups in which there is a high incidence of poverty, "blame the victim" theories have been very popular. Not surprisingly, one of the clearest statements of the theory that Indians are poor because they lack the individual characteristics that would enable them to avoid poverty comes from a statement by the BIA to a Congressional committee in 1969. The Bureau said that:

Most Indian families live in varying degrees of poverty that stem from various sources—cultural differences from the non-Indian society, lack of educational opportunities, and lack of development of reservation-based resources . . . aggravated by geographical isolation from the rest of society and a set of values . . . [unlike those of non-Indians].[12]

A consequence of this conception of the problem has been the view that Indians can only escape poverty by leaving the reservation and adopting White culture. Thus, the BIA for many years put much emphasis on the relocation program, which was designed to assist individual Indians to acquire job skills of relevance only in urban areas; the Bureau then helped them relocate to cities. While there is no doubt that the relocation program helped to increase the number of Indians in urban areas and while average incomes of urban Indians are somewhat higher than average incomes of Indians still living on reservations,[a] it was a failure for several reasons. These include the lost value of services provided by the BIA and IHS but the more important reasons center around the strong attachment Indians have to their culture and the reservation land base. A high proportion of relocated Indians returned to the reservation sooner or later; hence, such income gains as there were proved to be purely temporary for many persons. Also, there is general agreement that urban Indians suffer from a great degree of social disorganization and personal unhappiness; higher incomes have not necessarily meant a better life. Finally, the relocation policy neither produced a large number of White Indians nor alleviated the poverty of reservation Indians.

Poverty and Resources

A more realistic view of Indian poverty is that Indians are poor because they have been deprived of the resources needed to prevent poverty. This view is also well illustrated by a government statement. President Nixon in an important 1970 address on Indian affairs that is still the stated basis of the administration's Indian policy said that:

The first Americans—the Indians—are the most deprived and most isolated minority group in our nation. On virtually every scale of measurement—employment, income, education, health—the condition of the Indian people ranks at the bottom.

This condition is the heritage of centuries of injustice. From the time of their first contact with European settlers, the American Indians have been oppressed and brutalized, deprived of their ancestral lands and denied the opportunity to control their own destiny.[13]

It is obvious that traditionalists cannot live in a wholly traditional way, for the most part, because the reservations have reduced their land base to

[a] According to the 1970 census, urban Indian families had a median income in 1969 of $7,323, compared with $4,691 for rural nonfarm families, and $4,319 for rural farm families.

a fraction of what it once was and because former food sources (such as the buffalo for the Plains tribes) have been destroyed. Those reservation Indians willing to make a substantial adaptation to White ways likewise find it difficult to avoid poverty. For many decades the BIA aimed to convert Indians who had been primarily hunters to farmers, and many Indians today rely on ranching and farming for their main source of income. But the reservations typically lack adequate agricultural land and/or developed water resources. Further, the period during which the allotment policy was pursued by the BIA not only resulted in loss of much of the best land but also led to White leasing of much of the remaining Indian land on some reservations. Because the BIA handling of inheritance rules for Indian land led to a fantastically complicated ownership pattern in some places, land-holdings are often too small to permit economical use by Indian owners. While this situation has often frustrated Indians desiring to use their lands, the BIA has not infrequently found it possible to lease such lands to non-Indians. In this way Indians have lost control of lands still nominally belonging to them. [14] For a number of reasons, then, few reservations have sufficient resources to avoid extensive poverty for the Indians remaining on them.

Two Indian authors have recently made a thorough and carefully reasoned proposal for a restoration of Indian lands to an approximate national total of 100 million acres. [15] The national government has taken some steps in this direction; the 1970 presidential Indian address referred to above asked Congress to recognize that Taos Pueblo in New Mexico had title to Blue Lake, an area sacred to this tribe, and Congress approved this proposal later that year. Since then, a number of tribes, such as the Warm Springs Tribe of Oregon and the Havasupai Tribe, who live in the Grand Canyon, have had significant enlargements of their land base by congressional action. [16]

Recent Changes Affecting Indian Poverty

Within the context of the basic features of Indian communities and Indian-white relationships outlined above, we are now ready to discuss the extent to which federal antipoverty efforts of the last decade or so have affected the poverty of Indians. First, we want to look at available evidence on the extent of Indian poverty before and after the creation of the Economic Opportunity Act (keeping in mind the qualifications regarding the meaning of measures of poverty in dollar terms for native peoples.)

The major measure of poverty used by the national government as it planned the poverty program was the proportion of families with incomes below $3,000 a year. In 1960 over half of all Indian families (54.3 percent) compared with 49.4 percent of Negro families, 18.6 percent of White families, and 21.4 percent of all families, had had incomes this low in the previous year. Another measure, the median income of all persons with income, produced these results: Indians, $1,348 per person; Negroes, $1,519 per person; Whites, $3,027 per person; total population; $2,823 per person. By this measure Indian incomes were less than half (47.8 percent) of all incomes on an average basis.

The 1970 census did not collect data on a fully comparable basis with 1960, but it produced several measures of income. The proportion of all Indian *persons* with incomes less than the poverty level (calculated to take into account inflation, family size, and urban or rural residence) was 38.3 percent in 1969, compared with 35.0 percent for Negro persons, 10.9 percent for White persons, and 13.7 percent for all persons. The proportion of Indian *families* below the poverty level was 33.3 percent, compared with 29.8 percent for Negro families, 8.6 percent for White families, and 10.7 percent for all families. The spread between measures of the poverty of Indian families and of all families decreased from 32.9 percent in 1960 to 24.6 percent in 1970.

Another measure is median income of adult persons with income. For Indians adult means persons 16 years or older; for all others it means persons 14 years or older. Here the figures were: Indians, $2,603 per person; Negroes, $2,917 per person; Whites, $4,318 per person; total population, $4,108 per person. By this measure the average Indian income had increased to 63.4 percent of the average of all incomes. Thus, absolutely and relatively, in dollar terms Indian incomes increased significantly over the decade. However, Indians remain the poorest racial group in the country and there is still a very large gap between the incomes of Indians and those of whites.

We believe that government antipoverty efforts probably played some role in this limited reduction of poverty, but the precise effects of the Office of Economic Opportunity (OEO) are difficult to disentangle from the other changes going on at the same time. We hypothesize a number of changes during the last decade, with OEO playing a part in these changes.

By 1964, when the Economic Opportunity Act was passed, there was a substantial amount of agreement among tribal pragmatists over the nature and direction of Indian policy, and the tribal pragmatists were taking the initiative to press for governmental changes. Because traditionalists were much less visible to government officials than tribal pragmatists (and also almost completely invisible to the rest of the non-Indian world), and because the White Indians had ceased to make any organized presentation of their viewpoint and the urban traditionalists had not yet organized, Indian America seemed more unified than it was. As of 1964 the tribal pragmatists were basically agreed on a policy for Indian communities that was partly designed to overcome or at least ameliorate Indian poverty and that contained these elements; continuation of the existing special Indian legal status, including the preservation of reservations; specific rejection of termination; greater Indian control of the Bureau of Indian Affairs and Indian Health Service, and/or transfer of existing Indian programs to tribal councils and/or other Indian organizations; the augmentation of resources available to Indian communities, through an addition to the reservation land base and a variety of new governmental programs.[17]

Shifting Governmental Policies

Since the mid-1960s Indian policy, of which OEO programs are a part, has moved in the directions desired by the tribal pragmatists of this period. Such movement has partly reduced Indian poverty, but it has also produced a new mood of militance and the development of new policy positions among Indians visible to government and the general public. The high point for the tribal pragmatists, in a symbolic sense, came with the 1970 Indian address of President Nixon, in which he accepted their basic program. Calling his policy "self-determination without termination," the president called for an explicit rejection by Congress of termination, firm support for the special Indian legal status, Indian control and/or operation of BIA programs, the symbolic recognition that Blue Lake belonged to Taos Pueblo, and increased spending for existing Indian programs, including antipoverty programs. Indians themselves and the United States government moved some distance toward accomplishing these goals during the decade, although not as far or as fast as the tribal pragmatists wanted to move. Specific changes over the last decade have included:

1. Indian organizations embracing more than one tribe have increased substantially during the last decade, and the relative importance of non-Indians and/or organizations containing both Indians and non-Indians has declined; it is our hypothesis that most of the new organizations have represented mostly tribal pragmatists. The older White-Indian national groups (such as the Indian Rights Association of Philadelphia or the Association on American Indian Affairs of New York) are still in existence but are much less important. In addition to inter-tribal councils in several states and the Great Lakes region (where it was organized specifically to take advantage of OEO programs)[18] there are now a number of national all-Indian organizations; while the National Congress of American Indians goes back to 1943, most are quite recent. We know of at least 12 national pan-Indian groups, including the National Tribal Chairmen's Association, the National Indian Press Association, the North American Indian Women's Organization, the National Indian Education Association, and the American Indian Chamber of Commerce.

2. There has been an expansion of the Indian press, which now comprises a number of vigorous publications of various kinds.[19] At least two of the new publications, *Wassaja* (published by the Indian Historical Society of San Francisco) and *Akwesasne Notes*, the latter representing a traditionalist viewpoint, are nationwide and have attracted attention from a significant number of non-Indians. The Indian Historical Society also publishes the *Indian Historian*, a quarterly, *The Weewish Tree*, a children's magazine, and various books; in addition, it has sponsored two national Convocations of Indian Scholars and published the proceedings of these meetings. Other Indian publications include newspapers published by tribes or intertribal councils.

3. Resources available to Indians have also increased over the last decade in two other areas: the provision of legal services and the development of Indian-controlled formal education. For many decades Indian tribes could secure attorneys only in claims cases. Further, even if tribes could afford to hire attorneys for other purposes, they had to secure the consent of the Secretary of the Interior to hire a particular person. Few individual Indians could afford attorneys at all. In the last decade legal services attorneys have set up offices on many reservations as part of the poverty program, and several national Indian legal service organizations—the Institute for the Development of Indian Law, the Native American Rights Fund, and the Native American Legal Defense and Education Fund—have come into existence. The first of these publishes a monthly *Legislative Review* and an *Education Journal*, which provide information about what Congress and federal agencies are doing in Indian affairs and about educational developments. At least two law schools—the University of New Mexico, where OEO funding was critical, and the University of California at Los Angeles—have special programs for training Indians to be lawyers, and the University of New Mexico publishes an *Indian Law Newsletter*. The number of Indian lawyers has increased significantly, and no doubt will go on increasing.

In the field of education there has been a trend toward Indian control of education institutions at every level. A United States Senate committee (first chaired by Robert Kennedy and then by Edward Kennedy) studied Indian education in the late 1960s.[20] The president's 1970 Indian address endorsed Indian control of elementary and secondary schools, and Congress passed the Indian Education Act of 1972, providing limited funds for Indian-run educational programs. Morris Thompson, Commissioner of Indian Affairs, has stated recently that 14 former BIA schools "are now under contract to Indian people" and that the goal of the BIA is to greatly increase the options of Indian tribes to control their schools if that is their desire.[21] Indian-run schools are still available for only a minority of Indian children, but change is accelerating. There are now several Indian-controlled community colleges, D-Q University (an institution with a joint

Chicano-Indian board), and a number of Native American studies programs at non-Indian colleges and universities, including programs for training Indians in the health professions centered at the University of California, Berkeley, and the University of Oklahoma.

4. Government spending for Indian programs has increased substantially during the last ten or fifteen years. Expenditures on Indian programs
roughly doubled between 1960 and 1970 and have doubled again since 1970.
However, total expenditures for Indians are still under $1 billion a year.[22]
New money for Indian programs of the Office of Economic Opportunity
accounted for part of this increase, and other federal agencies have also
established Indian programs. Some of the new programs have been directed toward development of the resources of reservations. The Area
Redevelopment Administration (later Economic Development Administration) helped tribes to develop factories or increase jobs on the reservations in other ways, and the BIA shifted its efforts to some degree from
relocating Indians to cities toward economic development of the reservations. (As late as 1968 an economic study of Indian Americans concluded
that the BIA had begun efforts toward reservation economic development
so recently that it had very little data on factories on reservations.)[23] In a
policy statement in 1971 the commissioner of Indian affairs announced the
end of urban-directed economic policies and the beginning of a
reservation-directed economic development effort.

5. OEO programs, in particular, significantly strengthened tribal councils. This resulted partly from two decisions concerning Indian community
action made soon after the passage of the Economic Opportunity Act.
These were to emulate the BIA and IHS by dealing only with Indians on
reservations[b] and to designate tribal councils (or, in some cases, inter-tribal
councils) on reservations as community action agencies. The initial response of many tribal councils was encouraging. Many tribal pragmatists
were seeking increased government aid run by Indian organizations, and a
number of tribal councils had specific plans for dealing with poverty when
OEO was created or came up with them quickly. A study of Indian community action on six reservations during the first year of the EOA bears out
this point. Particularly at White Earth Reservation in Minnesota and Pine
Ridge Reservation in South Dakota, Indian development plans were
presented to OEO by tribal councils.[24]

The designation of tribal councils as community action agencies
strengthened these groups (and the tribal pragmatists who were primarily
represented on them) in several ways. First, there were new jobs; by the
end of the 1968 fiscal year, approximately 3,760 new positions were under

---

[b] Although there appears to be no legal basis for making this distinction the BIA has provided
services solely for reservation residents, and the IHS has followed a similar policy, although it
has been more willing to make exceptions than the BIA. See Levitan and Hetrick, *Big Brother's
Indian Programs*, p. 7; Sorkin, *American Indians and Federal Aid*.

the control of tribal or intertribal councils functioning as community action agencies.[25] For the first time in many cases, leaders of the reservation could be paid for working on tribal affairs, and they could control other jobs on the reservation.[c]

Further, OEO encouraged the tribal councils to seek funds from other government agencies and/or foundations or other private sources. OEO funded a unit at the University of Utah to give advice and provide consulting services to tribal councils to increase their effectiveness in seeking other funds. Not every tribal council became a community action agency; in fact, in 1968 only 63 tribal or inter-tribal groups were receiving CAA grants. However, OEO asserted that 80 percent of reservation Indians had some kind of involvement with OEO programs.[26]

The chief effect of OEO programs was probably to provide some immediate income to participants rather than to make basic changes that could affect the poverty of Indian communities. Studies of the poverty program on two reservations—in Nevada and Arizona—indicate that the pattern of distribution of these immediate benefits apparently had two results, both stemming from the fact that the jobs, houses, or other benefits went primarily to members of the tribal councils or their families or supporters.[27] First, the benefits did not necessarily go to the most needy persons. Second, this pattern of distribution tended to increase tensions between factions in the community. If these effects occurred elsewhere, they may be highly significant for societies that traditionally had strong values favoring equality and decision making by consensus.

OEO provided a substantial increase in funds under the clear control of Indians, in contrast with the greater expenditures at the same time by the BIA and IHS, which spent the additional moneys chiefly in standard ways. However, the greater flexibility provided by OEO was limited for Indian programs as it was for others; relatively early in the first decade of its existence, OEO spending stopped growing significantly. Congress and the Johnson administration also started reducing the proportion of OEO moneys available for programs locally initiated and innovative.[28] In brief, as with other antipoverty programs of the national government, there was never enough money to meet the stated goals of Indian community action, and money was especially tight for programs developed by Indians in partial response to the impetus provided by OEO.

Another effect of the decision to use tribal councils as community action agencies was to neglect urban Indians. The 1970 presidential address

[c] There is also an accelerating trend toward increasing the proportion of Indians in the BIA and IHS, especially in important administrative positions. This might be called a "reddening" of national Indian agencies, in some ways comparable to the "blackening" of urban bureaucracies described in chapter 13 of this book by Paul B. Fischer. "Indian preference" provisions applying to BIA employment, significantly expanded in 1972 to include promotion, were upheld by a unanimous United States Supreme Court in 1974. See *Morton v. Mancari*, 417 U.S. 535.

on Indian affairs pledged the government to fund a number of urban centers for Indians, and centers in such cities as Chicago and San Francisco were aided subsequently. As with OEO on reservations, the literature about antipoverty efforts among urban Indians is slight. There is an account of an abortive attempt to organize a neighborhood council among members of the Pottawatomi tribe living in Topeka, Kansas and in Los Angeles an Indian was added to the governing board of the Economic and Youth Opportunities Board of Greater Los Angeles, the chief umbrella community action agency. In neither case, apparently, did a significant program for Indians develop.[29]

Growing Militance

Antipoverty and other programs for Indians that were expanding at the same time were major elements in producing growing militance among Indians, although of course there were many other elements. A similar process has been identified as a cause of urban violence by blacks in the late 1960s. The elements in the situation that seem to be essentially the same as those producing black militance are these: the over-blown rhetoric of the poverty program itself, which promised not just the amelioration of poverty but its abolition; the lack of relation of many of the programs to the real causes of poverty; and the effect of providing support for tribal councils and encouraging them to seek funding for their own antipoverty plans when there was insufficient funding for such programs. In short, we hypothesize that the programs of the mid-1960s increased the gap between reality and expectation at the same time that some movement took place, and therefore produced anger rather than greater satisfaction. However, we also believe that there were elements in the Indian situation that differed from the situation of other groups. The example of black militance, which antedated the poverty program, seems obvious, although little formal contact between black and Indian groups has taken place and Indian groups have been reluctant to use the same rhetoric as black leaders. More important, we hypothesize that the new Indian militance developed partly out of conflicts within Indian communities that were heightened by the fact that OEO programs, in particular, strengthened tribal pragmatists, at the expense of traditionalists.

The new Indian militance took several forms. First, several new national or regional groups with programs going beyond those of the tribal pragmatist sprang up. One of the first of these was the National Indian Youth Council, which began before passage of the Economic Opportunity Act; the views of its leaders are given prominent attention in *The New Indians,* one of the first books to note and describe the new militance.[30] A number of similar groups came into existence during the last decade; among those known to us are United Native Americans of the San Francisco Bay Area, Indians of All Tribes, and the American Indian Movement (AIM). These groups were drawn largely from the ranks of urban Indians, and represented chiefly the views of urban traditionalists. A reasonable guess is that the number of urban traditionalists increased at the expense of both tribal pragmatists and (especially) White Indians and that the urban traditionalists also became more militant.

The new militance was expressed in several ways. There was a wave of sit-ins or other occupations, usually peaceful (and often with elements of humor not usually associated with militance among other groups). A summary of many of these sit-ins can be found in Vine Deloria's *God Is Red*.[31] The occupation of Alcatraz Island in 1969-70, of the BIA building in Washington, D.C. in the fall of 1972, and of the village of Wounded Knee on the Pine Ridge Reservation in the winter and spring of 1973 generated national attention. In early 1975 the Fairchild Electronics plant on the Navajo reservation was occupied briefly.

The new militance was directed, for the most part, against non-Indian agencies or officials, but in some cases reflected mainly antagonisms within Indian communities. Notable in this respect was the occupation of Wounded Knee, which began as a conflict on the Pine Ridge Reservation between the elected leadership of the tribal council and the traditional Oglala Sioux leaders, later involved the American Indian Movement, and subsequently developed into a bitter struggle for control of the tribal council.[32] There is currently conflict between the National Tribal Chairmen's Association and the alliance of reservation-based traditionalists with urban traditionalists. The demands of the militants became more extreme and gradually shifted to a position urging something like a return to an earlier stage of Indian-white relationships. Partly, there was disillusion with the slow implementation of "self-determination," combined with the realization that the Nixon administration intended to turn over operation of programs to a much greater extent than it intended to delegate policy initiation and policy formation. The militants began to ask for a restoration of tribal sovereignty in something like the sense in which Indian tribes had once known such self-government. For example, the document drawn up by the Trail of Broken Treaties, the group that planned what led to the occupation of the BIA building in 1972, asked for a return to relations with the national government on the basis of the treaty process and for the abolition of the BIA.[33] Also, at the height of the occupation of Wounded Knee the Oglala Sioux Nation was proclaimed and the assistance of the United Nations was sought. A 1974 book by Vine Deloria, Jr. argues that restoration of the status of nation-states is not impossible or impractical; there are several states in the world smaller in population and/or area than a number of Indian reservations, and there are many possible forms that such status could take.[34]

The Future of Indian Poverty

Predictions about the future of Indian poverty are difficult. Continuation of the present direction of change—toward slow augmentation of Indian resources and gradually increasing control over Indian affairs by Indians—or a significant acceleration of present trends appear about equally likely.

The effect on non-Indians of a rise in Indian incomes will probably be a significant factor in influencing the direction of change. Robert Levine and others have argued that the approximately $10 billion a year annual poverty gap for the nation as a whole is small in comparison with the total income of the country.[35] Certainly the poverty gap for Indians is very much smaller, and average tax rates would be altered by scarcely visible amounts if enough income were diverted to Indian communities to raise all members of those communities above the poverty level. It has been estimated that the adoption of the Nixon administration's Family Assistance Plan would have increased incomes among the Indian population by 72 percent, undoubtedly the largest percentage increase for any group.[36]

On the other hand, non-Indians living close to Indian reservations often find that they can still gain by securing Indian resources, just as their ancestors did. One example of this is the strip mining of Hopi-Navajo coal to provide fuel for power plants in the Four Corners area of the Southwest. In this case an Indian-owned resource is not being used directly for economic development of the reservation but is being depleted to aid non-Indian economic development.[37] Conflict between Indian and non-Indian users of water resources is acute in several places in the West. Moreover, many Indian groups and water lawyer William Veeder believe that a major crisis for Indian reservations that have had legal rights to yet-unutilized water resources is at hand. Veeder charges that taking of this water by government would amount to genocide, for the "very existence of the American Indians as a culture is being destroyed because without water, the Indian culture passes out of existence."[38]

Congress has recently enacted a law providing for the most comprehensive study of the legal status of Indians since a study by the Brookings Institution in the 1920s (which had an effect in helping to change federal Indian policy in the 1930s). A recently-appointed American Indian Policy Review Commission on which there is significant Indian representation has been charged, among other things, with making "a study and analysis of the Constitution, treaties, statutes, judicial interpretations, and Executive orders to determine the attributes of the unique relationship between the Federal Government and Indian tribes and the land and other resources they possess."[39] The new commission may well find ways of securing additional resources for Indian communities through more consistent enforcement of existing Indian rights or the strengthening of these rights. Continued antipoverty efforts by the federal government are assured; the new Headstart, Economic Opportunity and Community Partnership Act of 1974 specifically authorizes Native American programs.[40]

Notes

1. See the chapters by Richard L. Fogel and Dale Rogers Marshall in Dorothy Buckton James, ed. *Analyzing Poverty Policy* (Lexington, Mass.: Lexington Books, D.C. Heath and Co., 1975).

2. Michael Harrington, *The Other America* (Baltimore: Penguin Books, 1963).

3. See Robert K. Thomas, "Pan-Indianism," in Stuart Levine and Nancy Oestreich Lurie, eds., *The American Indian Today* (Baltimore: Penguin Books, 1965), pp. 128-140.

4. For example, see the statement by Sidney Mills, "I am a Yakima and Cherokee Indian, and a Man," in Alvin M. Josephy, Jr., *Red Power: The American Indians' Fight for Freedom* (New York: McGraw-Hill Book Co., 1971), pp. 81-85.

5. Vine Deloria, Jr., *Custer Died for your Sins* (New York: Macmillan, 1969); *We Talk, You Listen* (New York: Macmillan, 1970); *God is Red* (New York: Grosset and Dunlap, 1973); *Behind the Trail of Broken Treaties* (New York: Dell Publishing Co., 1974).

6. Jack D. Forbes, "The Anishinabe Liberation Movement," *Harvard Civil Rights–Civil Liberties Law Review*, vol. 8, no. 1 (January 1973), pp. 217-222. A similar classification of groups in a contemporary Chinese-American community is offered by Melford S. Weiss, *Valley City: A Chinese Community in America* (Cambridge: Schenkman Publishing Co., 1974).

7. Hazel Hertzberg, *The Search for an American Indian Identity* (Syracuse, N.Y.: Syracuse University Press, 1971).

8. Sources for understanding the legal status of American Indians include: Felix S. Cohen, *Handbook of Federal Indian Law* (Albuquerque: University of New Mexico Press, 1971); Monroe E. Price, *Law and the American Indian* (Indianapolis: Bobbs-Merrill Co., 1973); and Vine Deloria, Jr., *Of Utmost Good Faith* (San Francisco: Straight Arrow Books, 1971).

9. *Native American Church* v. *Navajo Tribal Council*, 272 F. 2d 131 (1959), cited in Jay Vincent White, *Taxing Those They Found Here* (Albuquerque: Institute for the Development of Indian Law, University of New Mexico, 1972), p. 41.

10. See U.S. Senate Committee on Interior and Insular Affairs, "Background Report on Public Law 280," Committee Print, 94th Congress, 1st Session (Washington, D.C.: U.S. Government Printing Office, 1975).

11. P-L 93-197. See "Menominees Restored as Recognized Tribe," Institute for the Development of Indian Law, *Legislative Review*, vol. 2, no. 7, pp. 4-5, 8.

12. "Economic Development of Indian Communities," in Joint Economic Committee, *Toward Economic Development for Native American Communities*, vol. 2, Committee Print, 91st Congress, 1st Session (Washington, D.C.: U.S. Government Printing Office, 1969), pp. 331-355.

13. Message to Congress on Indian Affairs, July 8, 1970. Among other places, this address can be found in Josephy, *Red Power*, pp. 213-230.

14. On the heirship problem, see Stephen A. Langone, "The Heirship Land Problem and its Effect on the Indian, the Tribe, and Effective Utilization," in Joint Economic Committee, *Toward Economic Development for Native American Communities*, pp. 519-548.

15. Kirke Kickingbird and Karen Ducheneaux, *One Hundred Million Acres* (New York: Macmillan, 1973).

16. Ibid., p. 17; and *Legislative Review*, vol. 3, no. 5, p. 12.

17. For a number of views by Indian organizations, such as the "Declaration of Indian Purpose" adopted by the American Indian Chicago Conference of 1961, the statement of the American Indian Task Force of November 1969, and the statement of the Indian members of the National Council on Indian Opportunity of January, 1970, see Josephy, *Red Power*.

18. Loretta Ellis, "Great Lakes Committee Organized for Action," Institute for the Development of Indian Law, *Education Journal*, vol. 2, no. 8 (1974), pp. 10-12.

19. There appears to be no national collection of the current Indian press, but most such publications are listed in *Index to Bibliographies and Resource Materials*, published by the National Indian Education Association, 3036 University Ave., S.E., Suite 3, Minneapolis, Minnesota 55414, in the spring of 1975.

20. The final report of this study is: *Indian Education: A National Tragedy–A National Challenge*, U.S. Senate Committee on Labor and Public Welfare, Report No. 91-501, 91st Congress, 1st Session (Washington, D.C.: U.S. Government Printing Office, 1969).

21. *Education Journal*, vol. 2, no. 8, pp. 7-9.

22. For expenditures during the 1960s, see Sar A. Levitan and Barbara Hetrick, *Big Brother's Indian Programs* (New York: McGraw-Hill, 1971), p. 22. For data to 1975, see *Legislative Review*, vol. 2, no. 9, pp. 1-3.

23. Alan L. Sorkin, *American Indians and Federal Aid* (Washington, D.C.: The Brookings Institution, 1971), p. 19.

24. Albert Jenny et al., *A Comprehensive Evaluation of OEO Community Action Programs on Six Selected American Indian Reservations* (McLean, Virginia: Human Sciences Research, 1966), pp. 289-359, 163-220.

25. Sar A. Levitan, *The Great Society's Poor Law* (Baltimore: The Johns Hopkins Press, 1969), p. 268.

26. Levitan, *The Great Society's Poor Law*, p. 266.

27. Ruth M. Houghton, "Reservation Politics and OEO Community Development, 1965-1971," in Ruth M. Houghton, ed., *Native American Politics: Power Relationships in the Western Great Basin Today* (Reno: Bureau of Governmental Research, 1973), pp. 33-39, and Robert L. Bee, "Tribal Leadership in the War on Poverty: A Case Study," *Social Science Quarterly*, vol. 50, no. 3 (December 1969), pp. 676-686; "Self-Help at Fort Yuma: A Critique," *Human Organization*, vol. 29, no. 3 (Fall 1970), pp. 155-161.

28. Robert Levine, *The Poor Ye Need Not Have With You* (Cambridge: M.I.T. Press, 1970), pp. 63-77.

29. Louis A. Zurcher, Jr., *Poverty Warriors* (Austin: University of Texas Press, 1970), pp. 268-331; Dale Rogers Marshall, *The Politics of Participation in Poverty* (Berkeley: University of California Press, 1971), p. 17.

30. Stan Steiner, *The New Indians* (New York: Harper and Row, 1968).

31. Deloria, *God Is Red*, pp. 12-22.

32. For the views of some Indian participants in these events see: Peter Blue Cloud, ed., *Alcatraz Is Not An Island* (Berkeley: Wingbow Press, 1972); *Trail of Broken Treaties: B.I.A. I'm Not Your Indian Anymore* (Rooseveltown, New York: Akwesasne Notes, 1973); *Voices from Wounded Knee* (Rooseveltown, N.Y.: Akwesasne Notes, 1973).

33. See Deloria, *God Is Red*, pp. 325-364.

34. Deloria, *Behind the Trail of Broken Treaties*.

35. Levine, *The Poor Ye Need Not Have With You*, pp. 8-9.

36. Levitan and Hetrick, *Big Brother's Indian Programs*, p. 107.

37. See Suzanne Gordon, *Black Mesa: The Angel of Death* (New York: John Day Co., 1973).

38. *The Native American Today: The Second Convocation of American Indian Scholars* (San Francisco: Indian Historian Press, 1974), p. 19.

See also William H. Veeder, "Federal Encroachment on Indian Water Rights and the Impairment of Reservation Development," in Joint Economic Committee, *Toward Economic Development for Native American Communities*, pp. 460-518.

39. P-L 93-580. See *Legislative Review*, vol. 3, no. 5, pp. 2-4.

40. P-L 93-644, Title VIII. See *Legislative Review*, vol. 3, no. 8, pp. 6-10.

13 Bureaucratic Segmentation and the Politics of Poverty: Observations from a Case Study

Paul B. Fischer

Introduction

Much of the literature analyzing bureaucratic behavior focuses on the formulation and character of the service delivery. The War on Poverty, for example, was publicized as a program to alter drastically the quality of welfare services to the poor partly through a maximization of client input. Political activity or community action was perceived as an innovative vehicle to upgrade those services.

The reality has been quite different. The antipoverty program has been more efficient in dealing with more latent bureaucratic functions, particularly job creation, than in the manifest function of dispensing services. Rather than fundamentally improving service output, the War on Poverty provided a tremendous expansion of opportunity for movement into bureaucratic structures. This phenomenon should not surprise anyone familiar with the development of municipal bureaucracies in the United States.

Part of the history of urban politics in America has involved the movement of ethnic groups into municipal bureaucracies followed by progressive segmentation of these bureaucracies into ethnic enclaves. The Irish police and fire departments have been part of many older municipalities since the nineteenth century. More recently Italians have dominated public works and general construction. Education and social welfare departments are filled with Jews. Although the dominant group and degree of ethnic segmentation varies from city to city, the process is general, particularly in the older urban areas east of the Mississippi.

Typically the process occurred when there was a favorable mix of circumstances. Resistance to ethnic incursion was minimal, potential expansion of services was great, and an available pool of eligible personnel were interested in that particular segment of the municipal government. The Irish arrived in eastern cities at a time of expansion of police forces. Ironically this growth was partly in response to an increase in crime caused by Irish immigrants. With the support of political machines the Irish were able to overcome fairly weak resistance and to dominate police and fire departments in the urban Northeast. Employment in city government was perceived as a valuable means for moving into the middle class and was eagerly sought by the newly arrived immigrant. An added asset was the absence of civil service regulations. Thus, bureaucratic employment was a flexible process, sensitive to political change and permitting upward movement at a rapid pace.

A century later a similar process took place involving the movement of Jews into the education and social welfare fields in large eastern cities. The New Deal provided the impetus. Jews were available, qualified, and motivated. As with the Irish in the nineteenth century, a symbiotic relationship between client and bureaucrat existed particularly in the public schools, which had in the prewar and early postwar period large numbers of Jewish students. In contrast to the Irish experience, the Jews had to deal with a Civil Service system that potentially could slow down ethnic segmentation. But their availability and qualifications in a time of great service expansion enabled them to overcome resistance from an entrenched Irish bureaucracy. By the early 1960s the public schools were flooded with Jewish teachers and administrators.

Thus, in the postwar period the bureaucracies of many older cities were divided between white ethnic groups competing with each other for larger budget allocations and more jobs from the city. These groups sometimes gained entry by overcoming entrenched resistance, but more frequently were available when new bureaucratic structures were created.

The major contention of this chapter is that the "blackening" of urban bureaucracies has followed the same general pattern as that of white ethnics. The vehicle used in this case is the antipoverty program of the sixties. Like the New Deal, the War on Poverty stimulated whole new areas of bureaucratic expansion acting as a job-creating mechanism and providing blacks with a significant segment of municipal government. Further, the chapter argues that the process was facilitated first by political circumstances of the sixties, which substituted racial for class criteria in the organization of the program, and second, by conditions within the black community that gave blacks a "head start" toward control in comparison with other potential program constituents.

A second major contention of the chapter is that the War on Poverty, like the expansion of other governmental areas, primarily served the interests of the middle class, in this case, a black middle class. The "blackening" of urban bureaucracies meant access for the upwardly mobile to positions with economic security and status. It also facilitated the institutionalization of influence formalizing political interaction between middle class blacks and whites and providing a platform for black political activity.

In contrast the chapter argues that racial segmentation of the antipoverty bureaucracy has little effect upon the relationship between middle class leadership and the black poor, a relationship fraught with mistrust, alienation, and a general questioning of leadership legitimacy. This problem has not been solved by putting blacks in upper level administrative positions, but rather has clarified for many blacks the danger inherent in cooptation and the basic limitations of the program's intent.

To examine these contentions a case study of Springfield, Massachusetts was undertaken. Its relatively small size (165,000) but significant and growing black population (18,000) provided easy access to relevant information within a setting displaying a growing amount of interracial political activity. The Springfield antipoverty program and the controversies surrounding it are also typical of many other municipalities.

In sum, the War on Poverty and the 'blackening' or urban bureaucracies are inextricably tied together and the purpose of this chapter is to explore those ties.

The War on Poverty and Bureaucratic Segmentation

In the years preceding the introduction of the antipoverty program in Springfield, black political leadership was centered primarily in protest organizations like the NAACP and CORE. They pursued integration ends through the courts and the streets, operating outside the formal structure of government. Few blacks penetrated into the municipal government itself, particularly the policy-making apparatus of the city bureaucracy. What positions did exist reflected the integration orientation of race relations at that time.

The intergroup relations coordinator, for example, as the executive officer of the Springfield Human Relations Commission, monitored compliance with equal opportunity legislation. Two blacks had middle level positions in the school department. Both were "old-timers," conservative and middle class. One was the first black teacher in Springfield and had worked her way up through the ranks. Neither was involved in deciding questions related to the school integration controversies of the sixties. Blacks were also members of advisory boards—voluntary, ad hoc, and powerless.

Blacks in government, then, were a small group having no mass support, no control over political or economic resources, and little influence upon city politics. Their very narrow slice of the city administration was the civil rights section, basically a one man operation.

The War on Poverty in Springfield, as in all urban areas, meant, if nothing else, a proliferation of government programs: Head Start, Concentrated Employment (CEP), Neighborhood Legal Services (NLS), Northern Educational Services (NES) and Model Cities to name a few. These were followed by an ever-increasing number of satellite operations, including the semi-independent nonprofit development corporations, many of whom were subcontractors, dependent on antipoverty funds for their minority enterprises, job training, and housing redevelopment programs.

To coordinate and supervise these efforts and to provide a major community input, the Springfield Action Commission (SAC) was created. Besides distributing funds and overseeing operations, SAC was an intermediary or "bridge" agency between the city government and client groups. This role was reflected in the makeup of the Board of Directors, which included government officials, business leaders, clients, and community action representatives.

The major beneficiaries of these programs particularly from the job creation perspective were blacks. All the program administrators were black as were most of their assistants. Although this chapter primarily is concerned with administrators it must be added that a large part of the support staff was black as well. Many of them were paraprofessionals and job trainees. This situation is not surprising, of course, but it must be remembered that a significant number of the poor in Springfield were white and Latin even in the model cities target areas. These groups were represented on policy boards and in lower level nonprofessional capacities but their administrative representation was nil. It is most interesting to consider the reasons for this dominance of black administrators. Some interviewing was done in this area but the reasons offered below are essentially speculative.

Definition of the Problem

It became politically expedient in the middle sixties to respond to growing unrest in impoverished black ghettos across the nation. Most Americans perceived the situation in terms of a "Black Revolt" rather than a violent uprising by an American underclass. Consequently the War on Poverty, a program theoretically defined and structured to deal with a class problem—that is, the poor, most of whom are white—became in reality a race problem directed primarily at blacks in northern urban centers where tensions and violence were manifest. It is true that much effort has been expended on the white poor, for example in Appalachia, but in the minds of most Americans poverty tended to mean black poverty.

This perception merged with and buttressed some of the stated goals and theories of the program. One was the "return-of-the-ethnic-political-machine" theory, which envisioned the Community Action Programs (CAPs) as the stimuli and nuclei for black urban political organizations providing services similar to those of traditional white ethnic organizations but within a bureaucratic framework. A related theory had the antipoverty program substituting for the ethnically based social welfare structures that had traditionally provided for specifically ethnic needs like the Jewish and Catholic philanthropic federations. Both of these goals illustrate the ethnic orientation built into the program by concerned governments.[1]

Although the black poor in Springfield were not the largest impoverished group, they were the most concentrated, living in a low-income housing project on an island in the Connecticut River and as part of a larger black ghetto in the core of the city. White poor on the other hand were more dispersed. Black concentration increased their visibility as poor to the larger community reaffirming racist stereotypes that tended to lump poverty and blackness together. But geographic concentration also enabled blacks to mobilize political support and to influence hiring practices for programs, many of which were focused on very specific geographic targets like model cities. The boundaries of these programs frequently paralleled the boundaries of black areas.

The definition of the program in racial terms by both federal and local governments, along with the concentration and visibility of the black poor in Springfield, provided two necessary conditions for the racial segmentation of the poverty bureaucracy.

Plight of the Civil Rights Movement

Ben Seligman, in *Aspects of Poverty* (published in the late 1960s) argues that the War on Poverty was in great part a response to the declining significance of the Civil Rights movement and the society's inability to quickly transform the rhetoric and expectations regarding integration into a reality.[2] The energy of the movement and its members had to be redirected. The definition of the program in racial terms permitted civil rights activists to redefine themselves as "poverty warriors." These ex-civil rights workers provided a large pool of potential administrators.

In Springfield the influence of civil rights organizations peaked during the school desegregation demonstrations in 1965. But the organizational structure and leadership cadre remained, a leadership that had accumulated much political experience interacting and negotiating with the white community, a leadership willing and available for employment in the War on Poverty.

At one time or another the administrators of the Model Cities program, Comprehensive Employment Program, and Northern Educational Services, as well as the president of the SAC Board were past NAACP presidents. During one recent period two ex-NAACP officials were competing for the position of executive director of SAC. Policy board membership, particularly the community representation segments, were filled with members of civil rights organizations. Negotiations between SAC and the local NAACP chapter took place early to decide on what proportion of the SAC Board should be composed of NAACP members. All of these activities illustrate that blacks as compared with whites and Latins had the advantage of an existing political structure and experienced leadership that could be effectively reoriented to move into and dominate the antipoverty program.

Contrasting Self-perceptions and Group Cohesiveness

The geographic concentration and its effects were reinforced by a growing sense of black identity in the community that provided some cohesion and liberated many of the black poor from the psychic burden of the poverty-failure syndrome providing a rationale for their situation that could stimulate political activity. "We are poor because we are Black." The reality of that concept was illustrated by the large pool of upwardly mobile, ambitious middle-class types that existed in the black community, frustrated from moving up through the usual channels, such as in business and government, because of racism. In other words, there existed a large number of "middle-class" poor.

In contrast the white poor were the whites left behind, the failures in a system structured for their success. Lacking a rationale to justify their failure, they remained a community apathetic and leaderless with little sense of group in a society whose cultural values ignored class cleavages.

The Latin poor, on the other hand, were more recent immigrants to Springfield and had not yet settled in. They were disoriented, dispersed, and too involved with survival to challenge black dominance of the antipoverty apparatus, particularly in the early years when their numbers were quite small.

"The mark of oppression" had been reversed. The motivated and the future oriented were to be found among the black rather than the white poor, creating a source of ambitious career bureaucrats.

All of the circumstances present for ethnic segmentation existed for black dominance of the antipoverty program. In the early years resistance from an entrenched bureaucracy was absent and expansion was greatest since the program was new and constructed from almost nothing. A pool of talent existed generated from a declining Civil Rights movement and a large number of middle class poor. But there were also great differences between the process of ethnic segmentation and black movement into the poverty bureaucracy. The absence of a civil service increased fluidity of movement, allowing blacks without very specific credentials access to administrative positions. But more important, the deliberate policies of the controlling government agencies, abetted by "racist stereotyping" by the white majority accelerated the racial segmentation of the poverty program by defining it as a "black program" reinforcing the already existing conditions contributing to that development.

The Black Middle Class, the Bureaucracy, and the Poor

After almost a decade since the initiation of the antipoverty effort in Springfield, a black bureaucracy is visible representing a segment of municipal government incomparably larger than the civil rights "sliver" of the early sixties. Blacks represent the upper levels of most of the remaining programs, which contrary to Nixon-Ford rhetoric is essentially the same Johnson package in a more benign posture, but still there. For many, the large number of black faces in administrative positions has been the prime indication of the success of the programs. The War on Poverty has moved blacks out of poverty and the evidence exists in the administration of the programs themselves. In reality "maximum feasible participation" of the poor has not been the operating rule. For many of the new antipoverty bureaucrats their movement to the position has been more "sideways" than "upward." The Model Cities director was an ex-school teacher, the manager of Northern Educational Services had a college degree and the executive director of SAC had been a planner. A few, like the director of the Comprehensive Employment program, have been marginally white collar, working as a foreman, in a Springfield factory. This is not to deny the important economic and status incentives available from these positions. For all, the economic pay-off was impressive—from $8,000 to $9,000 per year to $15,000 to $18,000 per year employment.

Of course, it is not unusual for recruitment of administrators to be focused upon the middle class since they have the education and experience needed. And it is also true that movement upward for the marginally middle class opened up positions below for the poor—a trickle-down effect of bureaucratic job creation. But in the end, after almost ten years, the only significant indication of success of the antipoverty program is the change in the numbers of middle class blacks in administrative positions. The War on Poverty never meant the poor would administer the programs but, at least publicly, neither did it mean to serve the interests of the middle class.

Aside from the economic incentives for the black middle class, political incentives existed as well. The control of economic resources, namely, the programs themselves and the services they provided, could be used to build political influence. For many of the middle class administrators, the antipoverty program was a potential vehicle for deeper penetration into the black lower class, an opportunity to legitimize themselves as representatives for the whole community after years of failure at the effort.

The Black Middle Class Before the Program

Up until 1950 and for a period of 30 years one man dominated politics in the Springfield black community, a pastor of the most prestigious black church and founder of the Dunbar League later to become the Urban League of Springfield. For a community of only 3,000 residents, many of whom traced their local lineage back 100 years, this black leader provided a "bridge" to the white community. Reflecting the middle class orientation of that population he did not push the white community very far. But toward the end of his reign the character of the black population changed. The bridge leader who was neither elected nor appointed by the community, but rather chosen by the white leadership to speak for blacks, came under heavy attack as an "Uncle Tom." For many of the newer residents, he represented the "overseer" in a northern version of plantation politics.

The period of "one man rule" was followed in the fifties and early sixties by an expanded leadership group centered in civil rights organizations committed to pressure politics rather than accommodation and theoretically, at least, to broadening and deepening political activity in the black community. In fact, the Civil Rights movement in Springfield never mobilized large numbers of community residents. Demonstrations included sizable contingents of white college students, many times outnumbering black participants. School integration for many was never a "real issue." Access to jobs, better housing, and an improved black community were more meaningful. But for the membership of the NAACP—mainly middle class with a sprinkling of school teachers, doctors, ministers, and businessmen—the important issues were racial imbalance, the integration of swimming pools and other public facilities, and the opening of quality housing in middle-class white areas, issues that would have direct and immediate consequences for these groups. As black demands became more community-centered the chapter became disoriented and began losing members. To lower class blacks, particularly the young, the NAACP was a relic good for running cotillions, tea parties, and fashion shows. Yet, the white community continued to identify the NAACP and its leaders as the primary spokesmen for the black community, reinforcing black lower-class resentment toward the black middle class and intensifying the controversy over legitimacy.

As a successor to civil rights activity, The War on Poverty provided a hoped-for sanction for middle class blacks to speak for the poor and to organize them as a constituency using jobs, contracts, and services as political resources. But once again the leadership as administrators were confronted with the same unresolvable dilemma, namely the pressures from below and above, from a skeptical and alienated community and a powerful but unreliable white power structure.

The Black Middle Class and the Problem of Cooptation

The dilemma of cooptation and the related problem of vulnerability are serious ones not only in black communities but in all dependencies white or black. But the antipoverty program using the rhetoric of power redistribution provided a quantum jump in the process, creating a leadership group now more dependent and vulnerable than before.

One example of this problem in Springfield occurred during the occupation of Springfield College by a group of black students demanding basic changes in the structure of the college and large increases in Negro enrollment. Although the occupation seemed to have the support of large segments of the black community, especially in the surrounding area, the occupation ended after intervention from black leaders. It is impossible, from newspaper accounts, to be sure of the motives of the leaders, but all were administrators of programs either sponsored or funded by government and corporate enterprises. All had, in the past, made militant-like speeches expressing sympathy with the student demands. Yet, possibly because of the sensitivity of their positions their actions indicated a reluctance to push the white community too far or to engage in disruptive tactics.

Some of the sponsors of Model Cities programs before the City Council included Northern Educational Services; Uplift, Incorporated; Comprehensive Employment; Dunbar Community Center; and the AIC center for Human Relations, all important leadership bases in the black community. The leaders of these programs took care not to endanger their futures by antagonizing governmental officials, since funds for model cities came from the federal government and was a department of the city government. Ironically, the more money poured into the black community by outside sources, the less well black leaders and administrators dealt independently with that larger community and the more constricted became their actions, results of the responsibilities of power and authority within the system. Alternatives to vulnerability allowed one to be independent, to antagonize and press the white community, but without the financial resources needed to affect change in the black community's economic life. This is part of the dilemma of minority group leaders and a characteristic of the continuing conflict between the powerless and the powerful.

Many times the bind between the conflicting pressures and the vulnerable position of the black administrator was resolved through the use of violent rhetoric and moderate behavior. The first was used when publically addressing the constituents and the authorities, the second when interacting in private. But as the pressure increased, the gap between the two became greater, creating confusion in the minds of black community clients and feeding their basic distrust of "so-called leaders." Although pressure

from below seems to have ebbed lately, during the late sixties, constituents, particularly the youth, constantly questioned the "good faith" of
the leadership, giving them the "Uncle Tom" treatment, as one bureaucrat
described it.[3]

Thus, the ability of the black bureaucracy to speak for the black community was severely limited by problems inherent in the antipoverty program as well as by basic imbalance in black-white political and economic
resources.

Saul Alinsky described the War on Poverty as suffocating and seduc-
tive, destroying the ability of community groups and leaders to make
significant changes.[4] Others were critical of the civil rights leaders who
could not act effectively as independent monitors of the antipoverty program, because of their own involvement in it.[5]

But, in all of this criticism there is an implication of calculated deliber-
ateness on the part of the programs' originators, which may not be accurate. The aging Civil Rights movement, as Earl Raab points out, was in the
process of having its "teeth drawn" in any case. For Raab, CAP was not a
"sellout" because it was never meant to be a "revolution."[6] But others
have gone further and questioned the whole phenomenon of cooptation.
Dale Rogers Marshall argues that CAPs and their satellites gave minority
organizations a new focus.

The assumption is that all moderates are militant who have been cooled down. The
limited evidence we have suggests many of the organizations involved had never
been militant. Instead, they have reached a higher level of activity than they ever
exhibited in the past.[7]

In Springfield perhaps much of the cooptation involved persons already
coopted into white middle-class society, in psychological if not in economic
terms. Yet, what alternative pool of administrators existed? The limits of
cooptation and vulnerability were real and did inhibit the political responsiveness of the program. But it also provided a focus for the anger and
alienation of the black poor, a public structure that could be referred to
whatever the limits of its effectiveness. And, for many, coopted blacks
were preferable to whites under any circumstance. Most of the black
bureaucrats in Springfield did reside in the ghetto, and if nothing else, had a
clear personal memory of what poverty was all about.

Conclusion

Ralph Kramer, in a comparative analysis of four CAPs in the San Francisco
area, isolates three sets of displacements that took place during the early
years. Social service concerns prevailed over community organization and
social action, the middle class displaced the poor, and ethnicity displaced

poverty.[8] Although the emphasis in the Springfield study was on bureaucratic behavior rather than on the behavior of CAPs, similar results were found.

It is beyond the scope of this chapter to focus on goal displacement but the larger study did examine in some detail the early conflicts over who would control model cities. Behind the control question was the issue of social welfare versus political participation. The mayor, threatened by the political potential of the program under independent control, moved it directly into the city administration. The remaining political activity has turned into a variant of old-fashioned ward politics with fierce competition among black bureaucrats, community organizations, and the nonprofit development corporations competing for economic rewards.

From the outset ethnicity replaced poverty as the central criteria for employment resulting in the black segmentation of the antipoverty bureaucracy in Springfield and conforming to the pattern of previous ethnic segmentation of other bureaucratic structures. The black claim on a significant portion of the social welfare apparatus has been institutionalized.

The existence of a sizable black bureaucracy provides a point of access into the black community for the city government and serves as visible proof of the city's good intentions in the area of race relations. Further, as the black population of Springfield increases and the white population continues to decline, such proof becomes essential.

As in the San Francisco case the program in Springfield has been good for the black middle class, reinvigorating the civil rights leadership, providing well-paying jobs, higher status, and increasing interaction with the white power structure where even greater rewards are available. It has made many of them bureaucrat-brokers, who, like the Irish "ward heelers" in the nineteenth century, negotiate for the dependent population with or without their support. The problems of cooptation and vulnerability inevitably raise questions about the legitimacy of that leadership and provide limits to the poor's acquiescence.

Blacks in bureaucracy are by definition antirevolutionary, an example of the homeostatic process of American politics in operation. To join the government is to be part of a system structured and committed to reform at its limits and the status quo at its roots. Of course, radical change rarely occurs within the context of a bureaucratic structure and the antipoverty program stands as a prime example. Bureaucratic norms and commitments take on a life of their own, and the well-being of the organization becomes the overriding concern. The improved welfare of the client then becomes a side effect of that process. Richard Cloward and Francis Fox Piven describe the process as follows:

. . . future prospects for social change will be increasingly shaped not by low-income influence, but by the expansionist forces of public bureaucrats. If the emerging programs successfully impart competitive skills, the bureaucracies pursuing their own enchantment may thereby succeed in raising low-income people into the middle class. In this way the clients of the bureaucracies can indeed be said to have increased their political influence.[9]

Thus, internal job creation, first for the black middle class, and then down the ladder, has proven to be the major result of the War on Poverty.

One area of potential difficulty for blacks in the social welfare bureaucracy is the growing pressure from competing client groups for a "slice of the pie." New York and other cities have witnessed fierce struggles between blacks and Latins in particular for access and control of programs. In Springfield the tension has increased as more impoverished Latins move in. Blacks are perceived by many of these new groups as the power structure to be pushed aside, a typical pattern of ethnic politics in America. As long as the problems are defined ethnically, this pattern will continue. Subsequent studies of black bureaucratic behavior must take this phenomenon into account.

Other changes more advantageous for black bureaucrats also are taking place. Follow-up studies of Springfield blacks administering poverty programs document the beginning of a bureaucratic nexus or "social welfare complex" developing with continual movement of individuals between government programs, nonprofit development corporations, large private businesses, and academia. One black leader began as an intergroup relations coordinator in the early sixties, then administered a job training program funded by a large corporation and now operates his own consulting firm. Another started as assistant director of Northern Educational Services and now runs an intergroup relations institute at American International College. Antipoverty program experience is opening up new opportunities and creating a personnel loop within a social welfare subsystem dominated by blacks. More extensive research in this area needs to begin for it represents a new dimension to the "blackening" of urban bureaucracies.

Notes

1. Richard Cloward, "Are the Poor Left Out'" in Chaim Waxman, ed., *Poverty: Power and Politics* (New York: Grosset and Dunlap, 1968), pp. 159-170.

2. Ben Seligman, *Aspects of Poverty* (New York: Thomas Y. Crowell, 1968), p. 293.

3. For a description of a similar problem in the Detroit antipoverty program see: Murray Seidler, "Some Participant Observer Reflections on

Detroit's Community Action Program," *Urban Affairs Quarterly*, V, No. 2, (December, 1969), p. 195.

4. Saul Alinsky, "The War on Poverty—Political Pornography," in Waxman, *Poverty: Power and Politics*, pp. 171-179.

5. Kenneth Clark and Jeanette Hopkins, *A Relevant War Against Poverty* (New York: Harper and Row, 1969), p. 253.

6. Earl Raab, "What War and Which Poverty," in Waxman, *Poverty: Power and Politics*, p. 241.

7. Dale Rogers Marshall, "Public Participation and the Politics of Poverty," *Urban Affairs Annual Reviews* (Beverly Hills: Sage Publications, 1971), Vol. V, pp. 474-475.

8. Ralph Kramer, *Participation of the Poor* (Englewood Cliffs, N.J.: Prentice-Hall, 1969), p. 237.

9. As quoted in Samuel Kravitz, "The Community Action Program in Perspective," in Warner Bloomberg and Henry Schmandt, eds., *Urban Poverty* (Beverly Hills: Sage Publications, 1970), p. 301.

14

The Impact of OEO Legal Services

Harry P. Stumpf,
Bernadyne Turpen,
and John Culver

Introduction

Poor people lack nearly everything except problems. Most noticeably, they lack money. Their economic condition also has political, social, and legal ramifications. The poor do not command political influence. They are regarded as second class citizens socially and their encounters with the legal system are usually involuntary. The legal system is not very appealing for them because they habitually emerge from it with even less than they had before. It is this legal aspect of poverty that is of concern here, specifically the attempt of one federal program to use the legal system as a vehicle for social change for the nation's impoverished.

Lawyers and the War on Poverty

Lawyers have long acknowledged their societal obligation to represent the unpopular and controversial client. Similarly, the legal profession, by virtue of its monopoly on the practice of law, has continually reminded itself and the public that justice shall have no price; that lawyers are mindful of their responsibility to represent those unable to afford the attorney's fees. Unfortunately, rather than the poor defining their legal needs, the general practice of the organized bar and private practitioners has been to define for them what legal problems should be handled free or on a reduced-fee basis.

The poor person who is behind in his credit payments, seeking a divorce, or having trouble establishing welfare eligibility is often passed from one lawyer to another before receiving help (if he ever does). Until the mid-1960s the only recourse available to the poor needing legal assistance, aside from those private practitioners devoting time to the indigent, was the traditional legal aid society, a private charity-oriented group of laymen and

Professor Stumpf wishes to acknowledge the kind permission of Sage Publications, Inc. to use portions of his book *Community Politics and Legal Services: The Other Side of the Law*, © 1975, in this chapter. The original research of OEO legal services was performed pursuant to a contract with offices of Economic Opportunity, Executive Office of the President, Washington, D.C. 20506. The opinions expressed herein are those of the authors and should not be construed as representing the opinions or policy of any agency of the United States government.

lawyers, understaffed, overworked and underfinanced. The goal of these societies in meeting the legal needs of the poor has been admirable but, for a variety of reasons including the desire to avoid litigation and controversial problems, never fulfilled.

As a remedy to the problems of the legal aid societies, the Legal Services Program (LSP) was created in 1965 as the legal arm of the War on Poverty. Borrowing heavily from the proposals set forth by Edgar S. and Jean C. Cahn in their landmark article, "The War on Poverty: A Civilian Perspective," the LSP was to offer a radically new approach in the delivery of civil legal services to the nation's impoverished.[1] While the LSPs were to duplicate most of what the established legal aid societies were doing, they were to do much more. The financial resources committed to the program allowed for the creation of new programs (preventive legal counseling and education, organizing consumer and tenant groups) and more staff attorneys than were ever feasible on the meager legal aid society budgets. Second, the constituent poor were to serve on the boards of directors, thus making the program more independent of local political control that often restricted the activities of the societies. This marked a dramatic shift from the traditional social service approach whereby programs for the poor were formulated and directed by the nonpoor. Third, the concept of neighborhood law offices was introduced. In the past, legal aid societies were usually confined to downtown offices in or near the courthouse, often far removed from the poverty pockets in a community. Under the new program neighborhood law offices would be strategically located in poverty areas. Finally, the new programs were to adopt an aggressive law reform orientation, filing class action suits and lobbying for changes in the laws that adversely affect the poor.

Implicit and at times explicit in the literature on the program is the assumption that the heart of the new departure in legal services was to be its law reform dimension. It is true that at the outset this aspect of program operations was down-played, that over the years national policy was not entirely consistent on the point, and in any case terms such as "law reform" or "aggressive, creative advocacy" were never clearly operationalized by program officials. But there is considerable evidence pointing to this aspect of the program as its chief goal.

In 1966 E. Clinton Bamberger, Jr., first LSP director, reaffirmed the LSP goal of accomplishing more than making legal counsel available to the poor. He asserted that "Our responsibility is to marshal the forces of law and the strength of lawyers to *combat the causes and effects of poverty*."[2] And in 1967 Mr. Bamberger's successor, Earl Johnson, Jr., echoed the credo:

. . . [T]he primary goal of the Legal Services Program should be law reform, to bring about changes in the structure of the world in which poor people live in order to provide a legal system in which the poor enjoy the same legal treatment as the rich.[3]

These are heady statements, but there is every indication that they were to be taken earnestly and that a serious attempt was made to implement this policy. Program annual evaluation reports covering the 1966-69 period continually used the law reform criterion as the chief benchmark for commending or criticizing local program operations. On the one hand, dozens of programs were phased out or significantly restructured in an attempt to enforce this orientation. On the other hand, programs with the deepest commitment to aggressive litigious activity on behalf of large groups of the poor (such as filing significant class actions in order to bring about major changes in the law) are most frequently cited as the "best" of OEO programs.

Of course it would be unduly narrow to measure program accomplishments and shortcomings solely in these terms. The program clearly employed a multifaceted approach that must also be considered. The impact the program has had all along the continuum of its activites, from service per se to possible unanticipated consequences must also be weighed in any final evaluation. But *legal change* and the *effects of such change on the poor* is the ultimate criterion by which the program's accomplishments can be fairly measured.

Accomplishments

If one were to define "equal justice under law" as the availability of competent legal counsel to every American who cannot afford it, one must recognize at the outset that we are light years away from achieving that goal. True, the Office of Economic Opportunity (OEO) legal services never contemplated such an ambitious undertaking, but it is useful to consider for a moment where we are along the volume of service scale.

In 1967 it was estimated that if the poverty population (then 16.5 percent) were afforded legal representation at the level of persons with annual incomes in excess of $10,000, over 137,000 attorneys (about 47 percent of all lawyers) would be needed to serve the poor.[4] In that year the OEO program was off and running with about 1,800 attorneys in the field. Approaching the problem a little differently, in 1970 there were 324,818 attorneys in the United States with directory listings (presumably in actual practice), a ratio of one for every 662 persons. Assuming the poor (numbering some 25.5 million in 1970, or 13 percent of the population) should be served by a like percentage of lawyers,[a] the task would require 42,225

---

[a] However, Silver has argued that the need of the poor for legal services, per client, may be as much as five times that required of a middle-class citizen. See Carol Ruth Silver, "Imminent

poverty practitioners. In fact, only some 3,000 OEO attorneys were at work in 1970, and even if we add 2,000 "movement" attorneys, the ratio of total poverty attorneys to the poverty population would be only about 1:5,000. If we further assume that the OEO cost of putting 3,000 lawyers in the field is about $60 million annually, it would take nearly $850 million each year to serve the need as above calculated, or nearly 15 times the funds now available. Such are the dimensions of the problem if defined just in terms of service. In these terms it is apparent that the legal services effort is but a drop in the bucket, the unmet need being immense. However, the program can have the other types of impact beneficial to the poor. Defining the problem a little more broadly, what have been these benefits or potential benefits?

The answer must depend on the perspective of the viewer and on a number of tentative judgments. Compared to where we were in 1964, one must conclude that the program has made a substantial *dent* in serving the poor. As shown in Table 14-1, expenditures are up sixteen-fold, the number of cases handled per thousand population has quadrupled and the total number of cases handled annually has jumped from some 380,000 to over a million. If measured only by the volume of research now devoted to law and poverty, public (or at least professional) awareness of the multiple problems in the field has significantly increased. Thousands of attorneys who heretofore gave the problem but fleeting attention have now been exposed, in law school or in the field, to the inequities of the legal system in relation to the poor, and though difficult to prove, the program has probably had significant spin-off effects in encouraging the practice of "public interest" and pro bono law in studying and experimenting with new forms of delivering legal services.[5] These are not trivial accomplishments and might be taken in and of themselves as sufficient justification for continuing the program. But what has been accomplished by way of legal change and how has this benefited the poor?

Program Orientation

Ten years of program history provide more than sufficient support for the proposition that from the majority of programs we can learn little about the impact of law reform activities because most programs practice almost exclusively traditional, case-by-case, band-aid law. This statement is not based on a systematic nationwide survey, but such very expensive research is probably unnecessary to establish the point. From case studies of

Failure of Legal Services," p. 220. Statistics on the distribution of attorneys are taken from Bette H. Sikes, Carla N. Carson, and Patricia Gorai, eds., *The 1971 Lawyer Statistical Report* (Chicago: American Bar Foundation, 1972), p. 6.

Table 14-1
Civil Legal Aid in the United States, 1964-71

	Offices with Paid Staff	New Cases Handled	Cases per Thousand Population	Gross Expenditures
1964	147	380,384[b] (172)[c]	2.8 (247)	$4,352,453
1971	616[a]	1,194,634 (349)	12.3 (297)	$75,312,375
% Increase	319	214	339	1630%

Source: National Legal Aid and Defender Association, Summary of Conference Proceedings, 1965 (Chicago, NLADA, 1965), pp. 84-99; and National Legal Aid and Defender Association, *1971 Statistics of Legal Assistance Work in the United States and Canada* (Chicago: NLADA, 1972). All figures have been corrected to exclude Canada and the Philippines; Puerto Rico is included.

[a]Includes branch offices in other cities, but not separate neighborhood offices.

[b]Only offices reporting number of cases and cost of operation.

[c]Figures in parentheses indicate number of offices reporting.

programs in several California communities, New Mexico, Illinois, Michigan, and New York, in addition to evaluation reports on programs in Colorado, Missouri, New Jersey, and so on, the findings have a resounding sameness—that Washington's attempts to structure local programs so as to insure their independence from local bar and community economic interests have largely failed.[6]

The reasons for this are not difficult to discern. At bottom, private practitioners are surrogates for the interests they represent, and these interests are largely those of the dominant economic and political forces in the community. Truly effective legal representation of the poor can pose a threat to such interests that can be (and generally has been) thwarted by keeping local programs under wraps.

Of the dozens of examples of mechanisms for community repression of aggressive programs one could cite, perhaps none makes the point more vividly than the role of the UCF—United Community Fund (variously labeled Community Chest, United Givers Fund, etc.). Typically headed by leading figures of business, finance, and industry, the UCF fund drive is that annual rite by which middle-class money is collected to fund middle-class projects of charity that largely reflect middle-class values.[b] Sac-

[b]The Boy Scouts, Girl Scouts, YMCA, and similar organizations that receive the bulk of UCF funds are anything but poverty oriented. A study in Omaha in 1967 found that only about 10 percent of the YMCA's clients had family incomes below the poverty level, though 40 percent had incomes above $10,000 per year. In Detroit, less than 5 percent of poverty families had any contact with organizations such as the Boy Scouts or the Catholic Youth Organiza-

rosanct and ostensibly above politics, it is actually the clearest embodiment of political power in the community. Experience with traditional legal aid forewarned OEO planners of the threat posed by United Fund interests, but whether by design or oversight, all community action programs (LSP being one) were required to produce a 20 percent nonfederal share, and in most instances this is provided through the United Fund. This convenient lever has been used in various ways to promote legal services conforming to community norms. In St. Louis and Oklahoma City UCF support was withdrawn when legal services brought suit against local government agencies.[c] And in Baton Rouge, United Givers cut off financial support to the legal services program in the face of pressure from the local police who were upset because program attorneys brought legal action to stop alleged ". . . unjustified police slayings of Negroes."[d]

In Albuquerque the UCF Board of Directors did not wait for such a suit. Rather, the indirect hint that legal advice might be offered to barrio residents in the face of possible police harrassment was sufficient, first to attempt unsuccessfully to dismiss the program's general counsel, then to withdraw some $24,000 in annual support of the program.[e] These funds were then redirected to support a Judicare program, which the Albuquerque Bar Association had been trying to establish since 1965.

The point is not merely that community interests pose serious threats to the effective legal representation of the poor; that is obvious. The more significant lesson from the UCF experience relates to the behavior of the

tion. Of the UCF in San Francisco, a black leader said, "Their idea of solving social problems is to give sailing lessons to the Campfire Girls." See "No Fun for Funds," *Newsweek* (December 22, 1969), p. 65.

[c] In Oklahoma City it was the local housing authority. See Paul R. Wieck, "Justice on the Defensive," Vol. 162, No. 8, *New Republic*, Western Edition (February 21, 1970), p. 12.

[d] "U.S. Continues Support of Legal Aid for the Poor," *Albuquerque Tribune*, January 15, 1970, p. B-8. The suit, brought in U.S. District Court, sought to enjoin police conduct and "to provide availability of police protection and treatment by police in a manner which does not discriminate on the basis of race and color." The action grew out of an incident in which three Negro youths were killed by police who claimed self-defense in pursuit of burglary suspects. The Shreveport, Lousiana *Journal*, on August 19, 1969, editorialized that such litigation ". . . stirs ill will between the races."

[e] The Albuquerque Committee on Social Action (COSA) circulated a bulletin that said: "The police are there to protect you. Do they? Or are they trying to scare you or embarrass you publicly? Or roughing you up for no reason?" It then mentioned that the Legal Aid Society "may be able to help," and gave neighborhood office numbers. The general counsel for the Albuquerque LSP said, "We didn't publish it, we didn't pass it out, but I don't disagree with a single thing in it." Protests from the Fraternal Order of Police (including implied requests not to support UCF) brought a strong disavowal of the COSA circular from the executive committee of the Board of Directors of the Legal Aid Society, to which Fitzpatrick took public exception. The board then met to fire him on grounds of insubordination. In a later meeting of the entire Legal Aid Society, Fitzpatrick's opponents on the board were voted out of office or resigned, whereupon UCF withdrew its $24,000 annual support. The series of incidents is related in Frank L. Dewey, "What Happened in Albuquerque," Vol. 28, No. 7, *Legal Aid Briefcase* (July, 1970), pp. 227-235.

local legal profession when legal services activities thrust the program into communitywide politics. In only a few communities has the local bar, or even significant organized portions thereof, come to the defense of the local program on grounds of an attorney's professional responsibility to his clients. While the bar is seldom hesitant to cite professional ethics in defense of its own interests, principles of professional responsibility tend to become subservient to larger community concerns, again underscoring the surrogate role lawyers play.

Another dimension of the problem is found in the nature of professions themselves. They are, by definition, closed systems characterized by the existence of a monopoly with respect to a highly developed body of knowledge. Other attributes include an insistence upon exclusive control over the use and application of such knowledge, the development and implementation of a philosophy concerning the proper allocation of services performed and the relation of that service to the larger society, and an emphasis on colleagueship by which the system is perpetuated.[7] Without ever explicitly saying so, however, the OEO effort directly challenged these professional prerogatives. "Maximum feasible participation" of the poor in legal services suggests that laymen will be setting priorities for legal strategies, that legal resources must be redistributed along more equitable lines—in short, that law is too important to be left entirely to lawyers. The evidence now available to us strongly suggests that the local legal fraternity has no intention of sharing its function as "gatekeeper to the halls of justice." In the main, local bar associations dominate local program activities, and these activities proceed in the traditional professional vein of highly individualized, case-by-case lawyering. Law reform, test cases, aggressive group representation? These are not a part of the traditional practice of law for most attorneys and are all but absent in most programs.

These professional considerations also help to explain the strong preference for Judicare among local bar associations. Judicare's emphasis on voluntarism and the individual case-by-case approach is clearly much more consistent with traditional professional mores than the neighborhood staff plan. That Judicare is much more costly than the conventional staffed program, that it holds little promise for changing the legal position of the poor, or that it provides grossly unequal service to potential clients are apparently minor considerations to most private attorneys, for truly effective legal representation for all citizens has never been a real goal of the legal profession, only a symbolic one.[8]

Hence, local bar control, in combination with community political and financial pressures, have pressed toward maintenance of the status quo such that for most communities we have little more than expanded old-line legal aid societies. Prophetically, Ken Pye came close to saying it all nine years ago when he concluded that, in spite of the new innovations in the

LSP experiment, it will be doomed because the needs of the poor will become lost in the political shuffle over local legal control of the program.[9]

Legal Change

Nevertheless, the OEO experience has included several programs whose activities provide a fair test of the proposition that an aggressive law reform approach can bring substantial benefits to the poor in the form of systemic change. If by change we mean alterations in the basic interrelationships of individuals and social classes,[10] for the poor this must mean a measurable improvement in their economic and political position vis-à-vis the middle class. Jerome Carlin, former coordinator of the San Francisco Neighborhood Legal Assistance Foundation, an LSP that did adopt an aggressive law reform strategy, saw his mission as one of finding "leverage points in the system" to force changes benefitting the poor. He observed:

The test for the efficacy of such activity was whether it would result in increasing the income or political bargaining power of a substantial number of poor persons. Litigation (with emphasis on class suits) and administrative and legislative advocacy were the principal tools.[11]

Based on the testimony of those experienced in the law reform struggle these past nine years one must conclude that the effort has been disappointing.[12] The welfare behemoth grinds on, there being scarcely any evidence that the thousands of suits brought to correct its injustices have significantly improved the economic position of its millions of recipients.[13] The housing situation for the poor is if anything *worse* than it was when legal services began,[14] and in fields such as consumer and education law whatever systemic change has been wrought has by all evidence been minimal. These are admittedly broad generalizations subject to confirmation by more empirical data than is presently at hand, but if the Legal Services Program has achieved significant change to benefit the poor this has yet to be shown. Certainly those who have worked in the movement and written about their experiences tend to substantiate this conclusion.[15] If they are largely correct, it is important to understand why. What are the dynamics of legal reform and how do such changes relate to broader economic or social change?

The OEO experience should cause social scientists and lawyers with a social engineering bent to pause to reconsider carefully some basic assumptions about our legal system. The early years at OEO were exciting times, reminiscent to some of the New Deal era. For the first time in our history funds were promised to mount a serious attack on poverty, and concepts to guide strategy and tactics were quickly and uncritically operationalized. Based in part on the misunderstood history of the civil rights movement, legal services strategists assumed (1) that with sufficient funds the stunning legislative and judicial victories in civil rights could be repeated on an even more massive scale in the field of law and poverty, and (2) that such policy changes could (and would) bring about material improvements in the livelihood of the poor. The implicit model was *Brown* v. *Board of Education*.[16] Neither of these assumptions is entirely wrong, just mostly so. As Goeffrey Hazard points out, one problem is that poverty differs from racial discrimination in critical ways, not the least of which is the ethical dimension. American society has never decided, even symbolically, that poverty is wrong and that market conditions helping to create and perpetuate it are legally correctable.[17] Additionally, the civil rights movement is not a particularly apt model for judicially induced change if the systemwide noncompliance with such decisions as *Brown* has been accurately reported.

The achievement of legal changes is substantially more arduous in general than OEO seems to have assumed, and it has proven especially difficult in the poverty field. Local courts are not organized either structurally or functionally for change but rather the opposite, the routinization of procedure and the perpetuation of existing substantive rules.[18] Nor are appellate courts oriented to change. In the teaching of law the great landmark cases are stressed; less attention is given to the fact that these are the exceptions. As Harold Rothwax noted, a great many issues in the field of law and poverty may be judicially resolved to benefit the poor only by holding certain rules and procedures unconstitutional, and courts are traditionally reluctant to do this.[19] When one adds to these factors the extremely slow pace at which litigation usually proceeds, combined with the high expense involved, one can begin to have an appreciation of the limits of judicial policy making as an instrument of change in the condition of poverty.

In many ways legislatively originated law reform seems to be the best hope for the poor, but here, too, the barriers are formidable. By definition legislatures are majority policy-making bodies, and poverty is not a problem of the majority. On the whole legislatures are not likely to enact major new policies to benefit the poor if such legislation involves a significant cost to the middle and upper classes, which is generally the only type of change that will be really significant. Both courts and legislatures, particularly the former, can correct procedural abuses perpetuated on the poor, and they have done so. But poverty is not principally a matter of procedure; it is a matter of income-distribution.

The Impact of Law Reform

More crucial than these considerations are the implications of legal change for meaningful improvement in the economic position of the poor. In spite of the many barriers to legal change, the fact is that legal services attorneys have been quite successful in bringing about a good many changes in the law, largely through adjudication. Recent decisions in welfare are but one example. Others may be cited in the areas of housing,[20] education,[21] and access to the judiciary.[22] The OEO experience suggests that the basic difficulty in the law reform strategy is not so much law reform itself. That, it would appear, is *comparatively* easy to bring about. The problem lies in translating changes in LAW into changes in law and in turning both into substantial material improvement for the poor.

Our social system is characterized by a diffusion of policy-making units. Legal change is policy change in but one of these units, while the others remain to frustrate the impact of a change in the Law. If welfare residency requirements are adjudged unconstitutional there is a battery of counter-vailing policy moves at other levels and in other jurisdictions, including but not limited to legislative or bureaucratic countermoves, which can be employed to thwart the judicial decision. If the legislature or judiciary should decree stiffer enforcement of building codes or usury laws, any benefits accruing to the poor can be more than offset by higher rents or more restricted access to credit. And if legal services attorneys should win a major judicial victory in the expansion of the right to counsel concept, such a legal change may carry muted or nonexistent benefits for the poor if states and local governments have neither the willingness nor the financial ability to provide such legal representation, and/or if our total attorney resources are insufficient for compliance.

It should not be assumed that noncompliance with a legislative, judicial, or administrative change in the law is always willful. More often than is commonly acknowledged, legal change is made with little or no attention given to whether resources are available in sufficient supply to make compliance possible or to whether other more basic changes are needed to render the initial policy shift effective. There are a great many laws now in existence that are all but meaningless because administrative resources are grossly inadequate for enforcement, or because the nature of the conduct to be regulated makes enforcement especially difficult, or because funds were never forthcoming to implement the policy. Housing codes, laws regulating certain personal conduct, and the now defunct war on poverty are examples. It might well be pointless for a court of law to raise the level of welfare benefits if public funds are not correspondingly forthcoming. Courts have no direct access to the public purse. All of these examples suggest the distance between what is desired and what is, between law and its mean-

ingful implementation, without ever mentioning the multitude of opportunities the system provides for willful noncompliance. In our haste to save
the poor, legally speaking, we seem to have forgotten a reality of our legal
system addressed by Karl Llewellyn:

Substantive law presents the problem of where officials *would like* to get with a
problem and of where they say they *are going* to get—either because they want to,
or because tradition forces them. But discussions of substantive law become so
easily misleading; one falls easily into thinking that because he would like to get
somewhere, he has arrived. If wishes were horses, then beggars would ride. If rules
were results, there would be little need for lawyers.[23]

This discussion only begins to suggest the complex interrelationship
between law reform and social reform. To employ legal change to induce
more fundamental changes in society is to put the cart before the horse.
Law is by and large a reflection of values implicit in the larger society, not
the reverse. The law reform approach really does not address the fundamental problem. Particularly is this true of poverty.

From the truism that poverty has important legal dimensions we cannot
(or should not) jump to the conclusion that its legal aspects are crucial or
that legal change can materially improve the economic position of the poor.
The appeal of legal reform is always the same: its simplicity. Change the
legal rule and you have changed (or begun to change) underlying social and
economic arrangements; if you want something done, order someone to do
it. With only this brief excursion into the problem, it should be clear that the
relationship is a great deal more complex than OEO assumed. The most
that can be said for legal change is that it may be used in conjunction with a
host of other policy instruments if directed social change is desired. And
until other forces can be brought into play, law alone can usually achieve
only very modest results.

This is not to argue the uselessness of the law reform strategy, only its
serious limitations. If the law reform approach is not likely to bring about
the dramatic results contemplated by its proponents, it is nonetheless the
only legal services strategy carrying any hope for change. The hope is that
by relieving the poor of the more oppressive policies and procedural
inequities of welfare, the police, the courts, and other agencies public and
private, a degree of improvement in the life of poverty is achieved. More
significantly, constant legal pressure can at times produce secondary results by serving as a catalyst for reform in institutional practices. In spite of
its limited resources, legal services has hardly been irrational in insisting on
a law reform approach. With all its limitations, this strategy is perhaps the
only one consistent with the other aims of the War On Poverty.

This analysis of the impact of OEO's law reform efforts admittedly (and
perhaps inevitably) emphasizes short-term results that are apparent at this

time. The conclusions reached may well understate more significant long range effects as well as cumulative spillover effects of a secondary nature. For example, it may be that we are in the early stages of fundamental changes in the practice of law (and perhaps legal education as well) in the United States due in part to our experience with OEO legal services. One might further speculate that the first major blow has been struck for equality of civil legal rights irrespective of wealth that may eventually result in, or at least contribute to, a marked improvement in the material position of the poor. But it requires an optimistic analyst to reach such speculative conclusions on the basis of the extremely scanty evidence now available. At least in the short run, if not over the long haul as well, one cannot fail to be impressed with the capacity of the political and social system to mount countervailing pressures sufficient to maintain the status quo of the poor. To be sure, change of the type we are discussing is incremental in nature, and it may be too early to make definitive statements about the ultimate impact of the OEO experiment. As has been so frequently noted, the massive opposition to aggressive lawyering by neighborhood offices may itself testify to the effectiveness of the enterprise these past ten years. But are we speaking of effectiveness in the sense of bringing about meaningful change for the poor, or only the perceived and rather vague threat of such change? In all likelihood, it is the latter. In any case it does not seem unfair to place the burden of proof on those who opt for a more optimistic appraisal of the legal services experience. If the program has had (or is likely to have) more extensive and fundamental ramifications for improving the legal, political, or economic status of the poor than this analysis suggests, it has yet to be shown.

Notes

1. Edgar S. and Jean C. Cahn, "The War on Poverty: A Civilian Perspective," Vol. 73, No. 8, *Yale Law Journal* (July, 1964), pp. 1317-1352.

2. Address of E. Clinton Bamberger, Jr. to the National Conference of Bar Presidents, Chicago, Illinois, February 19, 1966.

3. Address of Earl Johnson, Jr. to the Harvard Conference on Law and Poverty, Harvard Law School, March 17, 1967.

4. Carol Ruth Silver, "Imminent Failure of Legal Services for the Poor: Why and How to Limit Caseload," Vol. 46, No. 2, *Journal of Urban Law* (1969), p. 218.

5. For example, see Robert Borosage et al., "The New Public Interest Lawyers," Vol. 79, No. 6, *Yale Law Journal* (May, 1970), pp. 1069-1152. Some of the recent studies by the American Bar Foundation illustrate the point. For example, see Preble Stolz, "Insurance for Legal Services: A

Preliminary Study of Feasibility," Vol. 35, No. 3, *University of Chicago Law Review* (Spring, 1968), pp. 417-476; and Barlow F. Christensen, *Lawyers for People of Moderate Means* (Chicago: American Bar Foundation, 1970).

6. Some of these findings are reported in Harry P. Stumpf, Henry P. Schroerluke, and Forrest D. Dill, "The Legal Profession and Legal Services: Explorations in Local Bar Politics," Vol. 6, No. 1, *Law and Society Review* (August, 1971), pp. 47-67. See also Ted Finman, "OEO Legal Service Programs and the Pursuit of Social Change: The Relationship Between Programmed Ideology and Program Performance," Vol. 1971, No. 4, *Wisconsin Law Review*, pp. 1001-1084; and Lois R. Sincere, "Legal Representation and the Poor: Pressures and Prospects for Social Change" (unpublished research report, Department of Political Science, Northwestern University, March, 1968).

7. The reader may wish to compare this definition of professions with that of sociologists. For example, see Bernard Barber, "Some Problems in the Sociology of Professions," in *The Professions in America*, ed. by Kenneth S. Lynn (Boston: Beacon Press, 1965), pp. 17-19.

8. These conclusions are drawn by Leonard H. Goodman and Jacques Feuillan, *Alternative Approaches to the Provision of Legal Services for the Rural Poor: Judicare and the Decentralized Staff Program* (Washington: Bureau of Social Science Research, 1972).

9. A. Kenneth Pye, "The Role of Legal Services in the Antipoverty Program," Vol. 31, *Law and Contemporary Problems* (Winter, 1966), p. 246.

10. See Stuart S. Nagel, "Overview of Law and Social Change," Vol. 13, No. 4, *American Behavioral Scientist* (March-April, 1970), p. 486.

11. Jerome E. Carlin, "Storefront Lawyers in San Francisco," Vol. 7, No. 6, *Transaction* (April, 1970), pp. 66-67.

12. For example, see Carlin, "Storefront Lawyers"; Fred J. Heinstand, "The Politics of Poverty Law," in *With Justice for Some*, ed. by Bruce Wasserstein and Mark J. Green (Boston: Beacon Press, 1970), pp. 188-189; and Harold J. Rothwax, "The Law as an Instrument of Social Change," in *Justice and the Law in the Mobilization for Youth Experience*, ed. by Harold H. Weissman (New York: Association Press, 1969), pp. 137-144.

13. Some insights into the program's impact in welfare and housing may be found in Carlin, "Storefront Lawyers."

14. Ibid.

15. Supra, note 12.

16. 347 U.S. 483 (1954).

17. Goeffrey C. Hazard, Jr., "Social Justice Through Civil Justice,"

Vol. 36, No. 4, *University of Chicago Law Review* (Summer, 1969), pp. 705-707.

18. See Herbert Jacob, *Justice in America*, 2nd edition (Boston: Little Brown, 1972). Jacob argues that in the vast majority of cases, local courts are enforcing community norms (chapter 2).

19. Rothwax, "Law As An Instrument of Social Change," p. 141.

20. For example, see *Thorpe v. Housing Authority of the City of Durham*, 37 LW 4069.

21. *Serrano v. Priest*, No. L.A. 29820, Cal. Sup. Cit., Aug. 30, 1971.

22. *Boddie v. Connecticut*, 401 U.S. 371 (1971).

23. Karl N. Llewellyn, *The Bramble Bush: On Our Law and Its Study* (New York: Oceana, 1951), p. 18 (emphasis his).

15 The Supreme Court as Enunciator of Welfare Policy

Stephen L. Wasby

The area of welfare policy, broadly defined, is one in which the Supreme Court has begun to play a major role only in recent years. Once it had sustained the Social Security Act,[1] the Court was not much concerned with welfare policy until after initiation of the War on Poverty. Cases involving the poor, particularly those on welfare, finally began to reach the Court in some numbers in the late 1960s. This resulted from the work of lawyers in the Office of Economic Opportunity (OEO) Legal Services program who were willing to challenge statutes and regulations, and from the increasing militancy of welfare beneficiaries, particularly those in the National Welfare Rights Organization (NWRO).

Unlike many other areas where the Court's decisions have attracted attention, on welfare policy the Court generally has been able to rule only interstitially because of the mass of existing statutory language, primarily the Social Security Act as amended, and administrative regulations. This means that the Court has not written on a clean slate and has had less freedom to enunciate policy on welfare than in some other areas of policy making, for example, freedom of speech or criminal procedure. The largely statutory basis of the Court's welfare rulings means that its individual decisions generally have not been far-reaching. In addition, because Congress can reverse the Court simply by rewriting the statute, welfare recipients' fortunes are ultimately left largely in Congress' rather than the Supreme Court's hands.

Direction of Policy

The most important distinguishing feature of Supreme Court policy on welfare has been that, even during the supposedly liberal Warren Court, rulings did not always strongly support welfare beneficiaries' claims and were only mixed in their potential benefit to the poor. The appointment by President Nixon of four nominees to the Court provided a change in orientation in an even more conservative direction, one unfavorable to the poor. However, the Burger Court's policy direction on welfare did not represent a radical change from what had happened during the late Warren Court years. The idea of a *right* to welfare was never firmly established. Justice Brennan did talk in one case of the "important rights" involved in removing welfare benefits to which a person was statutorily entitled and suggested (in a footnote) that such benefits might be seen as a form of property rather than as charity. However, there was not much follow-through on this idea, which was clearly distasteful to President Nixon's appointees. They reinforced the older idea of welfare as charity, carrying with it relatively few rights.

Overall, the Supreme Court in the last half-dozen years had been willing to make state legislators follow the Social Security Act, to make them calculate benefits openly, and to enforce certain due process requirements. However, when the issue was forcing legislatures to spend money to raise the level of welfare benefits, the Court generally supported the states, not the welfare clients. The states were allowed much freedom to determine both *how much* money should be spent and *how* to spend it, even when it meant exclusion of some potential beneficiaries. Although it was the failure of social welfare agencies that led to the court cases, the Court seemed not very well suited for the supervisory task of making welfare bureaucracies perform their assigned duties.

Policy questions considered by the Court in the welfare area included exclusion from welfare of those eligible under the federal statutes, due process in denying benefits, and the amount of distribution of welfare funds, as well as the rights of illegitimates and consumer protection matters. As was suggested above, most of the Court's pronouncements in this area have involved not constitutional questions but statutory interpretation.

Statutory Interpretation

Several examples indicate the Court's interpretive function in the welfare area. In cases involving state attempts to disqualify AFDC recipients from receiving aid on grounds that they had a "man-in-the-house," the Supreme Court had to interpret the meaning of "parent" in the Social Security Act. In doing so it invalidated state regulations that had served to eliminate a number of AFDC (Aid to Families with Dependent Children) recipients from the welfare rolls.[2] The Court was also asked whether "continued absence" of the father for purposes of eligibility for AFDC benefits included a serviceman's presence overseas; the Court said that it did.[3] Delay in paying unemployment compensation benefits while employers appealed was struck down by the Court because of statutory language that benefits be paid "when due."[4] (Later, the Court basically maintained this position, but allowed the states to place somewhat more burden on the worker if he wished to continue receiving benefits.)[5] And the ruling that AFDC benefits did not have to be paid to unborn children turned on the meaning of the phrase "dependent child" in the statutes.[6]

Another statutory issue was whether Congress intended to preempt the field of welfare regulations from the states. In the absence of specific enabling provisions, the Court has generally refused to allow the states to narrow the categories of eligibility created by Congress. And the Court has also set aside certain rules for calculating expenses that have the same effect. For example, a state's uniform allowance for work-related expenses to be deducted from earned income was held improper, in spite of the state's interest in efficiency, unless the state provided an opportunity to challenge the allowance when expenses exceeded the uniform figure.[7] The Court has, however, granted the states considerable freedom to develop programs for those eligible. Thus, state work rules challenged as more restrictive than federal work incentive (WIN) guidelines were upheld, at least until Congress explicitly preempted the field.[8]

Constitutional Rulings

Not all the Court's welfare rulings involved only matters of statutory interpretation. Some constitutional questions came before the Court, and resulted in important rulings. One of them was the Warren Court's most important pro-beneficiary decision, *Shapiro* v. *Thompson*.[9] Here the Court invalidated durational residence requirements for receiving welfare benefits; such requirements interfered with the right to travel. This policy was later reinforced by the Burger Court in a unanimous ruling striking down a *15-year* residence requirement for aliens[10] and a nearly unanimous ruling overturning a one-year residence requirement for indigents for nonemergency hospitalization or medical care at a county hospital.[11] Justice Douglas, while agreeing with the latter disposition, questioned whether judicial rulings were sufficient to deal with the "enormous" economic and legal aspects of medical care. Other favorable constitutional rulings have occurred in the area of due process. Particularly important was the requirement that benefits not be terminated with a prior evidentiary hearing.[12] However, such due process decisions may be of little benefit to welfare recipients because daily administration of the laws can distort or negate judicial (or legislative) intention. An agency also can often reach its original result even if it uses proper procedure, giving the recipient only the benefit of delay. Although demanding "due process," the Court has not imposed rigorous procedural requirements. For example, doctors' written statements were allowed as "substantial evidence" in connection with disability claims although the claimants had no chance to cross-examine.[13]

Not only have some of the newer justices expressed a preference for flexible procedure, but others have seemed to take an attitude of "welfare recipients, go away," insisting that they take their complaints through HEW before coming to the court.[14] The Court has also been unwilling to accord public assistance recipients the same protections against searches of the home accorded to criminal suspects. When a social worker's "home visit" without a search warrant was challenged, the Court, although conceding that the social worker would have to report evidence of fraud and recognizing that refusal by the AFDC mother to grant admittance led to termination of benefits, decided in favor of the government.[15] The Court so ruled even though in earlier cases it had invalidated warrantless searches of a warehouse and an apartment building. Those cases were distinguished on the ground that in those situations refusal to allow the search was itself a criminal offense.[16]

The Court has been accused of reinforcing its conservative approach by avoiding certain procedural problems. For example, instead of invalidating certain procedures for determining disability benefits, the Court majority remanded them for reconsideration in light of new regulations, even though the dissenters claimed they were clearly improper.[17] A challenge to a rule that a spouse must be absent through desertion for six months before aid was available received comparable treatment,[18] the result of which is to exhaust the claimants before they are able to exhaust their remedies. More serious, the Court has hindered poor people's access to the courts. While the Court struck down the requirement that an indigent person must pay court fees to seek a divorce,[19] it later sustained the fee requirement of the federal bankruptcy act,[20] as well as Oregon's $25 fee required before one may contest in court the rulings of administrative agencies (including welfare departments.)[21] Such rulings make it difficult if not impossible for the impoverished to get a judge to help them resolve economic problems or obtain review of agency decisions lowering their welfare grants.

Welfare beneficiaries may be unable to recover funds due them even when they get a court to invalidate a regulation. The Supreme Court ruled in 1974 that, even when welfare payments had been improperly withheld, the Eleventh Amendment barred suits in federal court against a state (or state officials) for retroactive payment of the benefits—unless the state consented to the suit.[22] As the dissenters in this case argued, the states' incentives to violate the rules were reinforced, for the most that would now happen if the states lost in court was that they would have to make the proper payments in the future.

Benefit Levels

For the Court to eliminate residence requirements or to require due process is one thing. To demand that the states provide increased welfare benefits is quite another. When questions arose about legislative allocations of money for welfare benefits, the Court's stance was both very restrained and conservative. For example, the Court held, 4-3, that the Social Security Act's reduction in social security benefits to reflect workmen's compensation payments was acceptable; the justices made this decision in spite of the fact that people receiving other types of payments did not have their social security payments lowered. Here the Court also rejected the claim that social security payments, because financed in part by the worker's contributions, could not be reduced; the majority said there was no contractual right in such benefits,[23] a statement that flew in the face of the expectations of many Americans that they were *entitled* to the social security benefits toward which they had made contributions.

Another important case involved the congressional requirement that amounts used to determine welfare needs to be recalculated to show cost-of-living increases. Adopting what amounted to a policy of full disclosure but not full payment, the Court turned aside a challenge to New York's changes that had resulted in some families receiving less money.[24] To comply the state had only to *show* the true standard of need, although only a percentage of that amount might be *paid*. In this case Chief Justice Burger and Justice Black would not go even this far, taking the position that welfare recipients should have taken their case to HEW before coming to the courts.

At the same time, in a case that made clear that there was no chance the Burger Court would say there was a right to welfare, the Court also upheld a state-imposed maximum on the welfare grant any family could receive, even though each child in large families received less than those in small families.[25] Here Justice Stewart made references to the "inherent economies of scale" that allowed large families to subsist on less per child, but Justice Marshall, who argued that children cannot control the size of the family into which they are born, expressed the view that the Fourteenth Amendment's Equal Protection Clause has been emasculated in the welfare area. The majority's policy of leaving money decisions on welfare largely to the states was further reinforced in 1972. The policy of paying a lower percentage of needs for AFDC beneficiaries than for those in other aid categories was sustained, as were certain methods for calculating outside income even though they made many people ineligible for basic benefits or supplemental services like Medicaid.[26] In general, showing increasing deference to the states, the Court had adopted a position that provisions must *openly contravene* federal statutes and/or the United States Constitution before they would be invalidated.[27] In 1973, however, the Court did throw out Congress' 1971 Food Stamp program amendments that were aimed at "wealthy" college students and "communes" but that had made ineligible many others living in poverty,[28] on the ground that the legislation was improperly drawn.

At least among certain segments of the concerned public, there has been increased support for the position that welfare benefits are not merely a "privilege" but a right to be surrounded with protections.[29] In spite of this shift in attitudes, members of the Court, particularly Mr. Nixon's appointees, have continued to equate welfare benefits with "charity," and there appears little chance that the Burger Court will say there is a *right* to welfare.[30] The present Court's general orientation can also be clearly seen in Justice Blackmun's characterization of AFDC benefits as "charitable funds" and his reference to the social worker's investigation of the home as being a "gentle means, of limited extent and considerate application."[31]

Related Cases

In addition to its ruling dealing directly with welfare policy, the Court has also ruled on problems, such as alcoholism and illegitimacy, which take a particularly heavy toll among the poor. Thus, the Warren Court ruled that a state may not make it a crime merely to be a narcotics addict[32] and the Burger Court outlawed the "posting" of a person's name in public places for excessive drinking (on due process grounds).[33] However, punishing chronic alcoholics for public intoxication stemming from that disease was held to be acceptable by the late Warren Court.[34]

As to illegitimates' rights, the Court first upheld their right to sue to recover damages for their fathers' deaths.[35] However, the Court then sustained a law that deprived them of recovery when the father died without a will;[36] the law also prevented such children from inheriting even through the father's will if he could not have legally married the mother at the time of their conception. This decision was, however, based on the Court's deference to the states' power to make rules concerning the disposition of property, and was restricted to that field, as became clear shortly afterwards when the Court allowed recovery by illegitimates of damages for the father's death under a workmen's compensation statute.[37] State rules fencing out illegitimates from paternal or state support have also been thrown out;[38] the Court even invalidated part of the Social Security Act that deprived illegitimate children of disability insurance benefits unless they had been supported by the disabled wage earner before the disability, because there was no opportunity to prove dependency.[39] The Court also agreed that an AFDC mother did not have to tell her child's father's name or institute proceedings against him to continue receiving benefits.[40] However, the justices would not support an unmarried mother's demand for the initiation of criminal prosecution of the unmarried father for refusal to provide support, although the state honored such requests from married mothers.[41]

Also significant were rulings providing equality of treatment between the sexes. One required that when one unmarried parent died, surviving unmarried fathers were entitled to be treated equally with unwed mothers with respect to custody of children; the other, not involving illegitimates, invalidated a section of the Social Security Act in which widows but not widowers had been provided social security survivor's benefits while caring for minor children.[42]

Closely related to illegitimacy, of course, are the Court's rulings on contraception and abortion. The Warren Court had broken new ground by invalidating a Connecticut birth control statute that penalized the use of contraceptives, even by married couples. The Burger Court followed this up with a ruling striking down a Massachusetts law where use was not penalized but only married people could get material to prevent conception.[43] Then came the extremely controversial abortion rulings,[44] which struck down most state abortion statutes. Because of the extremely low danger to a woman's health from an abortion during the first trimester of pregnancy, the state's interest in her health was subordinate to the woman's right to determine—in connection with her physician—whether or not to have the abortion. After the first trimester, however, the state could prescribe the conditions under which abortions could take place.

Because the poor are most negatively affected by landlord-tenant and consumer law, recent cases on these subjects are of especial importance to them. The Court has not helped the poor tenant. By upholding an Oregon law allowing eviction for nonpayment of rent even when the landlord did not provide a habitable dwelling, the Court thus forced the tenant to sue separately to recover damages.[45] The Court has been somewhat more helpful to the consumer, but, as in the welfare area, the picture is mixed. The Court at first said that wage garnishment could not take place without notice to the debtor and a hearing,[46] a ruling soon extended to financial responsibility laws for drivers.[47] The Court also said that "confession of judgment" contract provisions (allowing a judgment for default on payment without a hearing) were invalid if a person signed such a provision without being fully aware of what was involved.[48] The "notice and hearing" rule was first extended to summary repossession of consumer goods,[49] but the Court virtually overruled itself two years later by allowing a creditor to repossess goods (to protect them) before a hearing, because the debtor had an opportunity to go to court to get the goods back.[50] Showing that the end of the line had come for the "notice and hearing" rule, the Court said in late 1974 that a privately owned utility company could terminate electric service for nonpayment without a hearing, in spite of the dissenters' arguments that as a regulated monopoly, the utility was required to utilize the same due process as a public agency would have to use.[51]

Conclusion

With respect to welfare policy, neither the Warren Court, which began to enunciate policy on the subject only in the late 1960s, nor the Burger Court was particularly generous or liberal toward the poor. However, the Warren Court's major ruling eliminating durational residence requirements was of substantial help to welfare recipients who might have moved from one state to another, and the Burger Court seemed willing to follow and reinforce that decision. However, on matters of procedure and particularly on the crucial matter of expenditures for welfare benefits, welfare recipients could expect little help—and a sour attitude—from the new members of the Court. If benefits were to be raised, the efforts would have to come from elsewhere than the nation's highest court.

What the future will bring in this relatively new area of Supreme Court policy is unclear. Many issues "working their way up" are yet to be presented to the Court. In spite of the feeling by some poverty lawyers that they should rely less on litigation if the result is to be "bad law," the Court will continue to receive many cases. Whether the Court will take the cases proferred to it is unclear. Because the Court retains virtually unlimited discretion to accept or reject cases, it is likely to avoid or delay deciding some important issues, particularly given its present complexion. Where cases are accepted, the majority's attitude toward the poor is not likely to be extremely charitable, and welfare recipients and others living in poverty certainly cannot count on consistent victories; those they achieve are not likely to be considerable magnitude. However, because the new members of the Court do not always vote together or always control the Court's policy output, the picture in the welfare/poverty area is likely to remain not wholly illiberal and somewhat uncertain.

Notes

1. Steward Machine v. Davis, 301 U.S. 548, and Helvering v. Davis, 301 U.S. 619 (1937).

2. King v. Smith, 392 U.S. 309 (1968); Lewis v. Martin, 397 U.S. 552 (1970).

3. Carleson v. Remillard, 406 U.S. 598 (1972).

4. California Department of Human Resources v. Java, 402 U.S. 121 (1971).

5. Dillard v. Industrial Commission of Virginia, 416 U.S. 783 (1974).

6. Burns v. Alcala, 43 L.W. 4374 (1975).

7. Shea v. Vialpando, 416 U.S. 251 (1974).

8. New York State Department of Social Services v. Dublino, 413 U.S. 405 (1973).

9. 394 U.S. 618 (1969).

10. Graham v. Richardson, 403 U.S. 365 (1971).

11. Memorial Hospital v. Maricopa County, 415 U.S. 250 (1974). Later in the year, however, the Court upheld a one-year residence requirement for obtaining divorces. Sosna v. Iowa, 42 L. Ed. 2d 532 (1975).

12. Goldberg v. Kelly, 397 U.S. 254; Wheeler v. Montgomery 397 U.S. 280 (1970).

13. Richardson v. Perales, 402 U.S. 389 (1971).

14. See Rosado v. Wyman, 397 U.S. 397 at 431 (1971) (Justice Black).

15. Wyman v. James, 400 U.S. 309 (1971).

16. See v. City of Seattle, 387 U.S. 541 (1967); Camara v. Municipal Court of San Francisco, 387 U.S. 523 (1967).

17. Richardson v. Wright, 405 U.S. 208 (1972).

18. Carter v. Stanton, 405 U.S. 669 (1972).

19. Boddie v. Connecticut, 401 U.S. 371 (1971).

20. U.S. v. Kras, 409 U.S. 434 (1973).

21. Ortwein v. Schwab, 401 U.S. 656 (1973).

22. Edelman v. Jordan, 451 U.S. 651 (1974).

23. Richardson v. Belcher, 404 U.S. 78 (1971).

24. Rosado v. Wyman, note 14, above.

25. Dandridge v. Williams, 397 U.S. 471 at 479-480 (1970).

26. Jefferson v. Hackney, 406 U.S. 535 (1972).

27. D. Carolyn Busch and Lee Edward Hartman, Jr., "Jefferson v. Hackney: Charting the Direction of the Nixon Court," *Public Welfare*, Vol. XXXI (Spring, 1973), p. 63.

28. U.S. Department of Agriculture v. Murray, 413 U.S. 508, and U.S. Department of Agriculture v. Moreno, 413 U.S. 528 (1973).

29. See Charles Reich, "The New Property," *Yale Law Journal*, Vol. LXXIII (April, 1964), pp. 738-878.

30. Samuel Krislov, "American Welfare Policy and the Supreme Court," *Current History*, Vol. 65 (July, 1973), p. 42.

31. 400 U.S. at 319.

32. Robinson v. California, 370 U.S. 660 (1962).

33. Wisconsin v. Constantineau, 400 U.S. 433 (1971).

214

34. Powell v. Texas, 392 U.S. 514 (1968).

35. Levy v. Louisiana, 391 U.S. 68; Glona v. American Guarantee and Liability Co., 391 U.S. 73 (1968).

36. Labine v. Vincent, 401 U.S. 532 (1970).

37. Weber v. Aetna Casualty & Surety Co., 406 U.S. 164 (1972).

38. Gomez v. Perez, 409 U.S. 535 (1973); New Jersey Welfare Rights Organization v. Cahill, 411 U.S. 619 (1973).

39. Jimenez v. Weinberger, 417 U.S. 628 (1974).

40. Meyers v. Juras, 404 U.S. 803 (1971); Carleson v. Taylor, 404 U.S. 980 (1971).

41. Linda R.S. v. Richard D., 411 U.S. 614 (1973).

42. Stanley v. Illinois, 405 U.S. 645 (1972); Weinberger v. Weisenfeld, 95 S. Ct. 1225 (1975).

43. Griswold v. Connecticut, 381 U.S. 479 (1965); Eisenstadt v. Baird, 405 U.S. 438 (1972).

44. Roe v. Wade, 410 U.S. 113 and Doe v. Bolton, 410 U.S. 179 (1973).

45. Lindsey v. Normet, 405 U.S. 56 (1972).

46. Sniadach v. Family Finance Corp., 395 U.S. 337 (1969). This ruling was reinforced in 1975 in North Georgia Finishing v. Di-Chem, 95 S. Ct. 719 (1975).

47. Bell v. Burson, 402 U.S. 535 (1971).

48. Swarb v. Lenox, 405 U.S. 191 (1972).

49. Fuentes v. Shevin, 407 U.S. 67 (1972).

50. Mitchell v. W.T. Grant Co., 416 U.S. 600 (1974).

51. Jackson v. Metropolitan Edison, 42 L. Ed. 2d 477 (1974).

16 How to Provide Legal Counsel for the Poor: Decision Theory

Stuart S. Nagel

Probably the most controversial issue in poverty law is that of how to provide legal counsel for the poor. The main purpose of this chapter is to apply a simple decision theory approach toward throwing some light on that issue.[1] The model goes out of its way to be simple in order to have wider applicability to other legal controversies than it would have if it required more sophisticated measurement of the relations between legal policy alternatives and policy goals.

Decision theory basically involves five steps: First, decide what goals or criteria one wishes to achieve. Second, decide what alternatives are available for different types of situations. Third, decide how the alternatives relate to the goals. Fourth, if it is not obvious which alternative bears the closest relation to the goals, one may have to weight the goals. Fifth, in light of the relations between the alternatives and the weighted goals, choose the best alternative for each situation, assuming only one alternative can be chosen.[a]

Listing Goals and Alternatives

Goals

Table 16-1 in a simplified form illustrates the application of these five steps to deciding how to provide legal counsel to the poor. Column one of the table lists four basic goals or criteria in random order on which agreement might be obtained among relevant policy makers. The first criterion is that if all other things are held constant (which is an "if" assumption that applies to all the criteria), then the best alternative is the one that is the least

---

[a] Where more than one alternative can be chosen, choose the top two or three or more until one's resources are exhausted. Where portions of an alternative can be chosen, the optimum mix may be capable of being determined by a form of linear programming. For further detail on elementary decision theory and linear programming, see G. Black, *The Application of Systems Analysis to Government Operations* (New York: Praeger, 1968); D. Miller and M. Starr, *Executive Decisions and Operations Research* (Englewood Cliffs, N.J.: Prentice-Hall, 1960), 1-102; and S. Nagel, "Choosing among Alternative Public Policies," Dolbeare (ed.), *Public Policy Evaluation* (Beverly Hills: Sage Publications, 1975).

Table 16-1
Goals, Alternatives, Relations, Weights, and Choices in Providing Legal Counsel for the Poor

		Alternatives					
		Civil			Criminal		
Goals	Weights	Volunteer	LSP	Judicare	Volunteer	Assigned	PD
1. Inexpensive	Less	+	–	–	+	+	–
2. Visible and accessible	More	–	+	–	+	+	+
3. Politically feasible	Less	+	–	+	+	–	+
4. Specialized competence and aggressive representation	More	–	+	–	–	–	+
Unweighted Summation of Pluses		2	2	1	3	2	3
Weighted Summation of Pluses		2–	2+	1–	3–	2–	3+

+ = Yes relative to the other alternatives.
– = No relative to the other alternatives.

expensive. Second, the best program is the one that is the most visible (e.g., storefront neighborhood office) and therefore accessible to the poor without being unprofessionally garish (e.g., no neon signs) in its visibility.

Third, the best program should be politically feasible, meaning that it should be capable of being adopted by the relevant legislative or other policy-making body. This partly means that the program should be inexpensive, but it also means that regardless of expense the program should only minimally antagonize powerful political forces. Fourth, the program should provide attorneys who are competent in poverty law matters and aggressive in representing their clients' immmediate class interests. Other goals could be added or these goals could be varied, but the decision methodology remains the same.

Alternatives

Table 16-1 indicates that the available alternatives differ depending on whether one is dealing with civil cases or criminal cases. The relations between the same alternatives and the goal-criteria may also be different between civil and criminal cases. For civil cases the main alternatives are (1) a list of volunteer attorneys maintained by the local bar association; (2) a salaried government lawyer as in an Office of Economic Opportunity (OEO) legal services program; or (3) a judicare system whereby indigent clients go to whatever attorney is willing to take their case, and the government then pays his fee. Assigned counsel is not legally possible in civil cases unless a court or legislature declares a constitutional or statutory right to counsel in civil cases that would authorize local judges to assign counsel.

For criminal cases the main alternatives are (1) a list of volunteer attorneys generally only nominally paid although more likely to be paid something than in civil cases; (2) assigned counsel generally on a rotation basis from a list of practicing attorneys in the county; or (3) a public defender who is analogous to the salaried government lawyer in civil cases. The judicare system for criminal cases is not politically feasible because local governments can satisfy their obligation to provide counsel to the poor so much more cheaply through volunteer or assigned counsel or through the mass production methods of the public defender. Other alternatives (or combinations of or variations on these alternatives) could be added without affecting the basic methodology.

In light of the above goals and alternatives, the problem for civil cases is basically: which is the best system among volunteer, salaried, or reimbursed legal counsel. For criminal cases: which is the best system among volunteer, assigned, or salaried legal counsel? Table 16-1 attempts to resolve this dual problem through the five-step methodology of elementary decision theory as previously described.

Relations Between Alternatives and Goals

Civil Cases

Proceeding down Column 3, one can say that volunteer counsel is inexpensive relative to the government salaried and judicare alternatives. For simplicity we insert a "+" on the first row of Column 2. If we were seeking a more sophisticated but possible unattainable analysis, we might try to express the relation in regression line slopes, or in degrees ranging from a +1.00 down to a −1.00, or in five categories corresponding to ++, +, 0, −, and −−. Volunteer counsel received a "−" on visibility compared to the fulltime storefront OEO government lawyer. Volunteer counsel, however, is politically feasible given the fact that it normally lacks wave-making activity and thus does not antagonize established interests. Its political feasibility is also higher in communities that have not had an OEO legal services program that volunteer counsel would replace, thereby possibly arousing opposition from the poor. Unfortunately, volunteer counsel tends to result in inexperienced lawyers, especially with regard to important appellate court work.

Proceeding down Column 4, one can say that a salaried government lawyer like those provided in the OEO legal services program is not as inexpensive as volunteer counsel (goal 1). The government lawyer is more visible (goal 2), but less politically feasible (goal 3). By being full time in poverty law work he is more likely to develop a specialized expertise and an empathy with the broader sociolegal problems of his clients (goal 4).

The judicare system is the most expensive of the three alternatives. It is not as visible as the Neighborhood Legal Services program especially if it is not aggressively publicized. It is, however, more politically feasible since it can obtain political support from many lawyers who will benefit financially from it without antagonizing economic interests that may feel threatened by an aggressive legal services program. The judicare system, though, does not result in specialized poverty lawyers pursuing the legal interests of the poor on a full-time basis.

Criminal Cases

Proceeding over to the criminal alternatives, volunteer counsel is relatively inexpensive for criminal cases as it is for civil cases although volunteer defense lawyers may receive some nominal payment, or full payment of out-of-pocket expenses, or even substantial payment as in the federal court system. Volunteer defense counsel is reasonably visible in the sense that arraigning magistrates are expected to inform indigent defendants of the availability of counsel as part of their right to counsel. Volunteer counsel is politically feasible given its lack of imposition on lawyers, inexpensiveness, and lack of trouble making. However, lack of experience on the part of attorneys who volunteer for criminal work to gain experience may be more harmful to criminal case clients that to civil clients since more is at stake and difficult trial work may be involved.

Assigned counsel in criminal cases is generally about as unpaid and as inexpensive as volunteer counsel. Assigned counsel also has about as much visibility in being called to the attention of indigent defendants by arraigning magistrates. It is, however, not so politically feasible mainly because lawyers generally do not like the idea of having to spend time representing nonpaying clients against the lawyers will. Even many conservative lawyers might therefore welcome having a salaried government lawyer available to relieve them of this unwelcome burden. Assigned counsel, like volunteer counsel, also tends to result in the appointment of attorneys who may not be experienced attorneys in other fields. Even experienced assigned counsel may lack enthusiasm given his other pressing law firm interests.

The public defender system is the most expensive of the three alternatives especially if it is adequately financed to handle aggressively its full caseload. Like volunteer and assigned counsel, it is about as visible and accessible as the arraigning magistrate makes it. A full-time public defender could, however, be made more accessible if indigent persons were allowed to consult with him before he is appointed to represent them, as is done in OEO civil programs. Such consulting and community education services could provide indigent persons with preventive advice that might keep them from getting into trouble. The public defender system is politically feasible for large communities that have enough indigent felony and misdemeanor cases to merit a full-time public defender. It may also be politically feasible for smaller communities if they would combine their caseloads to merit hiring a regional public defender. As a full-time criminal lawyer, the public defender is capable of developing a high level of expertise. Thus, he should score well on the criteria of specialized competence provided that his office is properly staffed and funded so that his expertise and potential aggressiveness will not be so diluted among so many cases.

Weighting and Choosing

Weighting

If for each alternative we add up the number of pluses on the goal criteria, then volunteer counsel for civil cases is tied with salaried LSP lawyer at about two points apiece. Likewise, volunteer counsel for criminal cases is tied with public defender at about three points apiece. To break these ties and also to make the whole scheme more meaningful it is necessary to weight the goals relative to each other.

Those associated with legal aid and defender work would probably weight the goals numbered two (visibility and accessibility) and four (specialized competence and aggressive representation) higher than the goals numbered one (inexpensiveness) and three (political feasibility). Others with a more conservative orientation might weight goals one and three more highly although they might recognize that effective representation for the poor is important for obtaining the respect of the poor for law and order.

Choosing

If goals two and four are given more weight, then the salaried legal services lawyer comes out ahead of volunteer counsel as a civil case alternative since the salaried government lawyer is plus on two and four and volunteer counsel is minus on two and four. Likewise, the salaried public defender lawyer comes out ahead of volunteer counsel in criminal cases since the public defender had at least the potentiality for being more visible and more aggressively competent than volunteer counsel.[b]

This analysis does not resolve the problem of what is the best way to provide legal counsel for the poor because others may not fully agree with this writer's listing of goals, alternatives, relations, and weights. The same method of analysis, however, can be applied by others using their own lists. In doing so, perhaps further insights will be generated on this important problem, and less emotion than has been the case in the past. It is especially hoped that this method of analysis and more sophisticated versions of it will be applied to other controversial legal policy problems that involve choosing or ranking conflicting policy alternatives.

The advantage of such a system of analysis is that it generally forces one to clarify and offer reasons for the goals, alternatives, relations, and weights involved in policy problems. Such clarifying and justifying can

---

[b] As an alternative to the system shown in Table 16-1 of using pluses and minuses to express the relations between each alternative and each goal, one could use 1's and 0's or more precise numbers like regression slopes if the data for generating them are available. As an alternative to the system of using "more" and "less" to express the weight of each goal, one could also use 1's and 0's or more precise numbers. With numbers for the relations and numbers for the weights, one could then calculate a summation score for each alternative equal to the sum of r times W for each goal, where r is the numerical relation between each alternative and each goal and W is the weight of the goal. Whichever policy alternative then has the highest summation score is the one logically to be preferred.

provide one with a much better understanding of policy problems, as well as provide more effective solutions. The key difficulties are determining and at least roughly measuring those four components, but the theoretical and practical results may be well worth the extra effort over a more intuitive muddling approach to policy problems.

Notes

1. For further detail on the issue of how to provide legal counsel for the poor in civil cases, see E. Jarmel, *Legal Representation of the Poor* (New York: Mathew Bender, 1972) part 1; H. Semmel, *Social Justice Through Law* 1-82 (Mineola, N.Y.: Foundation Press, 1970); and R. Levy et al., *Cases on Social Welfare and the Individual* 1423-1519 (Mineola, N.Y.: Foundation Press, 1971). In criminal cases see L. Silverstein, *Defense of the Poor: The National Report* (Boston: Little, Brown and Co., 1965); D. Oaks and W. Lehman, *Criminal Justice System and the Indigent* (Chicago: University of Chicago Press, 1968); and S. Nagel, "Effects of Alternative Types of Counsel on Criminal Procedure Treatment," 48 *Indiana Law Journal* (1973).

**Part V
Alternative Proposals**

17 Self-management: The Core of an Effective Program to Eliminate Poverty

Stephen M. Sachs

It is urgently necessary to develop an effective set of antipoverty programs in the United States that really will eliminate poverty. Efforts to do so to date have produced only isolated successes and have failed to make sufficient reductions in the level of poverty.[1]

There are many reasons why past programs have been ineffective including underfunding, inadequate and inaccurate planning, insufficient coordination, and inefficient administration.[2] Any new programs must deal with the full range of related problems, but it will not be enough simply to make present efforts more efficient. The basic emphasis of actual current policy is misdirected. In essence, programs to date have concentrated in practice upon providing services and limited subsidies that make poverty more bearable. What is needed is a program that will break the poverty cycle by dealing with the full range of fundamental problems that are economic, social, and psychological, as well as technical and administrative.

Providing Income: Two Approaches to the Basic Problem

The basic economic problem is to provide sufficient income to those who do not have it. This can be achieved by either of two methods—income maintenance or economic development utilizing an employment program supported by appropriate training and necessary services. Income maintenance in any form is expensive both initially and for the indefinite future, where employment programs, if properly set up, are only expensive to establish and soon pay their own way, contributing positively to the economy while providing employees with income in the form of wages. In contrast to schemes for income maintenance payments that continue economic and psychological dependency, appropriate employment systems provide economic and psychological independence. Partly for this reason an effective employment program would be far more politically acceptable for most Americans, including those who would be participants. If stated in proper terms, conservatives and liberals alike would give support to a work

"Self-Management: The Core of an Effective Program to Eliminate Poverty in the United States" is a shortened and updated version of the origional proposal presented in a paper given at the First National Conference on Workers' Self-Management, Boston, 1974.

225

program of "equal opportunity development" or "democratic capitalism," while many of those same people would oppose a continuation of "welfare handouts" or "the dole." Moreover, an antipoverty employment scheme could be expanded and coordinated to help alleviate the cronic unemployment in America, which runs at least 4 percent and is usually in excess of 6 percent. It is particularly important to reduce unemployment rates among young people in poor areas where unemployment rates run especially high. If satisfying, well-paying work can be provided for these young people, that in itself will do a great deal to break the poverty cycle.

This is not to say that an innovative employment program can, by itself, reach everyone who is in poverty. A supplementary income maintenance or insurance plan would have to be continued on a limited basis for those who are too old, sick, or otherwise handicapped to be employed, or who have been rebuffed in their attempts to get out of poverty for so long that it is too late for them to readjust. But with proper planning, training, and services the number of those nonemployable could be greatly reduced. Most old or handicapped people would prefer to work and would be psychologically and physically better off working, at least on a part-time basis, if appropriate jobs were available. Services such as day care centers, transportation, and housing would allow many to work who would not otherwise be able to do so. Proper prejob and on-the-job training and supervision would, in time, overcome many of the psychological and social problems that are sometimes limitations upon employability. The point is that while it is not the sole fruitful line of reform, an innovative employment program should be the core of a new antipoverty effort.

Psychological and Social Problems

The psychological and social spheres are extremely important aspects of the problem of overcoming poverty. Many of the poor are sufficiently alienated so that standard American employment schemes are often ineffective. For example, in an on-the-job training employment program for the poor in Indianapolis, over 80 percent of those hired lost their jobs within a short period of time.[3] No employment plan for overcoming poverty can succeed unless it overcomes the problem of alienation.[4] This is in part a matter of convincing the participants that the program will work and will be worthwhile. Participants must be shown clearly that the program will not be another failure bringing negative personal experiences. Mistrust of antipoverty programs is now very great among poor people as exemplified in the Indianapolis Model Cities Board elections of three years ago in which voter turnout was so low that there were a number of zero to zero ties, indicating that not even the candidates took the program seriously.[5] Therefore, to be successful, such a program must deal effectively with cultural manifestations of poverty including attitudes of hostility and mistrust toward established programs, institutions, and personnel.[6]

In order to overcome alienation, an antipoverty employment program must maximize the ability of the participants to identify with the program so that they will feel that it is their own project in which they are willing to make the commitment necessary for its success. This requires strong positive psychological and economic incentives and reenforcement and minimal generation of anxiety and insecurity. Those requirements can best be met in a program utilizing employee participation in profits and management that is preferable for a number of reasons including the following.

Self-management Plan

There is now ample evidence that employee participation in management and profits, if properly established and operated, does increase employee morale and identification with an organization, making work more satisfying, in part through giving workers a feeling that they, and what they do, matters to the enterprise, and that they have some control over the workplace in which they spend a considerable portion of their waking hours.[7] To the extent that employee moral and commitment is raised, there is an increase in the quality and quantity of work. When this is added to the increased information and feedback made available from discussion in decision making it leads to a significant increase in economic efficiency where participation of the work force is well coordinated.[8] Moreover, participation in decision making is an excellent teaching device,[9] especially when combined with job enrichment and enlargement,[10] for it increases employee understanding of the enterprise and leads to more knowledgeable, flexible, and adaptable employees, better able to meet changing needs in the enterprise, who are also qualified for a broader range of jobs should they seek employment elsewhere.

Since participation tends to be more effective in relatively small face-to-face units in which everyone knows, and can talk with, everyone else,[11] it is proposed that the program consist of a large number of small enterprises, each of which would in general employ no more than two or three hundred workers. Keeping the number of employees in each unit small will tend to maximize the ability of each employee to have his say while achieving high levels of identification with the enterprise, solidarity with the group, ease of communication, and knowledge of the operation. Where larger enterprises are desirable for economic or technological reasons, they should, so far as possible, be broken down into basic, self-governing units according to the logic of the division of labor. Each unit of the enterprise would elect representatives to the central board of directors of the enterprise as a whole.

Enterprises should only be established after careful economic investigation and planning, as would be done by any prudent investor considering a new venture. The choice of location and type of business should be made according to what will be economically viable and have a high chance of becoming self-sufficient, and what will best meet the needs of the intended participants and of the community or area where they will be located. Funding for such projects could come from any source including private foundations. However, only the federal government has enough resources to fund an effective program for the entire country.

Where there are a number of enterprises in the same area, they should be linked together with an umbrella organization directed by a board of directors, the majority of whose members would be elected by each of the member enterprises. Other members of the board would represent the community and the agency administering the program. The board would have a voice in and, where appropriate, control of, such matters as cooperation among the organizations in the program, general recruiting and development plans in the area, coordination and development of supporting services in the area. Such services as housing, day care centers, transportation, and medical facilities would be established as needed. They could be parts of individual enterprises or placed under the direction of the area board. In general, however, they would probably best be organized as additional enterprises contracting with individuals, enterprises, or the area board as appropriate. This would better fit them into the program as a whole and allow them to be of benefit to the community in general.

Each enterprise would be supported by on-the-job and by prejob training. This would require that initially supervisory staff and technical and professional personnel would be previously experienced at their jobs and would be hired primarily on the basis of their competence and potential to act as instructors in a self-management situation. It is extremely important that the participants learn to participate effectively and actively in decision making as well as acquire job competence. Therefore, prior training of the supervisory and instructional staff would be necessary including background in employee self-management and how to develop it. Emphasis would be placed upon the utilization of leadership styles that encourage participation. This has generally been proven to be a crucial factor in developing effective self-management[12] and would be even more critical in a situation in which many of the employees would be highly alienated at the commencement of the project.

Orientation of supervisory and instructional staff would also include acquainting them with the cultural, social, and psychological factors and problems that would create difficulties for many of the employees in adjusting to the project and in relating to the staff and to each other. Lack of such training of supervisors was estimated to be one of the primary reasons for the high rate of early termination of employment in the Indianapolis program.[13] In most instances employees were fired or resigned who might have succeeded had they been encouraged and otherwise assisted by empathizing foremen who understood their problems in adjusting to the job situation. Unfortunately, participants in the program were merely hired and placed on the job under foremen who were given no background about the people they were dealing with. Many of the supervisors quickly became annoyed with employees who were late or who worked poorly or learned slowly, thereby producing hostility, and/or insecurity that only perpetuated alienation and increased problems that in many cases could have been decreased and eventually overcome. The situation was especially difficult in instances in which there were cultural differences relating to diversity in ethnic background between foremen and employees in the program, especially where black employees were supervised by Appalachian whites who had recently advanced to the position of foremen.[14]

The entire project should be organized in terms of development toward self-sufficiency and independence: economically, managerially, socially, and psychologically. In the beginning the employees and the project would be heavily dependent upon the supervisory, technical, and instructional staff for information, training, administrative leadership, and supportive encouragement. As the employees adapted to the program, acquiring technical skills, knowledge of the operation and of the enterprise, and competency in participation in decision making and management, they would be given greater responsibility and voice in management. Similarly, at the beginning the enterprise would be economically dependent upon the funding agency, but as employees gained competence, the firm's income and efficiency would increase and it would soon become economically independent. As employees gained the necessary competence, they would begin to be promoted, replacing the original supervisory and technical personnel so far as practical[a] for efficient operation of the plant and continued educational competence of the project as a whole including quality training of new employees.

The project would be perpetuated to assist additional people as new positions opened up in the normal course of advancement and replacement of the original staff. Additional openings would become available as employees, having gained competence and experience to the point where they became able to enter the job market on favorable terms, decided to move out.

---

[a]Training and technical staff members released from one project would then be available to work on other, new projects, or could reenter the regular job market.

Although no competent and cooperative employees ought to be forced to leave the organization, the enterprise in cooperation with the area organization should make available and encourage continuing education that would make participants flexible in their ability to advance in the job market with the capability to adapt to changing needs of a dynamic economy. Such educational programs, which could be academic and avocational, as well as vocational, would be valuable to the personal satisfaction and self-management of the employees, and would thereby increase their identification with and support of the program. Moreover, continuing education would improve the efficiency of the enterprise and success of the project in three ways. First, it would increase employee knowledge of the operation of the enterprise and its environment, and improve their analytic and decision-making ability. Second, the flexibility of the workforce to adapt to changing production and work needs would be increased. Third, as employees became able to do a variety of jobs, their work could be made more interesting and hence more satisfying through job enrichment, enlargement, or rotation. This would be particularly beneficial for those doing dull or tedious work as it would limit the amount of time an employee would have to spend on the same boring or annoying task.[15]

Structure of Incentives

One of the most important educational factors in the program would be the system of economic incentives and reinforcements. In order to be effective, economic incentives need to be sufficiently great and must be received sufficiently often to be meaningful for the employee in his daily work. They should be structured in a way that will foster three basic goals necessary to the well-being and development of the employees and the success of the project. First, the system of pay should provide some feeling of secuirty. This can be accomplished through providing minimum salaries for all jobs that would be guaranteed except in cases involving disciplinary action. Minimums might be scaled to increase with seniority or other factors, but should always be high enough when taken together with the value of fringe benefits, including supportive services, to insure at least a minimally acceptable living standard for every employee, and total projected salaries should be sufficiently high to promote successful participation in management.[16] At the same time minimum salaries ought not to be so high that they interfere with the other incentives.

Second, the economic rewards ought to stimulate individual initiative and productiveness in terms of both quantity and quality. This can be achieved by paying workers for piecework or its equivalent whereever it is calculable, with adequate controls maintained to insure quality work and honest recording. This kind of incentive will be most effective if it is calculated regularly so as to give workers immediate feedback in their next paycheck. Such payments for individual work must be high enough to be effective stimulants but ought not to be so high as to encourage divisiveness, anti-institution attitudes, or cheating.

Third, economic returns should encourage solidarity, cooperation, and identification with the enterprise and the work unit. This can be achieved by profit sharing by employees on both the enterprise and work group levels. All workers should receive a share of the total profits and a share of the total enterprise profits should be divided among the personnel of each unit according to that unit's contribution to the whole operation. This could be calculated according to a unit's success in such activities as producing, selling, and saving money in relation to the plan, discounting factors that were not the result of a unit's doing.

To be effective, all such profit sharing payments need to be made often enough to connect work efficiency and bonuses in employees' minds. Payments should be made and calculated monthly if possible and must be made at least quarterly. Similarly, such payments need to be large enough to have the desired impact. If profits after other wages would be too low to provide meaningful bonuses, basic guarantees and/or piecework payments could be lowered to allow for larger bonuses.

In distributing profits, a number of factors must be taken into account. First, at least until workers learn about long-run planning problems and have faith in the long-run ability of the enterprise to benefit them, they are likely to ask that too large a proportion of the profits be paid out in bonuses leaving insufficient funds for future investment, improvement, expansion, and upkeep and replacement of equipment. To some extent this problem can be minimized by incorporating funds for improvement, replacement, and similar needs in planning the regular budget. Where this is insufficient, it is suggested that a levy be placed upon profits that are distributed as bonuses on a progressive scale as the percentage of bonuses to cost increases, with such levies being paid into special accounts, perhaps as contributions to the area board for its reserve, investment, and operating funds.

Second, care will have to be taken in structuring the organization and its decision making in harmony with the economic incentive system so as to establish a fair system for resolving and balancing interests. Incentives should not create conflict of interest situations for any employees, and the structure and range of incentives should be such that is it not a source of divisiveness.

Third, foresight is necessary in establishing and adjusting the wage, incentive, and profit making system to achieve and maintain a proper balance among security, individual incentive, unit solidarity, and identification with the enterprise and its workforce as a whole.

Fourth, economic incentives themselves should be only one of several motivational factors and should be balanced with moral, psychological, and social incentives developed from the beginning through leadership styles, orientation and instruction, supervision and counselling, and in the course of employee participation in management.

Finally, the wage structure raises important questions about funding. At its inception an enterprise will have to receive its capital funding and operational expenses from the area board or from the agency. As the enterprise becomes productive, its dependence upon outside funding will diminish until the operation is self-sufficient. But what happens if an enterprise is unable to meet its expenses including minimum salaries? To meet such contingencies, each enterprise and the area board should have reserve funds available that are included in its regular budgeting. In some instances loans might be provided if reserve funds were insufficient, but the area board, and beyond that the agency, would reserve the right to review the operation of any enterprise that became insolvent or was not properly self-managed. Such review should begin with an outside investigation in consultation with the enterprise's self management bodies. If such advice, perhaps supported by financial aid, did not adequately improve the operation of the enterprise, the reviewers could reorganize it, temporarily reducing or suspending self-management, as necessary, until the enterprise regained secure, self-sufficient operation. In extreme cases an enterprise could be closed down, but in such cases, the area board would have a responsibility to help relocate the employees.

Similarly, the agency, often acting through the area board, would have the responsibility for reviewing the operation of all enterprises in the program to insure that their activities were legal and proper. This would provide an outside channel for reviewing complaints of violation of rights of employees, particularly with regard to participation in management, that could not be settled satisfactorily by the enterprise's own adjudicative machinery.

Organization of Self-Management

Management of each enterprise should be based upon the basic and instrumental goals of the project. The fundamental aim of the program is to make possible personally satisfying economic, psychological, and social independence for the participants. This requires educational development in an economically efficient and profitable enterprise, with good working conditions and supportive services and activities, that promotes self-development and group cooperation. Employee management is particularly appropriate for these purposes since it is an effective means for achieving all of these ends if properly organized and operated. But, while these goals can all be met through self-management, the goals themselves are only compatable within certain limits. Beyond that point the goals conflict and must be balanced dynamically according to the needs of a changing situation. For example, to a large extent employee morale enhances economic efficiency, and economic efficiency, through profit sharing increases morale. Beyond a certain point, however, employees prefer less income to more work and other personal costs of economic efficiency. Maximum achievable economic efficiency will not be maximum job satisfaction and vice versa. On the one hand the results of self-management will be in large part determined by the way in which these goals are structured and balanced within it. On the other hand, industrial democracy can provide an excellent means for balancing those goals equitably in practice since it requires each participant to make his own priorities concerning his interests and then provides a forum for all concerned to discuss their views and achieve a reasonably equitable compromise. The fact that in many instances each individual is himself partly on each side of the issue, at least in principle, if not in the case at hand, seems to promote balanced judgments in most instances because most of the parties are concerned about resolution of issues rather than overwhelming the opposition.[17]

While self-management can be an excellent means for running an organization, it is not an end in itself. Like any other technique it can be misused or overdone, and it involves costs and risks. Holding meetings takes time that could otherwise be used for production or leisure; discussion of issues with all concerned delays decision making, therefore, self-management decisions require more lead time than do the dictates of a single administrator; discussions of issues also takes energy and may be frustrating if one appears to make no impact; if too much time is spent debating minor points, participants may be bored and alienated; and so on. All things considered, employee-management will produce more benefits than costs if properly utilized. The problem is how to organize it.

To begin with self-management itself involves the interaction of two opposed principles: independence and interdependence. It involves an individual's ability to control his own work situation, which means on the one hand to do his own job without interference and on the other hand to have a say about everyone else's work since it affects him. Delegation must be balanced with joint decision making. This is a complex problem involving such issues as the type of work and technology involved, the culture, psychology, and capability of the worker, the importance of coordinating the particular task or set of tasks with the work of others, and the value of independence in execution to the individual in the particular cases. Every instance is different but a rule of thumb can be stated. In general, important decisions, particularly involving policy, should be decided jointly by all those concerned and tasks that require coordination should be jointly organized by those involved, but tasks that can be carried out independently and minor instrumental decisions should be delegated. Since a primary goal of the project is to develop independence, delegation should be developed as far as is consistent with all the relevant factors in each instance, and this in turn will tend to increase the quality of joint decision making since independent participants have more to bring to joint decision making than dependent participants.

This leads directly to the second major point about self-management. Delegation does not deny review and joint decision making does not pre-empt supervision. In fact, a study of a number of similarly organized self-managed factories shows that economic efficiency was highest in those concerns in which there was both the highest level of actual employee participation in decision making and the greatest quantity of, and the greatest variety of, supervision.[18] While legislation should be joint, execution usually requires direction. Policy ought to be made jointly but the carrying out of that policy should be directed and overseen by supervisors responsible to those they are supervising and to whom they can feed back their observations and judgments.

Third, self-management involving either delegation or joint decision is applicable at every level of the enterprise from the individual task in the basic work group or unit through any intermediate organizational levels to the general management of the enterprise since all levels of the work process are relevant to the job of the individual employee. Beginning at the lowest level, each unit should be delegated maximum authority to govern its own affairs, but those issues that effect others directly outside the unit should be decided jointly at the next level up to the top of the organization. In enterprises of 200 to 300 persons this usually means two levels of organization for decision making. Each identifiable basic unit of work should have a unit council that would be a meeting of all the members of the unit if it is small enough, and of elected representatives if it is large. In addition, each unit would elect representatives to the board of directors of the enterprise. A president and other officers would be elected for each unit council by its entire membership, and the president and other officers of the board of directors should be elected by the entire membership of the enterprise. To keep the councils and the board representative, officers and representatives should serve relatively short terms of one, or at most, two years and should be subject to recall.

Parallel to the legislative structure should be an administrative staff headed by a general manager and including a manager for each unit. The general manager and unit managers would be ex-officio members of the board of directors and appropriate unit councils and would be ineligible to be elected officers of those bodies. Administrative staff meetings would be held by directors as necessary to coordinate administration, review operations, and prepare proposals for the councils and the board of directors. Similarly, nonadministrative personnel would have union organization and meetings to review procedures, discuss issues, and represent employees whose interests or grievances were not being met adequately by the self-managing bodies.[19]

Developing Self-Management

Since the project is an educational one, self-management would have to be developed over time. At the inception of an enterprise, the first set of managers would be appointed for a term of several years by the area council or by the agency. Thereafter, the managers would be elected by the employees, who would also have power to fire, but the first election of a general manager would have to be approved by the area board who perhaps would have at least a formal advisory voice in the selection of the general manager, thereafter.

At first, the managers with the area board or agency assistance, would hire the other staff, but later this would be done by an elected hiring committee. When the initial group of employees was assembled and, having finished prejob training, was ready to commence work supported by on-the-job training, a series of general and unit meetings would be held for orientation to the enterprise and preparation for electing representative bodies and officers after a short period. At first, the representative bodies would be advisory, but beginning at the earliest possible date they would be given authority in area after area as they gained competence and experience until all legislative authority was in the hands of the unit councils and board of directors with all important decisions subject to approval by the personnel of the entire enterprise. Similarly, committees to handle important matters requiring adjudication such as disciplinary problems, hiring, and promotions would be provided for and adequate safeguards and procedures established, including review procedures.[20]

Over time, then, the formal structure would be developed so that it would allow for total self-management. This is a necessity for the attainment of successful participation but an appropriate formal structure is not sufficient by itself to provide successful employee-management. It is also necessary that modes and styles of leadership and participation also be democratic in actual practice.

Democratic Styles of Participation and Leadership

Participation can only be successful to the extent that it is meaningful to the participants. First of all, they must believe that their participation is both effective and worthwhile. Employees must have real authority to decide important issues with the knowledge that those decisions will be carried out. They must have the belief that managers respect their views if the operation is to be a smooth one. This requires managers to encourage participation and to cooperate fully in collective discussion and decision making. This does not mean that managers should not be leaders, they must be if self-management is to succeed, for the managers, if they are capable, have competence, experience, and knowledge that few if any of the other participants have. Moreover, managers, too, are employees and human beings with personal needs for job satisfaction. They hold jobs that require delegation of authority and require taking initiative. But they should not attempt to monopolize that initiative. When taking leadership and making proposals, they should present alternatives and estimates and not merely espouse completed plans giving others little choice except to rubber stamp a fait accompli.[21]

Managers and technical personnel must also make available all necessary information for meaningful discussion and knowledgeable decision making. This means that, with the exception of properly confidential material, the files and books of the enterprise should be open to employee inspection and that there must be a frequently published employee-edited bulletin containing all relevant information and reports along with discussion of important issues. In addition, open meetings and discussions should be held to provide additional data and background information and to provide opportunity for employees to learn what the issues are really about and just how the plant actually operates. To make participation maximally effective, an education program should be provided so that employees can come to understand not only what the facts are, but what they mean. In addition, managers and others presenting information need to be careful to present it in a form in which it can be easily understood.[22]

In summary, what is needed for the core of an effective antipoverty program is an innovative employment scheme utilizing an educational program of employee managed, profit sharing, small enterprises supported by prejob and on-the-job training and appropriate services and after hour activities. Where feasible, such enterprises would be linked together in a communitywide area association engaged in a program of community development. The result of such a program should be to significantly reduce poverty in the United States while contributing to the general economy, improving and developing the concerned communities, and providing currently dependent and alienated poor people the opportunity to lead satisfying and independent lives.

The Politics of Establishment

If it is agreed that such a program would be an effective means for eliminating poverty in the United States the next question is how to establish it. While it is impossible to analyze this issue fully in a few lines, a number of central points need to be made.

Although it is extremely difficult to establish any adequate antipoverty program in the United States today,[23] a proposal of the type suggested here has a number of political advantages that if properly handled can more than overcome its liabilities. The first advantage is that by emphasizing the program as an economic development investment that would, after a short period, greatly reduce welfare and other government expenses while generating new tax revenue, the program could gain support from many Americans, both liberal and conservative.

Second, such a program could be favorable to organizations representing poor people, most of which favor locally controlled community development programs. In fact, there already exists some related community economic development efforts including some aspects of self-management such as those in the Brownsville area of Brooklyn, New York, and in Eastern Kentucky.[24] The unusually high level of successes of these development programs are strong precedents for the current proposal, especially as there are an increasing number of antipoverty workers in Washington who are becoming interested in developmental approaches to poverty.[25]

Third, if such a program is linked with reducing unemployment in general, it should be possible to gain strong labor backing, particularly if one emphasizes the need for union activity in the newly established enterprises as indicated above.

Fourth, business objections could be minimized by pointing out that the new development of relatively small local businesses will produce more new buying power than competition. Ideological objections can be headed off by indicating that such a program of "democratic capitalism" is merely an extension of such existing public programs as "black capitalism" that have received support from business.

Fifth, where a few years ago the idea of workplace democracy was unthinkable, it is currently gaining popularity in the United States as indicated by the rapid growth of the organization, People for Self-Management, and the utilization of various forms of employee participation in management by a growing number of major firms such as Proctor and Gambel.[26] More and more American companies have become interested in employee participation as a means of overcoming the ill effects of increasing dissatisfaction among workers.

In conclusion, a program along the lines suggested here has great practical potential and is capable of gaining necessary political support.

What is necessary now is to attempt to gain sufficient funding for pilot projects from public and private agencies while building public and professional interest.

Notes

1. Kenneth Clark and Jeanette Hopkins, *A Relevant War Against Poverty* (New York: Harper and Row, 1970); and Joseph Kershaw, *Government Action Against Poverty* (Chicago: Markam, 1970).

2. Ibid.; Alan Batchelder, *The Economics of Poverty* (New York: John Wiley and Sons, 1971); Theodore Marmor, *Poverty Policy* (Chicago: Aldine-Atherton, 1971); and George Shipman, *Designing Program Action Against Urban Poverty* (University: University of Alabama Press, 1971).

3. Interview and discussions with CAAP personnel, February to June, 1970 as part of research concerning poverty problems and programs in the Indianapolis area, 1970-72, hereafter referred to as Indianapolis Poverty Research.

4. Alienation in the sense of Emile Durkheim, *Suicide* (Glencoe: Free Press, 1951) and *The Division of Labor* (Glencoe: Pree Press, 1969).

5. Indianapolis Poverty Research.

6. Oscar Lewis, *The Children of Sanchez* (New York: Vintage Books, 1963), especially the introduction, pp. xxv to xxx.

7. Paul Blumberg, *Industrial Democracy: The Sociology of Participation* (New York: Schocken Books, 1968), particularly Chapters 5 and 6; International Labor Organization, *Co-operation in Industry* (Geneva: I.L.O., 1951), pp. 9-10; Bernard Bass, "Greater Productivity and Satisfaction Through Self Planning," and Boydan Kovcic, "Some Trends in the Development of Self-Management," papers presented at the First International Sociological Conference on Participation and Self-Management, Dubrovnik, 1972; Terence Mitchell, "Motivation and Participation an Integration," in *Participation and Self-Management* (Zagreb: Reports of the First International Sociological Conference on Participation and Self-Management held at Dubrovnik, 1972), Vol. IV, pp. 159-178; Ichak Adizes, Industrial Democracy: Yugoslav Style (New York: Free Press, 1971), Chapter 8.

8. Gerard Kester, "Towards a Participative Malta," in *Participation and Self-Management*, Vol. V, pp. 133-142; Sven E. Kock, Supervision and Effective and Ineffective Hospital Wards," in Ibid., Vol. IV, pp. 191-201; and Janez Jerovsek, "Self-Management in Yugoslav Enterprises," in Ibid., Vol. I, pp. 113-122.

9. Ichak Adizes, "The Role of Management in Democratic

(Communal) Organizational Structures" (Santa Barbara: Paper presented to the Center for Democratic Institutions, 1972), Section 5.

10. Gerald Susman, "Decision Making at the Work Place Under Varying Conditions of Environmental Complexity," *Participation and Self-Management*, Vol. V, pp. 191-202.

11. This was strongly demonstrated in examining self-managed units of varying size during field research into self-managed institutions in Yugoslavia, December, 1972 to November, 1973, hereafter cited as Self-Management Research.

12. Adizes, "The Role of Management in Democratic (Communal) Organizational Structures."

13. Interview with CAAP personnel February to June 1970, Indianapolis Poverty Research.

14. Ibid.

15. Susman, "Decision Making," pp. 191-202.

16. Robert Cox, Kenneth Walker, and L. Greyfie de Bellecombe, "Worker Participation in Management," in *International Institute for Labor Studies Bulletin*, No. 2 (1967), pp. 22-23. In addition, minimum salaries would have to meet the standards of minimum wage laws which are generally so low as not to affect the necessary calculations.

17. Stephen Sachs, "Problems in Building Successful Organizational Democracy" (Chicago: American Political Science Association Meeting, 1974), pp. 4-6; Adizes, *Industrial Democracy*, Chapters 4-7.

18. Janez Jerovsek, "Self-Management System in Yugoslav Enterprises," *Participation and Self-Management*, Vol. 2, pp. 113-122.

19. Concerning the important role of a union in a self-managed enterprise see Sachs, "Problems in Building Successful Organizational Democracy," pp. 27-29.

20. Adizes, *Industrial Democracy*, Chapter 6.

21. Adizes, "The Role of Management in Democratic (Communal) Organizational Structures," Sections 7 and 8.

22. Self-Management Research.

23. Dorothy James, *Poverty, Politics and Change* (Englewood Cliffs, N.J.: Prentice-Hall, 1972), Chapter 7.

24. "Mountain Capitalism and Political Efforts Make Knox County a Rare Anti-Poverty Success," *Louisville Courier Journal* (June 11, 1972), p. A10.

25. Personal communications with people from Federal agencies concerned with poverty attending the First National Conference on Workers' Self-Management, Boston, 1974.

26. Michael Brower, "Relationships Between Organizational Democracy, Productivity and the Quality of Life" (Chicago: American Political Science Association Meeting, 1974); and Blumberg, *Industrial Democracy*, Chapters 5 and 6.

18

National Income and Services Policy in the United States

Marian Lief Palley and Howard A. Palley

Introduction

We have in the United States a long tradition of fragmented, and nonintegrative social welfare services and income policy. These programs have frequently evolved in such a haphazard, unplanned fashion, that many critics suggest rather strongly that the present social welfare system does not effectively service those people in need. What we have is a myriad of uncoordinated national, state, and local income and service programs that assist individuals differentially and inequitably. The availability, as well as the quality, of most income transfer and service programs varies from state to state and even within states.

We also have, in the United States, social conditions that are characterized by extreme disparities between affluence and poverty and economic deprivation. United States Bureau of the Census data indicates that in 1970 the wealthiest fifth of the nation's families received 41.6 percent of all incomes, while the poorest 20 percent of American families received only 5.5 percent of the nation's income (see Table 18-1). The United States Bureau of the Census also reported that in 1973, 23 million people were living in consumer units with incomes that fell below the official poverty level of $4,540 for a family of four in an urban setting. This group represented 11 percent of the total population.

In spite of our nation's aggregate affluence and potential ability to provide for greater economic equity between groups, American public policy makers have not accepted the notion of an economic "floor" authorized by statute and related to the provision of the "physical and social necessities" required for attainment of individual welfare. We believe that a society which has the economic resources to alleviate extreme poverty for 11 percent of its population has the responsibility to do so. The existing income and service programs have not been sufficient to achieve such a goal. A coordinated income and services program with a statutorily authorized economic "floor" would foster the elimination of extreme economic deprivation. Achieving such a goal would require additional federal revenues, and a bureaucracy to develop and administer the program. This, in turn, would necessitate the expansion of tax revenues so as to enable government to provide income transfer payments and social welfare services to those in need.

241

Table 18-1
Family Income Distribution in the United States, 1970

Families Ranked from Lowest to Highest	Percentage Distribution of Income Received
Lowest fifth	5.5
Second fifth	12.0
Third fifth	17.4
Top fifth	41.6
Top five percent	14.4

Source: U.S. Department of Commerce, Bureau of the Census, *Current Population Reports*, Series P-60, No. 80, "Income in 1970 of Families and Persons in the United States," (Washington, D.C.: U.S. Government Printing Office, 1971), p. 28.

The thesis of this chapter is two-fold: First, it is our contention that what is required to cope adequately with the problems of inequitable distribution of goods and services in the United States is an integrated national income and services policy. Second, it is necessary to develop the political will to achieve such a goal in the face of the constraint of the American political system's strong predisposition against planning and lack of budgetary commitment to social programming.

The Constraints of Social Values

American social welfare programs are predicated on the assumption that changes in the life and conditions of the poor can be accomplished without broad scale economic and social change. This belief rests upon the assumption that American society will remain basically unchanged in terms of its economic and social structure. However, the large-scale social and economic problems associated with modern industrial society may require major shifts in public policy.

As technology alters industrial labor needs, some people with skills appropriate for yesterday's market no longer have skills that are needed for today's market. This phenomenom is referred to as technological unemployment. Thus, if there is wholesale adoption of teaching machines in American colleges and universities, many college professors would become technologically unemployed. Similarly rural in-migrants to the large metropolitan areas have difficulty coping with our industrial society. The underlying conditions that have made these people poor are not receiving sufficient attention. For example, the poor people of Appalachia require more than public assistance. The towns and counties in which they live need viable economic bases. Once there is a viable economic base with employment opportunities, then the effects of poverty of the region can be brought under control. Only then will these areas be able to provide the education and training for their children that is necessary for them to be able to compete in the American market economy.

William Ryan in his book *Blaming the Victim* has suggested that Americans "blame the victim" in the sense that the poor are seen as being responsible for their own poverty. This assumption of personal fault fits well with our market economy and market-oriented values. If poor people are seen as causing their own condition, why reorient our system to help them out of their poverty? This belief leads one to assume that people will not change even if we tamper with the system.

In American society, personal income and industrial profit are seen as very positive societal values. On the other hand inputs for public assistance, social services, public housing education, and the like, are often looked upon as costs rather than viewed as investment in economic and social resources that might in the long term strengthen the basic fabric of the American democratic system. This attitude is reinforced by our tendency to "blame the victim." Can policies that often treat poverty as problems of individuals in need of rehabilitation in order to provide a "better fit" into society be adequate to cope with the extreme poverty of 11 percent of the American population?

Any substantial change in the conditions that maintain poverty in the United States would require a reorientation of social and political attitudes. We would have to begin by assuming that poverty is not primarily the fault of the individual poor, but that there were serious systemic causes of poverty. Also, we must learn to value the individual's worth. For example, a child receiving public assistance payments should be given the proper eucation, motivation, and prospects for future success, which will enable him to contribute as an adult to the general welfare of our society. As long as we indicate an individual's worth in this nation with a surrogate cash measure, social programs will not be enacted that would permit this child to develop his individual potential. That is, we have an almost total neglect of social "utilities" of worth that strengthen the fabric of a nation. For instance, in terms of society as a whole, the contribution of the aged within the family and within the community has been undermined by their financial marginality and the limited community resources made available to them.

Given these underlying values and attitudes of many Americans, it is not surprising that we have inherited a series of disparate social welfare programs supported by a rather haphazard system of national grants-in-aid to the states and localities. This condition has been reinforced by the nonplanning predisposition prevalent in American domestic politics. We have had no central plan in American politics, and thus we have reacted to specific problems only as we have been able to raise the necessary consciousness among the policy makers to pressure for programs. At the present time, however, many political leaders seem to be cognizant of the need for more adequate national social welfare policies in order to meet income and services needs.

The Setting

Services

Some political leaders, who have commitments to budgetary constraint in the areas of income and services policy, have recently sought to reduce the scope of national social welfare programs. However, they have not been able to facilitate major reductions in expenditure levels because of apparent widespread recognition of social need. Thus, in the early 1970s the Nixon administration sought to restrict the scope of the free and reduced-priced school lunch program and the public assistance-related social services program by narrowing eligibility standards for participation. His administration also sought to eliminate some newer social programs. Such actions led critics of the Nixon administration to assert that the administration sought to dismantle the social welfare sector. The Ford administration, while similarly concerned with the expansion of federal initiative in welfare areas and the increased budgetary demands of social programs, has in general not sought to restrict eligibility to social welfare programs as a mechanism of budgetary constraint. Neither has the current national administration sought major curtailment of existing social programs.

In spite of executive concerns with the cost of income and service programs, political recognition of the need for income and service programs is reflected in the fact that the national expenditure level for social welfare programs has not declined during the 1970s. In spite of the Nixon White House attempts to reduce the scope of existing national social welfare programs, the aggregate budget outlays for social welfare income maintenance and services were not reduced. Rather, what happened was that some specific program areas had their budgets slashed. For example, the $1.1 billion (fiscal 1973) Emergency Employment Assistance program was discontinued, the Vocational Rehabilitation program was reduced from $676 million in fiscal 1973 to $650 million in fiscal 1974, and the Community Action program was largely dismantled.[1] Similarly, although the advent of congressional legislation in 1972 placed a ceiling on the uses of federal funds for social services that are related to public assistance at a maximum of $2.5 billion a year, this level of spending did not constitute a reduction in the size of federal outlay for these services for fiscal 1973.

Federal outlays for these public assistance-related social services increased substantially in the first half of the decade of the 1970s. In fiscal 1971 the federal outlay for these services was $690 million. In 1972 and 1973 the federal funds expended in this area by the states increased sharply. In part, the phenomenal increase in costs was related to the "use" that welfare administrators made of Title IV A and Title VI (of the Social Security Act) funds in order to finance state and local social service programs that could not be funded as adequately from other sources. The decision to apply such national revenue to social service development was the result of the unavailability of other revenue sources that would enable states and localities to provide adequate social services—in areas such as day care, family planning, or foster care. Limitations on the amount of social services money available to the states on a matching-grant basis, as well as on the uses of the available funds were intended to "put a lid" on such expenditures for social services. The 1972 legislation restricted more completely the delivery of social services to those people who were recipients of public welfare services or who were applicants for such assistance.

In terms of the social policy goal of establishing an income and services "floor," the "lid" on federal expenditures, and the restrictions regarding eligibility for services, were inappropriate. They were inappropriate because services provided were not sufficient to cope with the conditions of inequitable distribution of income and services throughout the United States that limit the opportunities for personal development of many Americans. Also, it appears that the integrated development of such an adequate social service policy would require a clearer national role in the development of social service standards and priorities. However, the 1972 legislation indicated the goals of a "floor" of income and services and a stronger national role in establishing federal standards and federal priorities concerning social services policy were not accepted as matters of national policy.

A more recent federal law has modified national social services policy to some degree. In 1974 the Social Services and Child Support Amendments (Title XX of the Social Security Act) were passed by Congress and signed into law by President Ford. These new amendments, which went into effect on October 1, 1975, modify some of the constraints that had been imposed by earlier federal law.

Perhaps, most significantly, this law repealed a requirement of the previous social service amendments whereby 90 percent of federal funding for most social services had to be used for actual welfare recipients or applicants for assistance. The present law provides that state expenditures for social services received by welfare recipients or applicants must be at least equal to 50 percent of federal matching funds received by the state for all services. States can now provide services to families with incomes of up to 115 percent of the state's median income—although fee schedules for receipt of the services being federally funded are required under the provision of the law for some categories of higher income social services consumers. This provision means that more persons of modest income who are not eligible for public assistance may receive social services under state programs that are largely federally funded. The 1974 amendments have not, however, provided for coordination and integration of social service delivery either at a national level or at the level of the various states. For example, although child care services, health support services, and training services at the state level may all receive federal funds under Title XX, such services are not necessarily provided in every state, nor is the distribution of such services nationally coordinated.

In addition, the federal government provides substantial funds to the states for many of the services that the states provide that are not funded by Title XX—such as medicaid, food stamps, and school breakfast and lunch programs. The funding is shared most often on the basis of federal-state matching grants-in-aid or specific project formula grants. States do not have to accept federal funds for programs. They can choose not to provide a specific service. Also, states have considerable discretion in determining the extent to which a service is provided and thereby the effect of a service on a target population. As a result of these conditions, the range of services as well as the level of service delivery will vary from state to state.

In addition to the funds made available to states by grants-in-aid and formula grants, some "untied" federal revenues are provided to states and localities as a result of general revenue sharing. The services provided the citizens of states through the use of these funds (whether they are used for social services or for other projects) have very few restrictions and very little administrative or legislative oversight attached to them. Thus, variability in both the quantity and quality of services available to citizens of the 50 separate states have been reinforced through the general revenue sharing program.

Funding for services at the federal level has been increased significantly during the 1970s. This has occurred in spite of the attempts by some political leaders to limit the scope of such spending, and to limit the number of individuals eligible for such services. Federal revenues usually are distributed to states that have established service programs eligible for federal funding. To date the federal government has not played an important role in requiring states to provide services, in requiring that adequate levels of service be provided, and in mandating that available services be distributed equitably. Thus, establishment of a national "floor" of services that would be nationally administered has not occurred. National involvement in the service area, however, has greatly increased during the 1970s.

Income Maintenance

A national income policy, which would provide for national minimum income payments, has been developing incrementally in the 1970s. In this section there is a consideration of stages of development of a national income policy, as well as a consideration of some recent proposals for the establishment of such a policy.

Our income maintenance system is based upon the two-pronged approach of the Social Security Act of 1935: public assistance and social insurance. Social insurance provides insurance payments for the eligible aged, eligible disabled, survivors of eligible recipients, and for many of the unemployed. Except with regard to the unemployed, the social insurance program is nationally administered. However, this program provides variable payments related to earned income and years of employment, and does not provide an adequate income floor for many recipients. The public assistance titles of the Social Security Act, as they were originally conceived, and as they were amended in the 1950s and 1960s, provided that states received federal grants-in-aid to fund public assistance payments to the needy. The categories of needy were aged, blind, disabled, and families with dependent children of limited financial resources. Resource standards for eligibility were determined by the states. In the public assistance programs payments as well as eligibility have varied from state to state. Even where payment levels have been relatively high in this system, given the increasing cost of living, they have been far from adequate.

Changes in this system have been made as a result of the enactment of the Social Security Amendments of 1972. Under this legislation state programs to aid the aged, blind, and the disabled have been replaced by a new federal program—the Supplementary Security Income Program (SSI)—that provides a minimum income for these three groups of eligible recipients. The states can, however, supplement the federal income grants, and at the present time 33 states make optional supplemental payments to individuals above the federal payment level. In July 1974 the federal payment level for an eligible person with no other income was $1,752 per year.

Broader income policy proposals are in the political atmosphere, although to date Congress has been only partially infected by this particular virus. Income policy approaches were greatly in vogue in the 1960s.

Guaranteed income proposals were offered by Milton Friedman, Robert Lampman, Edward Schwartz, Robert Theobold, and other policy analysts.[2] While these proposals had no legislative fruition, they stimulated a number of family assistance plan proposals that would have provided a national base income for most poor persons in American society, as well as some subsidy for moderately poor families with an employed head of household. SSI provides a national minimum income for those eligible. It does not provide coverage for the vast majority of the poor because they are not aged, not blind, nor disabled.

As a result of the limited national income maintenance policy that has been enacted, there has been some impetus to the discussion of the need for a national income policy that would benefit all of the poor. In fact, since the enactment of SSI, there has been increased concern by members of both the national welfare bureaucracy and Congress with the alteration of our means-tested income maintenance programs. As a result of this concern by decision makers with national income policy, it might be useful to review two of the most widely discussed "incomes" approaches. These proposals indicate the likely form that a national income policy will take. One of these proposals originated within the U.S. Department of Health, Education, and Welfare. The other proposal was developed by the Joint Economic Committee of Congress. Both of these proposals would establish a national income floor of $3,600 for a family of four.

Casper Weinberger, Secretary of Health, Education, and Welfare has suggested a basic national income maintenance program that would replace current programs such as the Food Stamp Program and that would eliminate the federal-state Aid to Families with Dependent Children program (AFDC). Under this proposal a family of four with no income would receive a federal payment of $3,600. If a family earns income, the benefits derived from this program would be reduced by 50 percent. For example, a family of four with an earned income of $2,000 a year would receive a benefit of $2,600, resulting in a total income of $4,600. Though the published version of this proposal is vague in many of its details, the proposal itself reflects recognition of the need for a national "incomes" policy. In fact, Secretary Weinberger has commented that, inasmuch as the problems relating to poverty are both chronic and national in scope, they are no more solvable at the state level than were the conditions that led to the establishment of the Social Security System in 1935.[3]

A more complex proposal has been developed by the Subcommittee on Fiscal Policy of the Joint Economic Committee of Congress under the chairmanship of then Congresswoman Martha Griffiths. The Griffiths' proposal provides basic federal benefits of $3,600 for a family of four with no other income. Part of the Griffiths' income benefit would be received through a tax credit structure. Rather than the current income tax personal exemptions of $750 per person, any person permanently living in the United States or otherwise required to file a federal income tax form would be entitled to a $225 annual per person tax credit against income tax liability. The unused credits would be paid to the filer—producing a "negative income tax" effect. In addition, the Griffiths' plan provides that for individuals or families with limited or no income an Allowance for Basic Living Expenses (ABLE) be granted. The allowance for a married couple with two children and no other source of income would be $2,700 ($2,050 for a married couple, and $325 for the first and second dependent child). Thus, a family of four having no other income, using the formula established under the Griffiths' plan, would receive $3,600 from the federal government—$2,700 ABLE payment and $900 in unused tax credits.

This plan would seek to eliminate federal participation in the AFDC program and to terminate the food stamp program in much the same manner as the Weinberger proposal. In addition, the Griffiths' plan would limit the scope of SSI by including more SSI participants in the ABLE program. Also, just as the Weinberger proposal would reduce assistance by 50 percent for each dollar of earned income less social security taxes paid, so too would this plan incorporate a 50 percent payment reduction mechanism. Other provisions of this proposal are 100 percent deductions of veteran pensions, farm subsidy payments, and federal tax refunds. Also, beyond the twenty-sixth week of Unemployment Insurance, the ABLE program would meet the needs of the long-term unemployed and supplement benefits received prior to that time after a 67 percent reduction for Unemployment Insurance payments.[4]

The provisions of the Griffiths' plan, as well as the thrust of the Weinberger proposal would act to reduce the scope of the existing federal-state programs and to establish firmly a federal "incomes" policy. Also, either proposal would provide for a broadened federal "incomes" floor while reducing the financial burdens borne by the states and localities to assist the poor. Both plans would include the working poor as well as the nonworking poor as potential recipients of federal income transfer payments. Thus, a greater portion of those people who live in consumer units with annual incomes that fall below the poverty level would be granted financial assistance.

Proposal

Most of the states and localities have been generally unable or unwilling to provide for adequate income and service programs for the poor. In part their unwillingness to develop such programs has been caused by their limited fiscal capabilities. These limitations are due in part to a lack of willingness on the part of elected decision makers to appropriate available funds for large scale public welfare programs. It is also the result of the limited revenue sources (generated through taxation and bonded indebtedness) available to these governmental jurisdictions. Given these restraints on state and local action, the type of program that could best deal with the problem of maldistribution of income and services in the United States would, we believe, be a national income and services policy. Given these constraints on state and local action to meet the income and service needs of low-income groups, the proposal for a national income and services policy falls increasingly within the realm of the politically possible.

As the previous section indicated, at least two forms of the national income component are under legislative discussion as of 1975. Neither of these two recommendations would require a change in the basic market mechanism of the economy, although some economic redistribution of income to the poor would result. Following this redistribution, more people would be given a chance to participate fully in American society. In order to achieve this goal they must first achieve a basic level of human health and dignity that is not provided by the present unfocused, unplanned, and fragmented income maintenance and service delivery system.

We have a legislative tradition to move ahead with such a program. The Social Security Act of 1935, though it established assistance titles that left most authority to the states, established a national base for social insurance (with the exception of unemployment insurance). Certainly we ought to have the legislative ingenuity to develop additional national income and services programs. We were, for example, willing to place the income maintenance provisions of Old Age Assistance (OAA), Aid to the Blind (AB), and Aid to the Permanently and Totally Disabled (APTD) titles under national jurisdiction beginning January 1974.[5] Certainly, the same logic could be used for nationalizing the major public assistance category, AFDC, at a level commensurate with human health and decency. Also, regardless of whether one considers the income level proposed by Weinberger and Griffiths adequate or inadequate, both of these income maintenance proposals address the *need* for a "national income policy."

As far as the services component of this proposal is concerned, there may be more problems involved in actualizing a national integration of service delivery. Problems may arise from the "vested interests" of the separate bureaucracies in the national and state governments that will, in all likelihood, exert all of their influence to try to retain the status quo regarding the delivery of "their" services.

A new national income and services policy should have to adhere to four critieria.

1. There should be national determination of nationwide standards of eligibility.

2. There should be national determination of adequate income mainte-nance payment levels and adequate availability of services.

3. There should be national program enforcement by federal staffs.

4. There should be integrative policies coordinating income maintenance and services policies with educational, health, recreational, and housing policies.

By adhering to these four criteria a "floor" in terms of meeting physical and social needs of residents of the United States would be established. Services and income would become comparable in the various states and localities and basic levels of human health and dignity might be better met.

Conclusion

In order to achieve a more equitable distribution of available resources, a statutorily authorized economic "floor" related to the provision of physi-cal and social necessities would be required for the attainment of individual welfare.[6] Such a standard would provide us with a rough idea of equality in that the material base of society would be put at a level agreed to be commensurate with the development and realization of the individual's potential. A program of this nature would involve increased public sector expenditures and a redirection of public spending priorities.

Inasmuch as the states and localities cannot perform this task adequately, we believe that the best mechanism to achieve this ideal would be a national income and services policy. Concerning its actualization, perhaps the thought of the late Robert Kennedy should be recalled: "You see things as they are and ask why. But I dream things that never were and ask why not."

Notes

1. Data derived from *The Budget of the United States, Fiscal Year, 1974, Appendix* (Washington, D.C.: U.S. Government Printing Office, 1973), pp. 131-144; Jules H. Berman, "The Federal Budget for 1974," *Washington Bulletin*, 23 (Feburary 26, 1973), 14.

2. For a useful summary of some of these proposals see Helen O. Nichol, "Guaranteed Income Maintenance," *Welfare in Review*, 19 (April, 1966), 1-10.

3. *The New York Times*, October 27, 1974, 46.

4. U.S. Congress, Joint Economic Committee, *A Model Income Supplement Program*, Staff Study prepared for the use of the Subcommit-

tee on Fiscal Policy, 93rd Cong., 2nd sess., 1974, Study Paper 16, *Studies in Public Welfare*; Also see Jules H. Berman, "Welfare Reform—Current Proposals," *Washington Bulletin*, 24 (January 13, 1975), 1-4.

5. See U.S. Publ. L. 92-603 (1972).

6. A.B. Atkinson, *Poverty in Britain and the Reform of Social Security* (Cambridge, U.K.: University Press, 1969), 15-16.

Index

Index

Abortion, 211
Accessibility of legal services to the poor, 216, 217, 220
Activists, the poor, 139-140
Administration on Aging, 45ff
Administrative Coordination, 78-82
Administrative Procedures Act (APA), 96
Administrative rule making, 95, 96
Affluence, 241
Aged, definition of, 42-43
Aggressive legal representation of the poor, 220
Aid to Families with Dependent Children (AFDC), 37, 206, 208, 209, 210
  Caseloads, 58, 59, 61, 63, 65, 68, 69, 70, 71
Aiken, Michael, 11, 17
Alaska, 97
Albuquerque Bar Association, 196
Alcoholism, 210
Alford, Robert, 4, 11, 15, 17, 19
Alienation, 226, 227, 228, 229, 233
Alinsky, Saul, 119, 186
Allison, Graham, 8, 17
Allotment Act (Indian), 161
Alternatives, choosing among in public policies, 215-221
  Weighting, 219-220
American Association of Retired Persons, 44
American Indian Policy Review Commission, 172-173
American Indians, definition, 158
American Medical Association, 48
Anderson, Janell, 17
Appalachia, 146
Appellate court work, 218
Arkansas, 91
Assigned legal counsel, 216, 217, 219
Attorneys, 215-221
  Assigned, 216, 217, 219
  Government, 216-218
  Judicare, 216-218
  Legal services, 220
  Public defender, 216-220
  Volunteer, 216-220
Austin, David, 17

Bamberger, E. Clinton, Jr., 192
Banfield, Edward, 4, 14, 103
Bardach, Gene, 10, 17
Benefit levels, 208-210, 212
Berk, Richard, 15
Black capitalism, 237

Black cooptation, 186, 188
Black middle class and poverty program, 183, 184, 185, 187
Black Panthers, 116, 118
"Blame the victim" theory of poverty, 162-163
Brookings Institution, The, 14, 19, 107
Brown, Charles, 106
Browning, Rufus, 3, 16, 17
Brown v. Board of Education, 199
Bullock, Charles, 4, 15
Bureau of the Budget, 76, 78, 81
Bureau of Indian Affairs, 162
Burger Court, 205, 207, 209, 210, 211, 212

Cahn, Edgar S., 192
Cahn, Jean C., 192
California, 89
Calkins, Susannah, 19
Caputo, David, 14, 19
Carlin, Jerome, 198
Caseworkers, 39
Charity, welfare as, 206, 210
Chavez, Cesar, 118
Checkpoint agreements, 78-80
Choosing among public policies, 215-221
Civil cases, 217-221
Civil Rights Movement, poverty program 183
Clark, Peter B., incentive theory of, 117
Class action suit, 192, 193
Class interests, 217
Cloward, Richard, 4, 146-147, 187
Code of Federal Regulations (CFR), 96
Cole, Richard, 5, 11, 14, 18, 19
Community Action Agencies (CAAS), 145-154
  Indian, 168-170
  rural, 151-154
Community Action Program (CAP), 84-85, 86, 94, 95, 125-129, 180, 186
  Problems of evaluating, 127-131
Community Development Revenue Sharing, 104, 106, 107, 237
Community education services, 219
Community organizing, 93, 95, 146, 148, 149, 150, 151, 152
Community power structures, 145, 148-149, 152, 153
Concentrated Employment Program in Springfield, Mass., 179
Congress, United States, 102, 104, 106, 205, 206-207, 209-210

255

256

About the Contributors

Robert B. Albritton received the Ph.D. from Northwestern University (1975) and is Assistant Professor of Political Science at Virginia Polytechnic Institute and State University. He has published articles in the area of welfare policy.

James E. Anderson received the Ph.D. from the University of Texas (1960) and is Professor of Political Science at the University of Houston. He is an editor of the *Policy Studies Journal* for economic regulation issues. Especially interested in public policy formation and administration, his published works include numerous articles, and several books including: *Politics and the Economy* (1966) and *Public Policy-Making* (1975).

Lawrence Neil Bailis received the Ph.D. from Harvard University (1972) and is Assistant Professor of Political Science and Assistant to the Director of the Graduate Program in Urban Social and Environmental Policy at Tufts University. He also serves as Director of Social Policy Analysis for the Contract Research Corporation. He is the author of *Bread or Justice: Grassroots Organizing in the Welfare Rights Movement* (1974), and several articles on poverty, welfare, and community organization.

Joseph A. Cepuran received the Ph.D. from the University of Iowa (1973) and is Assistant Professor of Political Science at the University of Michigan, Dearborn. He has held positions with institutes at the University of Virginia, University of Iowa and the University of Wisconsin. He has published articles in the area of welfare politics, welfare administration and local labor relations.

Terry L. Christensen received the Ph.D. from the University of North Carolina (1970) and is Assistant Professor of Political Science at San Jose State University. He specializes in urban politics and interest groups and has written several articles on urban growth policy, local uses of federal revenue sharing funds and voter turnout in city elections.

John H. Culver received the Ph.D. from the University of New Mexico (1975). He is a lecturer of Political Science at the California Polytechnic State University.

Frederick R. Eisele received the Ph.D. from New York University (1972) and is Assistant Professor of Social Policy in the Division of Community Development, College of Human Development and Associate Chairman of the Gerontology Center at Pennsylvania State University. He edited a special issue on the "Political Consequences of Aging" for *The Annals of the American Academy of Political and Social Sciences* (1974).

Paul B. Fischer received the Ph.D. from the University of Massachusetts (1971) and is Assistant Professor of Politics and Fellow of the Robert Wood Institute of Local and Regional Affairs, Lake Forest College. He is presently involved in research comparing the impact of metropolitan political structures on the quality of local services delivery systems in Toronto and Chicago.

Richard L. Fogel received the M.A. from the University of Sussex, England (1967), and the M.P.A. from the University of Pittsburgh (1968). As an audit manager with the U.S. General Accounting Office he is responsible for GAO's review of the programs of the Federal Bureau of Investigation and the Law Enforcement Assistance Administration. Previously he directed a major portion of GAO's reviews of welfare programs. He has written several articles on program evaluation.

William J. Hagens received the M.A. from Wayne State University (1971) and is a research analyst with the Office of Program Research, Washington State House of Representatives, a former legal services lobbyist with Pierce County Legal Assistance Foundation, Tacoma, Washington, a consultant to Michigan State Legislature, and the author of several articles on legislative behavior.

Dale Rogers Marshall received the Ph.D. from the University of California—Los Angeles (1969) and is Associate Professor of Political Science at the University of California at Davis, and a member of the Executive Council of the American Political Science Association and Editorial Board of *The American Political Science Review*. She is the author of several articles and a book, *The Politics of Participation in Poverty* (1971), and co-author of *A Guide to Participation: Field Work, Role Playing Cases and Other Forms* (1973).

Stuart S. Nagel received the J.D. from the Northwestern University Law School (1958) and the Ph.D. from Northwestern University (1961). He is Professor of Political Science at the University of Illinois and a member of the Illinois bar. He is Secretary-Treasurer and Journal Coordinator of the Policy Studies Organization. He has also been an attorney to the Office of Economic Opportunity, Lawyers Constitutional Defense Committee in Mississippi, National Labor Relations Board, and the U.S. Senate Subcommittee on Administrative Practice and Procedure. He is the author or editor of numerous articles and books including: *Policy Studies and the*

Social Sciences (1975), *Policy Studies in America and Elsewhere* (1975), *Improving the Legal Process: Effects of Alternatives* (1975), *Environmental Politics* (1974); *The Rights of the Accused: In Law and Action* (1972); and *The Legal Process from a Behavioral Perspective* (1969).

Howard A. Palley received the Ph.D. from Syracuse University (1964) and is Associate Professor at the School of Social Work and Community Planning, University of Maryland. He is the author of numerous articles on welfare-related problems and has co-authored several articles with Marian Lief Palley. They are presently working on a book tentatively titled: *Urban Politics: A Study of Linkages*.

Marian Lief Palley received the Ph.D. from New York University (1966) and is Associate Professor of Political Science at the University of Delaware. She is the co-author of several articles on welfare-related problems with Howard A. Palley. She has also edited two issues of the *American Behavioral Scientist* dealing with welfare problems. In addition she is co-author of *Tradition and Change in American Party Politics* (1975) and *The Politics of Social Change* (1971).

Leonard Rubin received the M.A. from the University of California at Berkeley (1958) and has worked in applied social research in various government agencies and in private contract research. He has been involved in research and has published numerous articles in such areas as the politics of South Asia, higher education and foreign areas studies, the employment problems of disadvantaged youth, welfare and other issues in poverty law, and economic and social problems of the aged, especially those related to racial disadvantage.

Elmer R. Rusco received the Ph.D. from the University of California at Berkeley (1960) and is Professor of Political Science and Director of the Bureau of Governmental Research at the University of Nevada, Reno. His published research includes studies of poverty, Nevada law regarding Indians, and *Good Time Coming? Black Nevadans in the Nineteenth Century* (1975). He is also a member of the Indian Rights Committee of the American Civil Liberties Union.

Mary Kiehl Rusco received the M.A. from the University of Nebraska (1956). She is an archeologist with the Nevada State Museum who has been employed in community development studies by the Inter-Tribal Council of Nevada. Her published research includes a study of Indian-fur trapper interaction in the Great Basin. She is also co-author of *Communication and Community Organization on Nevada Indian Reservations* (1970).

Stephen M. Sachs received the Ph.D. from the University of Chicago (1968) and is Assistant Professor of Political Science at Indiana University-Purdue University, Indianapolis. He engaged in three years of research into poverty problems, programs and policy in Indianapolis from 1970-72 and undertook a year of comparative field research in Yugoslavia in 1972-73. He organized the Conference for a Relevant Social Science in 1971 and has been active in the development of People for Self-Management. His publications include a number of papers concerning poverty and self-management.

Richard D. Shingles received the Ph.D. from the University of Minnesota (1973) and is Assistant Professor of Political Science at Virginia Polytechnic Institute and State University. His interests and research include the political behavior of minorities and the poor, impact analysis and political methodology.

Harry P. Stumpf received the Ph.D. from Northwestern University (1964) and is Professor of Political Science at the University of New Mexico. He has also taught at the University of Wisconsin and the University of Minnesota. He is the author of numerous articles on legal and poverty questions. His forthcoming book is *Community Politics and Legal Services* (1975).

Bernadyne Turpen received the Ph.D. from the University of New Mexico (1975) and is Assistant Professor of Political Science at Rutgers University. She is working in the area of law and poverty politics.

Stephen L. Wasby received the Ph.D. from the University of Oregon (1962) and is Professor of Political Science, Southern Illinois University at Carbondale. He is an editor of the *Policy Studies Journal* for free speech and civil liberties issues, and a staff editor of the *Justice System Journal*. He is the author of numerous articles on the United States Supreme Court and several books including: *The Impact of the U.S. Supreme Court: Some Perspectives* (1970), and the forthcoming *Continuity and Change: From the Warren Court to the Berger Court*.

About the Editor

Dorothy Buckton James received the M.A. and the Ph.D. from Columbia University and is Professor of Political Science and head of the Political Science Department at Virginia Polytechnic Institute and State University. Dr. James is an editor of the *Policy Studies Journal* for welfare and poverty issues and is a member of the editorial board of the *Political Science Reviewer*. She is the author of numerous articles on the contemporary American Presidency and on poverty and welfare policy and has written several books including *The Contemporary Presidency*, (2nd ed. 1974); *Poverty Politics and Change* (1972); and *Outside Looking In* (1972).